ALEX H

MAYBE

AN INSIGHT INTO THE EPIC STRUGGLES AND
TRIUMPHS THAT DEFINE MODERN
POLAR EXPLORATION

Happy Birthday John,

All the best,

Alen H

Maybe

First published in the UK in 2013 by Tricorn Books
Updated in 2018

ISBN: 978-0957343580

Published by Tricorn Books
Aspex Gallery, 42 The Vulcan Building
Gunwharf Quays, Portsmouth, PO1 3BF

www.tricornbooks.co.uk
www.alexhibbert.com
Instagram/Twitter @alexhibbert

A CIP catalogue record for this book is available
from the British Library.

Printed and bound in the United Kingdom

For my family.

ABOUT THE AUTHOR

Alex Hibbert was born in 1986, was educated at Canford School and read Biological Sciences at the University of Oxford. Following his graduation, he developed and undertook numerous expeditions in the mountainous and cold regions of the world. Upon completion of the record-breaking Tiso Trans Greenland expedition, he trained in the Royal Marines Officer batch before re-entering the exploration world as an expedition leader, international speaker, author and commentator. His wilderness and wildlife photography has also received widespread acclaim and he licenses his photographs via a global network of cooperatives.

CONTENTS

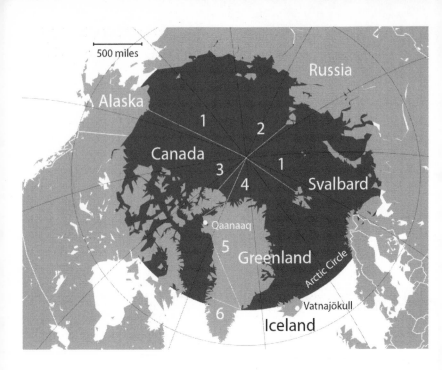

1. The winter Arctic Ocean crossing route of Wally Herbert in 1968/9.

2. The Russian route from Cape Arktichevsky to the Geographic North Pole.

3. The Canadian route from Ward Hunt Island to the Geographic North Pole.

4. The Dark Ice Project route from Qaanaaq, Greenland to the Geographic North Pole.

5. The return crossing route of The Long Haul expedition in 2008.

6. The East-West speed crossing route in 2011.

Ellesmere Island

Alert

Lincoln Sea

Kane Basin

Etah

Qaanaaq

Greenland

Thule

Baffin Bay

Above: The Nares Strait   Below: Iceland in winter

Iceland

Vatnajökull

Höfn

Reykjavik

Kirkjubæjarklaustur

CHAPTER ONE

I looked towards the horizon and then glanced across at George with an expression combining both unbridled excitement and bewilderment at the bizarre concept that another reality existed outside our cold, white wilderness. After 113 days and nearly 1400 miles without any external support, we had become entirely immersed in our featureless surroundings. Now, flying towards us, was the first evidence of the outside world we had seen in nearly four months. Our chartered helicopter, not a low-cost or simple prospect in the Arctic, was en route and I hoped the pilot had spotted us: two black dots on the white expanse of the Hahn Glacier. Even the simple task of transmitting our GPS location to the helicopter office had been an effort for me after the dizzying experience of completing the final hundred miles on nothing more than a flapjack a day.

The noise grew louder and I saw the helicopter deviate to one side. Had he seen us? Were the coordinates we gave recorded correctly? Was he about to turn around and fly back to Tasiilaq, the Inuit village, empty of his intended cargo? I had dreamed of this final moment for so long that I did not truly believe it would actually happen. A month into the expedition and I had been worried about our pace and the viability of our unprecedentedly long journey. A week from the end and with the loss of our final two depots of supplies, we had stared potential failure in the face. Having set a new unsupported distance record and fought for those final, crevassed miles to the coast, I was now so keen to get home that I did the only thing I could: I fired a green flare into the blue sky to make sure Hans, our pilot, had seen us.

He had spotted us. George and I clipped down the last of the straps to make sure all of our equipment was securely fastened to the sledges. From experience, I knew that pilots who flew expedition charters and landed on icecaps preferred to land very close in order to minimise the time taken to load up the aircraft. With potentially unstable ice and notoriously unpredictable weather conditions, it could be fatal for a helicopter or ski plane to be caught miles away from its base if a storm arrived. Time was of the essence.

The roar of the rotors and violent downdraft became ever stronger as he neared our final camp and in a flurry of snow and hurricane-like wind, the helicopter touched down with a thump. We knew the pilot had to reduce the engine speed before we could open the side doors and in those few moments of waiting, the tension broke completely. It really was over.

'That is the best thing ever! Wahoooo!' screamed George over the deafening sound of the engine. Hans, with both of us in an exhausted and weak state, helped us to lift the sledges and skis into the fuselage and I lifted my boot off the snow surface for the last time and into the helicopter, as if in slow motion. It was such an intense moment for me. Over four years of obsessively hard work, disappointment, setback, frustration and disapproving doubters had been worth it. We were vindicated. We had done it. We had skied further than anyone in history without resupply or support.

George had been a lucky find for me. Drafted in at short notice, when prior commitments forced the withdrawal of other companions, we both took a risk in putting faith in each others' abilities just five weeks before we were due to fly north. What became abundantly clear though, even a few days into the journey, was that I had struck gold. George's mix of enthusiasm, positivity, tolerance, athleticism and sheer toughness was unbeatable. It simply did not matter that it was his first icecap expedition and only my second. We learned fast and created a satisfyingly efficient system which allowed us to break one of the major, undiluted polar records which had stood since 2000: the unsupported polar distance record.

Little else about the expedition had been so fortuitous or gone so smoothly, however. My journey from enthusiastic teenager to polar traveller had been multi-faceted and hard won. I had turned from a boy with an idea, with very little in terms of practical ability, naïve certainly, into someone who knew his potential. Potential is the key word here because success is a very different beast – one that is dependent on so many things in such a brutal and unpredictable theatre. Storms, equipment breakage, injury, animal attack, and the list goes on, can spell an end to an otherwise well-constructed plan, executed by a competent team. For me, it had been a formative period. I had decided to take on a lifestyle which was unheard of for people of my age, and the 'profession' had inherent difficulties. Now, even a few years on, unsupported, full-distance expeditions in the Polar Regions have resisted the surge of commercialisation and popularisation that have been, in my view, the trivialising scourge of flagship mountains such as Everest and also the last degrees (just sixty nautical miles) to the Poles.

•

A last degree is a term that describes a short ski, usually in the most stable and benign time of the year from an arbitrary point, across sixty miles to a Pole, either South or North. Comparing a sixty or a hundred day unsupported expedition to a weeklong ski-tour with a professional tour-guide is impossible. For that reason, it is not really necessary to involve such expeditions in discussion; they do not have the same basic demands of skill, experience and robustness. I am the first to emphasise that there is nothing wrong with novice or entry-level polar tourism – it is inevitable in the modern day and it is not for an individual to judge worthiness – but they should not be considered in the same stable.

•

There is no doubt that genuine humility is not a common characteristic of polar travellers. An immense confidence in oneself is needed to pull an expedition together, knock the doubters and reject the sheer fear of facing the cold wilderness. Every man or woman, when faced with the ice, is instantly humbled in the presence of such an overwhelming and unbreakable force of nature; any suggestion or mention of the words 'conquered the Arctic' or 'tamed the Antarctic' are laughable. However, the knowledge that you are capable of creating the complex framework that is an expedition plan, with the constituent logistics, vision and coordination, requires a deep confidence in your own ability. Call it confidence, call it arrogance, call it stubbornness; expeditions simply do not happen without it.

The 'Tiso Trans Greenland', or 'The Long Haul', which was the end result of the four-year saga that comprised the start of my polar career, was the product of a refusal to give in and also the time during which I learned the skills to support my passion. Training and research can only do so much and beyond that I had to test myself. The expedition, which I completed after 1374 miles and 113 days on the ice with George Bullard, gave me that all-important springboard. We succeeded – genuinely – against all the odds, given our young age and the raised eyebrows of the exploration establishment.

Following on from that hard fought record, I spent my own period of time, only a year, training as a Royal Marines Officer – cut short by both a maddening series of injuries, many of which were a result of starting training only weeks after 'The Long Haul', and a growing realisation that the 'Corps' was going to frustrate me professionally.

My original plans involved tapping into my love of precision, teamwork and high standards whilst undertaking serious work, working through the military hierarchy over an entire career. However, after being exposed to that environment first-hand, the frustration predicted by my selection board Colonel did indeed materialise. Despite being the theoretical home of independent thinking and innovation in the Armed Forces, I found myself constantly banging my head against a brick wall, even in the very early stages of my career. Common sense made way for strict adherence to procedure and academic prowess was measured through learning facts parrot-fashion.

I suppose I came to realise what it really meant to hand over control over my purpose, identity and destiny to a system, which knew me only as 30030310. I felt that, counter to all my hopes and expectations, it was a retrograde step in my life, despite the things I had learnt. It sounds odd, but I found it was actually the lazy option. My career path, daily duties and even mealtimes were laid out before me. All this, was despite the fact that the course is considered the most arduous in the world for conventional combat troops.

I craved flexibility and a blank canvas. Using the impetus of a series of irritating and at times, humiliating injuries, I made the move outside the Corps. After the requisite withdrawal symptoms associated with leaving such an all-consuming institution, the real world opened up before me.

At the age of twenty-three, I returned to the polar world, full-time, unleashed, refreshed and hungry. I was launched into a world where I no longer had a monthly salary to rely on and as I filled in the form to register as self-employed, I was under no illusions as to what I was letting myself in for. The recession was biting and everyone was cutting back. I knew that, not only to survive but also to grow rapidly and thrive, I had to create a commercial side to my lifestyle, and fast.

Equal to the trepidation, which accompanies setting out into the world without being under the umbrella of a large organisation, was the satisfaction of knowing my success or failure would be entirely dependent on my ability and hard work. Self-employment is so pure and transparent – there is nowhere to hide. I like that; make it work and the world is yours. Let even the slightest bit of laziness or apathy creep in and you sink; it is wonderfully Darwinian and very real. I was abundantly aware that I was not wired in a way that would allow me to be a cog in a large machine. Any fears of self-employment being lonely or isolated were quickly stamped out by the sheer number of people my activities brought me into contact with.

I wanted to get back out on the ice again and even though my success on 'The Long Haul' meant that I had a track record and that sponsors may potentially be easier to find, I had to build a business. This is the critical difference between the person who can only afford to travel, climb or ski at weekends and on annual holiday and the person who becomes a full-time professional and is, therefore, able to strive for more notable goals. Remarkably, there are some individuals, climbers especially, who have risen to the top

13

of their sport despite having full-time office jobs. Given the time-pressures of polar travel and knowing my own personality, I felt the need to have the freedom to focus one hundred per cent on my goals: a list of major expeditions that I keep close to my chest but which seems to become longer, not shorter as time goes on. Such is the magnetic draw of the icecaps and the ambitions they represent for me. This, combined with my inherent impatience, is a package that can be at once as great a flaw as it is an asset. If used positively I firmly believe it is the latter.

The clear direction for me was to build a multi-faceted commercial plan, which could absorb market fluctuations and the unforeseen aspects of self-employed polar travel. This commercial plan was three-fold: firstly involving the growth of my photographic collection with the global leaders Getty Images (to later transfer to photographic cooperatives); secondly a move towards writing and thirdly, but most significantly, developing a series of regular public speaking engagements. In theory this mix was a perfect fit, allowing me to work very intensely on a small number of short projects and then freeing up plenty of time for training, planning and being creative at envisaging new ideas and strategies. The writing and speaking would go some way to satisfying my academic thirst.

Since speaking at corporate events and the like would be the backbone of my income and is not exactly an under-saturated market place, I would need to bring something new to the table. My youth was a noteworthy feature in an industry dominated by those twenty years my senior, but I did not want it to define me. Rather, I wanted my travels and performances to stand on their merits regardless of my age; besides, my youth would not last forever. A career whose unique selling point vanishes at the age of thirty would be a bad one indeed. Instead of relying on a raft of speaking agencies, which, apart from a special few, are routinely full of promises rather than results, I spoke directly to those in London and further afield and slowly built a client-base. These companies, and the individuals who staffed them, became far more than a source of income and some of my most fulfilling experiences off the ice have been in the company of those who have generously supported me and what I was trying to communicate.

14

In order to try and pay back some of the confidence these people had in me, I worked hard to make what I could offer as valuable as possible. It made life harder for myself, but I was determined not to fall into the trap that dozens of speakers, often long retired from the careers that fuelled their speaking, fall into of delivering the same tired speech regardless of the audience. I thought it my duty to do more – the end result is not for me to judge; I resolved to plan each talk from scratch. Some elements and themes are, inevitably, used more than once but I found it far more stimulating and enjoyable to try and match what I said to those who were due to listen.

It might sound strange to discuss something so entirely at odds with the raw ingredients of polar travel – smart, inner-city locations and lavish dinners with leaders of countless industries – but it satisfies the thirst I have for breadth. Many will be happy with a life in the outdoors without an academic element stemming from writing for both the page and auditorium. For me, far from being an attempt to cash-in on polar travel, it was a stimulating half of the whole. Those without this desire will see the mountains or rivers or other wild places as an end in themselves and that makes perfect sense.

It is true that being a champion 100m sprinter, for example, might not necessarily make someone a world-class, after-dinner speaker, but I wanted to work equally hard on all aspects of my lifestyle. I say lifestyle here, and not job or profession, because I really feel that I was slowly gaining the privilege of making a living from something I love, not having to will each and every weekend to come before dreading a Monday morning.

Whilst not a hero-worshipper by nature, those whom I admire most have excelled in a number of arenas with multiple talents, for example, Sir Peter Scott, a conservationist and artist, and Fridtjof Nansen, a diplomat, Nobel laureate, scientist and possibly the greatest polar explorer of them all. My personal desire, and the thing I always strive for, is to excel as a complete human being and not one that sacrifices all else for a narrow channel of success. For a person to be rounded and have breadth, which allows a varied perspective on the complexities of life, he or she should not neglect a constituent aspect of existence – be it the arts, language, philosophy, diplomacy or perhaps the sciences – humans do love to categorise the uncategorisable after all. We all have strengths in some areas and weaknesses in others but it is all too easy to write off those that do not come easily to us. Perhaps it is these fruits higher up in the tree that can lead to more and maybe even a fuller understanding of another.

Following a frenetic period of time setting up my business, writing and navigating the unfamiliar waters of book publishing with my first book, *The Long Haul*, and guiding a 350-mile journey in Greenland, I had a yearning for the ice. Months were threatening to become years. Following 'The Long Haul' expedition, I did genuinely wonder if I could, or wanted to, face such ordeals again. I did; polar travel is both a primal and cerebral passion for me and far more than a passing interest, a tick-box on an adventure bucket list or a launch pad for a comfortable retirement on the speaking circuit. My time in the Royal Marines and writing had meant a hiatus in expeditions that I was determined to put an end to.

Having teamed up with the foremost sports sponsorship agency in the City of London in 2010, the hunt was on for major funding for a series of landmark expeditions in the Far North and South. As with so many things in life and contrary to my natural impatience for action, sponsorship is a waiting game. The big prize was not to land neatly on my lap after a few meetings and I was not willing to sell out my guiding principles to expedite the process. I had confidence in the track-record and also in the personal commitment of the agency's Chief Executive and Directors and so concentrated on what I could achieve personally, via my own contacts.

Polar expedition skills are not like riding a bike and are not set in stone; they are constantly evolving and improving. This makes it vital to be out on the ice regularly – plying the trade and staying sharp. I was conscious that some individuals had fallen into a cyclical spiral of not raising enough funds and then just waiting for the next year and hoping for the best. Decades can be lost that way and I told myself, 'That will never be me'.

The truth is that polar expeditions are a mammoth expense, from high five to low seven figures and only deep sea and space exploration exert a greater burden on the wallet. This pressure is increasing in a financial climate in which there is progressively less funding available. This is not a good situation but one truth is clear to me: in the face of an obstacle, in this case not an open lead of water or a crevasse but a lack of critical cash, you can either roll over or you can fight. No-one can magically change the recent tendencies of companies and corporations to divert their dwindling sponsorship budgets towards celebrity endorsement or publicity stunts. That is how they sometimes maximise their marketing reach and that is ultimately what they need. Sponsorship is not a donation or a gift of kindness; it is a business deal and complaining achieves nothing. The announcement of the London 2012 Olympics was another sure sign that being in search of major funding when not an Olympian was going to get even tougher post-2008.

During the late winter of 2010 I had been in Finse, Norway, with polar and mountain guide and head guide for Pirhuk, Matt Spenceley. Matt had been part of my expedition world since my teenage years and was my main link back to the rest of civilisation during 'The Long Haul'. Exceptionally experienced and a talented ice climber, he was closing in on his IFMGA qualification at the age of only thirty and we were co-guiding a cold-weather training course.

●

I made a very clear decision very early on in my career to minimise the guiding I undertook. The few who make the leap of making polar travel their full-time vocation often opt to guide novices on trips, which range from sightseeing tours to mini-expeditions. Whilst I guide on occasions when specifically asked for, this is not my way.

Guiding can provide a regular, though modest income stream and 'paid-for' time on the ice. It is also rewarding, as I have found during my own guiding experiences, and I count former clients amongst my friends. But, and there is a big but, I think the time-constraints and repetitive nature of the journeys can send one into a different mind-set, one I did not wish to enter. There is little career progression or scalability in polar guiding. Also, it allows the world of commercialism, which I knowingly embrace whilst thousands of miles from the icecaps, to actually set foot on the ice itself. This was most dramatically proven to me during an exchange with Paul Walker of Tangent Expeditions, the only British organisation to compete with Matt Spenceley's company, Pirhuk (the company name being Greenlandic for soft snow flakes) in offering guided expeditions in the mountains and on the icecap of Greenland.

Paul is a regular fixture at the London adventure travel fairs, whilst Matt is conspicuously absent, preferring to spend almost every waking hour in the mountains. Paul and I were known to each other since the mid-2000s. I had noticed, following my 'Long Haul' expedition and prior to undertaking any guiding whatsoever, that I was on the receiving end of an email circular, presumably to other outdoors-people, asking for guides. Each time one of these emails arrived, the common theme was that the position was unpaid, or 'voluntary'.

I did not seek out guiding work with Tangent since the little I do is either through direct requests or occasionally via Matt. I did however take exception to the notion that a guide, the professional safety-barrier which every client relies on for their survival, was of zero value to Tangent. I took this up with Paul via email and he defended his position vehemently on the grounds that such positions are sought after and allow aspirants to gain guiding experience.

My position is clear – a person should not be gaining experience whilst guiding or even assistant-guiding paying customers. They should train privately, at their own expense or the expense of the guiding company who wishes to use them in future. It was, in my mind, a plea with a purely financial motivation and, above all, the premise is dangerous. The end results and client experiences are well documented online.

•

Finse is a polar training Mecca. Nestled in the mountains near the famous Hardangervidda plateau, it is a night train away from Oslo and is home to only a few dozen, hardy Norwegians. Almost every great European polar explorer of the Pioneering Age trained, at least briefly, in the snowy regions leading out from Finse. The small hotel, usefully stocked with outrageously priced beer, was adorned with photographs of Nansen, Scott and countless others.

Our teams, whom we were training up for various icecap trips, had settled into a daily routine of sledging through the undulating hills and so Matt and I skied a little ahead to chat. The conversation moved through to dream expeditions. Matt had always been one to talk about other people's journeys and modestly kept his own ambitions close to his chest. Indeed, he is one of the real mountaineers and outdoorsmen who value spending time in the wilderness and ranges, not just appearing every once in a while to add a non-taxing but famous peak to his CV. Matt loved speed and efficiency and so we talked about the speed record for crossing Greenland by the 'standard' route from near Isortoq/Nagtivit on the East Coast to 'Point 660' on the west side. It was at this point that the seed of an idea began to grow and my next polar objective began to take shape.

The record had not been beaten for some years and it was not really something that had appeared on my radar until then. I am a firm believer in the journey being everything for an expedition, not the subtext of who does it or why. I admit to finding teams who side-line their actual route and instead concentrate on the age, gender or medical history of the team a little tiresome and perhaps even irrelevant. This often occurs when the reality dawns on an expedition that their geographical intentions are highly unoriginal or not challenging enough to garner press attention without an extra media hook. These are steps backwards in my view, not forwards.

Speed could certainly be seen as fitting into one of these targets of questionable value. As our conversation continued, however, the pure athletic challenge of travelling faster grew on me. After all, the basis of it was not all that different to trying to ski **further**, where speed means far less as an end in itself. I had reservations about skiing the accepted route, one of 'only' 350 miles and over ice that was not untrodden. In order to compare speeds, though, it had to be this way and the appeal grew, mainly in terms of the opportunity to improve systems and routines, which are universally vital on all my expeditions.

Matt wondered whether the staggeringly fast record of eight days and nine hours to cover the 350 miles, set in 2002, could be done without sledges at all, just using a rucksack. My opinion was very strongly in opposition to this theoretically faster tactic. When George and I had been scheming our lightning fast dash to the West Coast and back to begin our return leg in 2008, we had pondered this exact question. At what point does it become faster to ski with a rucksack instead of a sledge? Sledges were designed for a reason: as an energy-saving method of transporting large loads over snow. When light enough, they glide and more critically, take much of the weight off the feet of the hauler, allowing them to ski more fluidly and with greater speed. Skiing with an enormous rucksack, albeit without a sledge, is a laborious, painful and ungainly affair. Since a 350-mile crossing of an ice sheet is a long way beyond taking a daysack with you on a weekend hill walk, I felt sledges were still the way to go.

After our return from the snowy peaks and valleys of Norway, I let the matter of the speed record drop as I had more elaborate plans afoot for expeditions in the vicinity of the two Poles. I was conscious of the fact that my original plans in the mid-2000s were, in fact, not for expeditions in Greenland, the second largest ice sheet on Earth. 'The Long Haul' was the lucky product of a number of other projects, which had to be delayed due to funding shortfalls. As such, and perhaps one of the reasons why I initially shelved the speed-crossing concept was because of a reluctance to be typecast as a Greenland expedition leader, as opposed to a polar traveller.

The financial constraints showed no signs of abating and I knew I simply had to get on the ice. Having rationalised the situation and the opportunities I had in my own head, I dusted off the notes and calculations I had made after the Norway training week and fixed my eyes on speed.

The calibre of those who had previously held the speed record was fearsome and the project was as far from a 'consolation project' as you could imagine. World-famous Norwegian, Sjur Mørdre and a stable of some of the other finest Scandinavian long distance skiers had previously held the record. Even in the 1990s, when interest had only just begun to build, the first expedition across my proposed route with speed as its main aim was over twice as fast as 'normal' for experienced and capable skiers which is twenty-five to thirty-five days, weather dependent.

Having fixed on the goal, I then focused on the detail. It had always been a real shame in my eyes that I had not been able to embark on a fully-fledged expedition with Andrew 'Wilki' Wilkinson. Having first met not long after my sixteenth birthday in 2002, on a Royal Marines selection course, we had hatched a number of polar plans. Despite being one of the four-man team that had worked together for nearly four years to make the 'Journey South 2007' a reality, it was not to be. After our likely source of funding fell through late in the day at the advent of the global credit crisis, our timings slipped and the three older members of the team had to defer to the commitments of work and family.

Now, to my delight and having switched careers from serving as an officer in a unit associated with the Royal Marines to teaching modern languages at a Berkshire boarding school, Wilki agreed to work with me on the project. His mountaineering exploits had continued to grow since his summit of Everest as part of an independent team in 2007. Aside from climbing highly technical rock routes with, amongst others, Matt Spenceley, he had completed the large bulk of a route on K2 before pneumonia forced him to retreat. I could tell this disappointment had fired him up even more than ever for another big trip.

Weather was always going to be a critical component of our attempt to cross the icecap at speed. All previous fast crossings had been undertaken in the post-summer months of August and September. Greenland and indeed all regions of the polar world fail to conform to temperate ideas of the four seasons. In the case of this, the second largest ice sheet on Earth, winter sets in with a vengeance in December, the sea ice slowly forming on the fjords and then drifting out to sea. The coastal mountains and the icecap itself accumulates a thick snow blanket. When the days lengthen in the new year, spring arrives in March; shortly after this, the ice reaches its greatest extent. The warmth provides enough energy for a gradual breakup to begin. Regardless, March through to the first days of May remain the golden time for travel, with enough sun to illuminate a full day of skiing, hauling or dog sledding and with the most consolidated and reliable ice to travel and camp on.

A typically and increasingly early summer is bad news for polar expeditioners. The sea ice breaks, the crevasse snow bridges thin and collapse and a network of deadly, fast flowing melt streams, resembling the veins on a giant leaf, covers the coastal areas. The summer is defined by the weeks before and after the 21st June solstice and afterwards, as the days shorten, conditions rapidly cool again. This means that summer expeditions, few though they are in number, are over by the end of July.

August brings with it the signs of changes to come and the melt actually reduces, gradually leaving the icecap scarred by vast swathes of open crevassing and drying melt-systems. The scale of this annual event is too breathtaking for words. Water still flows in vast quantities, mostly into the deep bellies of crevasses or their more sinister cousins, moulins. These monsters are vertical sinkhole shafts which can drop a mile or more to the bottom of the icecap, allowing the melt water to escape, then lubricating the mobile icecap on the rocky ground far below. Moulins occur very suddenly and the only warning when travelling at ground level is a crescendo in the roar of water flowing beyond a particular mound of ice.

The cooling season, beginning in August, intensifies into October and November. The temperature drops and storms become more common as the gradient of temperature between night and day becomes more pronounced. Given all this, speed crossings where every second is vital and efficiency is everything, have tended to be attempted in that post-summer cool down. Melt becomes less pronounced, weather is as predictable and settled as can be hoped for and the surface tends to be at its flattest and most sastrugi-free due to the time elapsed since the last major snows fell.

Across this accepted standard route, the one that I was so uneasy about conforming with, there also used to be a magic bonus, which aided the early fast times that became the modern benchmark. Bizarrely for a place as barren and hostile as the icecap region of the greatest area of permanent ice in the northern hemisphere, Skanska worked in tandem with Volkswagen for a few years after the millennium to create the 'Aurora' ice road on which they could test vehicles. Due to the permanent movement of the very active Russell Glacier, this ice road required endless labour. It is an area of heavily crevassed ice, flowing at speed from the icecap towards the sea or lowlands and approaching 'Point 660', the west coast start or finish point of a crossing. In order to drive vehicles on the glacier, the crevasses had to be filled in with snow and the worst of the solid ice humps smoothed out. As soon as this was achieved for the miles of route snaking its way east, the ice would move and undo all the work. This meant that the road had to be maintained from scratch each year, at great cost, and only a few months after its creation it would be destroyed by the might of nature.

Luckily for some of those early teams, the expedition season meshed very neatly with the ice road season and so they could expect a helping hand through this glaciated region which is notorious for being the most frustrating and dangerous on the route. Alas, and unsurprisingly, the sheer hassle and cost of the ice road meant it was abandoned in 2005. Volkswagen's original plans had been for a hundred-mile ice road onto the icecap where a semi-permanent base would be built for staff. From various reports and the evidence left, only rickety huts along the route were ever created and the general feeling about the project was one of dismay and that it represented a desecration of the pristine polar environment. The ice road crumbled over the subsequent years and the last evidence of its existence is now long gone. It does, however, due to the lack of public information of its former whereabouts and even its existence, now hold something of a mystical status amongst expeditioners, almost like the yellow brick road.

The only significance of this was that we knew most of the fastest crossings, and indeed the record, had taken place when the ice road was of use. The Russell Glacier, being far more unpredictable than the Nagtivit Glacier on the east side of the icecap, was the crux on which most expeditions succeeded or failed. We knew that the pure crossing, using only route-finding skill and a ladle-load of nerve, would be a tall order if the record were to fall. Also, times had changed and the acceptable crossing season, due to melt and weather changes, no longer ran from March until September. Post-2008 expeditions now, essentially, had to choose to go pre-melt or post-melt. This meant March and April or August and early September; there was not a great deal of choice or room to spare!

Simply put, the spring window meant fairly flat glacier surfaces with thick snow, high winds and cold temperatures, often down below thirty degrees below zero. The after-summer window meant open crevasses, residual melt water but milder temperatures and a faster, flatter plateau. It was a trade off and most previous teams had opted for the latter or the in between months of June and July when it had been feasible. The time of the year when I would make my attempt was decided by two crucial factors; firstly, when I thought we would have the best chance of success and secondly, when I would be able to secure the time of a top quality teammate. This brings us back to Wilki and following his career shift, we found a spare slot in the spring season around late April. The call had been made; take the risk of storms and deep snow in return for reduced melt and flattish glaciers.

CHAPTER TWO

It was wonderful to be able to immerse myself fully in expeditions once more. Aside from the endless emails and phone calls which allow the potential of the project to come to life, the most energising part is without doubt sourcing the equipment, testing, modifying and making a slick, lightweight system. We could not have picked an expedition more at odds with 'The Long Haul' with respect to equipment. Really, the only similarities were that we would be on skis and on an icecap. Everything else had to change. Besides, I had learned a lot of lessons since 2008 both the hard way and also by thinking through problems laterally. This satisfied my desire to buck what I saw as the trend for self-styled, 'innovative explorers' to behave like sheep and copy previous expeditions in every aspect – route, clothing and even rhetoric.

The key to success on a speed crossing is to streamline every system that leads to pace whilst not compromising on the fundamentals that ensure survival. Basically, this means having a skiing and hauling system, shelter and sleeping plan, and nutrition. Get these right and you are in with a fighting chance. The truth was then, and is now, that you do not ski three times as fast as a competent, 'normal' crossing expedition by accident. Every act must be deliberate and optimised. Whilst Wilki concentrated on other aspects of the planning, I broke down my own accepted polar routine into pieces and built it up again to suit a highly athletic, all-or-nothing expedition. Throughout, I studied the reports and articles written by those super-speedy Scandinavians who preceded us.

Instead of 5,600kcal per day, which had staved off life-threatening weight-loss until the final week of 'The Long Haul', I settled on 8,600kcal. It was, in fact, vastly less energy than we anticipated burning as we skied each day. As what we hoped would be a sub-nine-day expedition, weight loss was not a primary

25

concern – pace combined with endurance was. Weight of food no longer had to conform to the brutal one kilogram per person per day limit we had in 2008. But equally, taking 12,000kcal per day would be a total waste since a body unused to such an onslaught cannot effectively absorb so much.

Nutrition and human physiology plays an enormous part in the preparation of any athlete, whether for polar travel or a conventional sport. I had learned a great deal from my biological studies at university and so, with the input of experts in the field, took a keen interest in making sure that up-to-date thinking benefitted my team and that what we found out through experience could be channelled back.

•

Science and expeditions have an uneasy relationship. The earliest expeditions often integrated cartography, biology and meteorology, amongst many other disciplines, in a time when large gaps in knowledge existed. This attracted patronage but, as now, could serve to divide motivations. Often geographical ambitions could frustrate an expedition scientist and the need to haul heavy rock samples in some cases contributed to slow progress and even the deaths of sledging parties.

Today, scientific expeditions are fairly distinct from exploratory ventures. They have large logistic support from ships and aircraft to rely on and attract central government or private funding which independents can only dream of. There is a habit of trying to 'tack on' a dubious scientific message to a brochure in order to generate sympathy and more funding but the outcomes are usually academically lightweight or so flawed that the data is useless.

It is regrettable that so often the wool is pulled over the eyes of the public, the media who feed them information and those who stump up the cash for these pseudo-scientific adventure holidays. It is not possible to push boundaries physically whilst undertaking meaningful science – they are mutually exclusive and there should be a time and place for both in isolation from each other.

It reminds me of the political world where clearly impossible or devious statements are issued in the hope that those on the receiving end are too lazy or incapable to notice. As in the tiny expedition world, where inexplicable attempts are made at both ends of the spectrum, the same dystopian positions are peddled by the political left and right – the former living in a dream world and the latter in a miserable one. Moderation and reason are the solution in both arenas.

•

Besides the food, which would comprise nearly one and a half kilos of flapjack per day plus salami, cheese, butter and freeze-dried food, our normal shared and personal equipment would be kept to a minimum. Once it was collated and each item confirmed as being vital, it was to be loaded into perhaps the most significant part of the ensemble, the sledges. Whilst by no means a brand-new tactic, our speed on the crucial 280-mile mid-section of the icecap needed a low-friction sledge. We decided on lightweight and flexible plastic sledges from Snowsled (Roger Daynes had previously made our enormous sledges for 'The Long Haul') which were as light as physically possible, but also available in small sizes for short expeditions.

The sledge undersides were still flat, apart from the shallow runners and therefore, had a large surface area which would drag on the snowy surface. To limit this, I decided to raise the whole sledge up on skis. This would hopefully give us an injection of speed and fatigue our bodies a little more slowly. The major challenge was manufacturing such a thing – not an off-the-shelf product by any means. The skis and frame would need to be removable in order to allow us to tackle the rough, glaciated ice on both coasts where even the most robust undercarriage would be ripped apart within minutes. Using initiative, some prototypes and the decades of engineering experience my father had amassed, we finally had a sledge on skis; the aluminium frame mounted two children's cross-country skis underneath, with nut and bolt attachments to the sledge underside.

All that was left to do, with the technicalities resolved and kit packed, was to have a send-off with our friends, family and supporters. Although the time had flown by, it had been a few weeks over three years since I had embarked on a 'career expedition', i.e. not a trip as a guide or purely for training: an expedition that would be opened-up to an audience and the outcome of which would form part of the evidence by which I would be judged by both my contemporaries and the wider community. With that comes a little more pressure and it almost inevitably involves an event of some sort prior to setting off.

I love parties, but I loathe organising them. The complexities, unknowns and often-unreliable professional partners may sound like a story about organising expeditions. Launch parties, by contrast and in my experience, have an unfortunate habit of eating up much of the vital time set aside for preparing for the actual journey and can grow into unwieldy behemoths in their own right. For this reason, my respect for the ease with which Tina Fotherby had run our press launch for 'The Long Haul' predecessor, 'Journey South 2007', was even further heightened. That launch was a calm, serene swan of an event with furious paddling beneath the surface.

In response to this, I had decided to go for a lower-key event for the upcoming expedition, in a private gallery above the centuries-old 'Cross Keys' pub in London's Chelsea, not far from the Thames and only a ten-minute stroll over the bridge from my flat. The organisation was reasonably smooth and the event began well as guests arrived and mingled; there were a mixture of friends and family, both Wilki's and mine, our business contacts and those of my assistant, Carmen. It became clear before long, however, that even with a vastly simplified menu to ease stress on the kitchen, orders became backed up to around a ninety-minute delay; all was not well.

The sting in the tail for the evening luckily occurred after most guests had begun to head homewards. As the events manager beckoned me over to the bar to wrap up the evening, I was informed that a charge of a thousand pounds would be applied to my credit card to cover the shortfall in spending for the party, which had a minimum spend. According to him, with a likely motivation I do not need to spell out, the guests had bought, on average, less than a pint of beer each over more than five hours, during which time most ordered food – a highly improbable situation as most would agree and not what my guests' handfuls of receipts suggested. Weeks of dialogue ensued which resulted mostly in my being squarely fobbed off with a rather smug set of responses from the 'Cross Keys' before escalation towards legal action became my only option. Rather predictably, shortly before I took the legal plunge, the pub made an offer of settlement and the matter closed. My run of luck, or rather bad luck, with expedition events was unabated.

Tellingly and perhaps as a signal of why the bizarre behaviour had occurred in the first place, the manager was no longer in his post a few weeks later. Not too long after, the pub was closed with annual debts of hundreds of thousands, a matter which was widely reported in the local press. I was torn; the 'Cross Keys' was overflowing with history and character and had been a regular haunt with a former girlfriend. On the other hand, I could not help but feel a slight sense of satisfaction that the greed and indifferent arrogance of a few individuals had not prevailed. At any rate, a line was drawn and we were able to get on with more important matters and mercifully, the vast majority of guests was never aware of any of the conflict.

All set, ready and trained to the maximum, Wilki and I flew to the now-familiar Greenlandic East Coast at the end of the first week of April 2011. Weather delays are part of life in the Arctic, especially if you wish to fly anywhere, and I had always remembered the words of a local Inuit man who was about to exit the plane onto the snowy runway outside. A small group of wealthy tourists, who had decided to visit this frontier corner of the world, were jostling to be the first to the steps, like a scene more fitting to JFK airport in New York. The man quietly and calmly said, in unusually good English (English is taught, at best, as a third language in Greenland, after their local Greenlandic dialect and Danish), 'Welcome to Greenland my friends. Your impatience will get you nowhere here. Things happen at the speed they are meant to.' The hectic pushing stopped at once and the group stepped onto the slippery ground with faces like naughty schoolchildren.

This lesson was to take on an enormous significance for Wilki, myself and another couple of groups over the upcoming weeks. Although I had become accustomed to having to be patient with the weather, not something that comes naturally to me or to the helicopters that are slaves to it, there are limits.

After a twenty-minute helicopter shuttle to Tasiilaq, the larger settlement in the area and where we would base ourselves until the big 'off', the usually wide smile of the Tyrolean, Robert Peroni, who met us, had been replaced with a knowing glumness. Robert had become a regular part of my travels in the Greenlandic Arctic; he has been living there for over thirty years, following a career as a mountaineer. He had proved to be a man equally capable of both incredible knowledge and kindness and also of a somewhat vague and comedic personality. What was never in doubt, however, was his honesty and Robert did not look happy. He runs a guesthouse in the village which, whilst basic, serves as a welcoming hub for expeditions and visitors from around the world. As he drove us up the steep, icy hill from the helipad to his guesthouse in his somewhat tired Land Rover Defender, he explained that they had been engulfed with a persistent low-pressure system, which showed no signs of moving on.

Our helicopter shuttle came as a surprise to him as flights had been out of the question for days, paralysing the inter-village flow of local Greenlanders. Wilki and I relied on that one helicopter to fly our charter across the fjords to our start point, the Nagtivit Glacier and we soon realised we were not alone. An Italian expedition had been waiting for a week and a photographer and his assistant a similar time. The atmosphere was despondent as each day lost meant less chance of a successful trip – for the Italians to cross the icecap and for Murray Fredericks, the photographer, to capture his images. It also meant an ever-increasing bill to be paid. Greenland is not cheap; everything from the local and imported food to the hot water costs dearly.

What followed was twenty days of thumb-twiddling, hopeful weather-forecast checks, overpriced wine-drinking and ski-mountaineering trips into the beautiful coastline surrounding Tasiilaq to get our frustrated muscles working. It did not escape me that this existence for twenty days would have been seen by many, or even most, to be nigh on perfection for an adventurous holiday. Our expectations were different, however, and the time passed slowly, like purgatory.

Finally, it became apparent that we had run out of time for two reasons. Wilki had a day job to get back to and the date was approaching by which we could not be sure of getting him home in time for this. Secondly and more seriously, a late April start would have meant the West Coast would have had too much time to melt in the near twenty-four hour sun and would be a maze of melt rivers and vertical ice dead-ends by early May.

In the meantime, expedition permits in Greenland were becoming a headache. The Greenland expeditions office, which, since 'The Long Haul', had taken over responsibility for expedition permits from the Danish Polar Centre, has been changing its rules on permits almost each successive year to keep up with the ever-changing nature of the icecap. Their motivation is, understandably, to limit the number of dangerous rescue missions launched should a team get into difficulty. In 2011, permit holders after mid-May would be required to show proof, a bank guarantee, that they could cover the cost of a rescue mission not covered under the terms on their insurance. From 2012 onwards this bond is required for all permits at any time of year. There had evidently been, as I heard from the helicopter charter team and the expeditions office, a number of expensive air evacuations by people who had simply 'given up' on their expeditions when they found the demands of the icecap too great. With their insurance refusing to pay up with no obvious medical cause for abandonment, the cost was being met by the government; this is clearly not an ethical situation.

I have written extensively over the past few years about the dramatic reduction in the availability of expedition insurance and the strict terms on which it is now granted, largely due to this rampant increase in claims by novice teams who find themselves out of their depth. This was tragically illustrated in the 2013 spring season. Completely on the side of the insurance companies, I have long suggested that permits should be more difficult to attain and that people should take more responsibility for their decisions.

This would lead to insurers regaining confidence that expeditions are lower risk than at present.

This nervousness has rolled over into the process of getting permits, closely linked to insurance, as you cannot have one without the other. Large fees are now charged for permits to discourage time-wasting or the uncommitted and the bonds are charged for the time of the year when melting is a high risk. Recently though, frostbite suffered by teams early in the spring of 2011 has led to the start time for expeditions moving from 1st April to 15th April. To my mind this is a major error as it pushes teams further towards the melt season and an expedition should not set off if it is not prepared for storms with temperatures below minus thirty-five degrees. I advocate going early instead of late; cold is better than melt.

I have been in dialogue with the Greenland office about this and hope that there will be flexibility as the dust settles and things calm. The main insurers for Greenland expeditions already request one team member has previous experience of a crossing or highly similar experience elsewhere. I think this is very sensible and that they, and the expedition office could go even further, placing constraints and steeper premiums on novice teams and then offering 'no claims' deals with more relaxed time-windows for those proven to be self-reliant and experienced. The icecap is not a playground and it will continue to kill the underprepared, just as Mont Blanc does in the Alps.

Permit issues aside, the upshot of our spring attempt was that Wilki and I had to return home to England, expedition-less and feeling very sad. We were fit, focused and raring to go but one of the inescapable facets of the Arctic had not even allowed us to begin. To rub salt into the wound, the day of our flight to Iceland, my birthday, was blue and sunny without a breath of wind. It was perfect for an insertion flight to the glacier. However, our chance was over for the time being at least.

A few months later, already planning a 'take two' for the speed record attempt and with a raft of equipment tweaks we decided on our new expedition dates. Our insurers, who were understanding and brilliant throughout, agreed to defer our insurance to later in the year with no additional premium.

After yet another debate with ourselves and after re-researching the data collected prior to the initial spring attempt, we reasoned that whilst the spring was probably the optimum time of year post-2010 to make a fast crossing, we could still have a serious crack at the sub-nine day record in summer. We set a provisional launch date of 10th August, strictly post-summer and actually some way into the looming pre-winter season. This could only be a good thing as the melt lakes and streams would, hopefully, begin to empty and freeze up, hardening to a point at which they could be negotiated quickly on skis. What was certain, though, was that the icescape left behind after the summer-melt would be scarred, tortured and mangled like a battlefield.

Expeditions had to be complete by mid-September to comply with the permit. This was not a particular bother, though, since storms tend to begin to build as the winter approaches and these would instantly ruin the advantage of stable polar high pressure typical in the summer. Early was best, although not too early – a difficult balancing act and one that could not be predicted. We would either get it right or we would be caught out.

My last memory of Greenland in the summer was dazed and confused following 'The Long Haul' expedition. George and I had walked like ghosts around the village of Tasiilaq, taking in the thoroughly unfamiliar sights of people, bright colours and plentiful food. Apart from the remarkable lack of snow and open fjords which contrasted with the white landscape and solid sea ice of the months before we set off, it was warm enough not to wear a down jacket and if you let your guard down for a second, a swarm of midges would descend. Without doubt it was less picturesque than during the cold months but it was not this slim halo of mountains and settlements we were aiming for; we had our sights set, once again, on the vast expanse of icecap within.

A bizarre thought as we flew over the loose pack ice was that my own perspective of scale had shifted; this 350-mile crossing seemed almost bite-size compared to the near 700-mile route we forged in 2008. I banished the dangerous idea immediately, for although the shorter route is considered 'standard', it is highly technical in areas when tackled out of season. This distance in absolute terms is also highly demanding, regardless of past yardsticks.

The route was, in fact, the same as the one I guided fit and switched-on but still novice clients across the year before, but needless to say, it was to be made infinitely more dangerous and daunting by the remorseless time limits we set ourselves. Decisions would need to be made fast and under pressure and our minds and bodies would fatigue at a rate neither of us had experienced before, despite both having endured some of the most unrelenting military courses in existence. Still, it was what we desired. We were both highly motivated by the chase against the clock – for myself as an important show of skill for my growing polar CV and for Wilki mostly because a crossing at standard pace would not have presented a sufficient challenge.

This time we took the helicopter out of the equation, both to reduce costs and the risk of another false start. Fjords were navigable by boat in August and had been since early summer so we took advantage of the situation. Lars, a local hunter whom I had met a few times previously, ferried us and our equipment from Kulusuk to Tasiilaq, expertly weaving his small glass-fibre boat through the floating remnants of sea ice. As the boat slowed and then sped up, flicking left and right through the rock-hard maze of ice, I watched the waves caused by the engine wash up against it with its endless shapes and colours. It was almost hypnotic and my passion for the place was instantly reignited. Enormously keen to spread my net wide across the frozen regions of the world, Greenland as my 'first' would always be that little bit special.

The sea fog closed in slightly despite beautiful blue skies visible above and Lars, having travelled the route countless times, navigated mostly blind on pure memory. He knew exactly when to err left or right to avoid rocks just under the surface and when to move further out to sea in order to take advantage of clearer ice-free water.

We arrived at our launch point of Tasiilaq. Much of our equipment had been left in storage here since the spring, but after lugging the additional supplies up the steep rocky shore, we went to fetch a Land Rover from Robert Peroni, passing an enormous vertebra bone on the ground, most likely from a minke whale.

Mercifully, our stay in Tasiilaq lasted only long enough to check that our food and equipment had survived storage and soon we were nearing the hour agreed with Lars to meet again on the shoreline and begin our journey. It would have made sense to travel straight from Kulusuk, where the aircraft lands, to our glacial start point at Nagtivit. The route would have been slightly shorter and more direct than going via Tasiilaq but we had gear to collect and the direct line would have involved a riskier path further out to sea.

In keeping with the practical and refreshingly independent way in which even the modern Inuit live, there were no lifejackets or health and safety notices. GPS and radio were installed, but if we had the misfortune to get ourselves into trouble, the situation could become fatal without any warning.

The ice concentrations in the sea change daily and are dependent on the wind and the currents. One day the fjords could be choked up with ice and the coastal waters clear and then the next day the opposite. As it happened for us, the reasonably clear waters near the settlements were left behind as we motored at speed to the west. Soon, instead of rushing along with the wind in our hair, we were weaving our way through dense sea ice in low visibility. Regularly, we would reach a dead end and would need to retreat in order to try another way. Other times, a confident bump of a small ice chunk with the bow of the boat would create a way through, although the resounding booms these collisions made through the hull were more than a little unsettling.

Whilst the majority of the barriers in the way were the remaining survivors of the sea ice from the previous winter, their fresh-water big brothers were also around every turn: icebergs. These calve off from the numerous glaciers that protrude into the sea between the jagged mountains and high cliffs. As we rounded the final headland before making straight for the glacier, the fog miraculously cleared within seconds, leaving an azure blue sea under clear skies. The sheer scale of icebergs never fails to astound, no matter how familiar a sight they are. Some were half a mile in length, the height of a cathedral and in every shape imaginable.

Wilki and I were scanning the horizon for the glacier snout, something I had only ever previously seen in the spring when the sea was frozen and the glacier hard to distinguish from the white landscape. Lars, evidently, was not; he called out enthusiastically that he had spotted something. Both Wilki and I span round to see what was of such interest to Lars and immediately spotted a large fountain of water being blown ten feet clear of the water, only a few boat lengths away. What followed was the silent and graceful movement of a minke whale as it swam behind us. This was by far the closest encounter I had ever had with a great whale and it was hard not to be thoroughly awe-struck.

Again and again the whale would break the surface of the calm sea, exhale forcefully with a loud puff and then slide smoothly back beneath the water. Lars was not on the water that day to hunt, despite the seal-hooks and pools of blood on the cabin floor, which were a permanent reminder of his main occupation. It was obvious by his gestures and intent study of the movement of the whale that he saw it in a different light to us. It was a source of food, resources and income for him and on another day would have become his quarry.

•

All of a sudden I felt a rush of naïve inadequacy – it struck me I had an entirely different outlook to the people I respected most in this environment. My greatest desire from the first days of my polar career was to distance myself from the cosseted Western lifestyle and make conscious decisions to integrate and learn from the local people of the Polar Regions, rather than be the perpetual fish out of water in the cold places of the world. At this moment I felt a thousand miles away from Lars, Georg Utuaq and the others I had come to know and enjoy the companionship of over the years. Our minds worked in different ways and this was an added impetus for me to listen and learn more than ever before. I suppose at the core of this desire to integrate (as much as is possible for a nonresident) was not a desire to be 'at one' with anything or any such sentimental or spiritual concepts, but to be divorced in action, not just in my own mind, from those who have given the British a bad name.

It is a sad fact that the British are the first to be ridiculed in many of the polar and Nordic countries, where living off the land, ice and wildlife or at least existing with relative comfort in a snow-covered setting is normal. Our colonial past means that over the centuries the British, and to a lesser extent other nations under-qualified in all things cold, have often steam-rolled their way into situations they cannot deal with, usually woefully underprepared and lacking almost every skill necessary. In exploration history, there seemed to be an inexplicable confidence that simply coming from a particular country was strength in itself. A relish for unnecessary suffering and even a pride in incompetence seemed de rigour. Often, this ended in tragedy not only for those wilfully employed, but also for the locals who were forced to support large, siege-like expeditions. This says nothing of the regularly conquest-hungry behaviour and downright abuse of native people by some men on early expeditions, which is an eternal shame on our countries. These episodes, decades or even centuries ago, should, to all intents and purposes, be left where they belong – in the past. Life moves on and we should not be held responsible for the behaviour of our ancestors. However, this expansionist arrogance and practical incompetence typical of the old imperial nations, Great Britain at the forefront, has left an ugly legacy.

For our part, there is still a ferocious British hunger for adventure by travellers. The media and the public often have an unquenchable relish for some sort of perceived historical and innate superiority. Let us be clear, save for residents/natives of a few select nations on Earth, the ability to travel efficiently and safely in the cold regions has to be learnt. We have no natural talent for it and what is left of our ancient survival instinct and intuitive resourcefulness is quickly extinguished by our soft and comfortable formative years with central heating and packaged food. On the flip side, there is a sad relish amongst a few other groups around the world to beat us now with the same stick that should have been reserved for those who behaved badly in the past. The danger is that the few ensure that the remainder continue to be tarred with this brush. What results is a stalemate, with British expeditions coming up against an automatic barrier of scepticism from abroad but equally, many actually conform to the stereotype and reinforce it. How do we move on from this?

My message to those in the expedition community, myself included, and to those who wish to understand more about us is: I believe there is a clear and present danger in Great Britain, and perhaps in other countries, that the exploration or high-end expedition community is at breaking point. It is true in my mind, and other people's that the scramble for funding and profile in this country in particular and the resultant massive over-supply of announcements of near-identical ventures, most of which never occur, will cause the very foundations to crumble. In short, the noise we are making vastly overshadows and drowns out the actual quantity of meaningful, novel and progressive endeavour we are currently bringing to bear. The internet and the ease with which a project with zero basis can appear credible may explain this rise, but it is the person not the machine to blame here.

A stark example is the minor scandal caused online in 2012 by novice Brit, Tim Williamson announcing a vast solo expedition from Resolute Bay to the North Pole and back, without a tent or skis. This was not an April Fool's joke and he even netted a sponsor, until this sponsor called me out of the blue to ask for a reality-check and just days afterwards, the expedition website was quietly retired. In response to the torrent of righteous derision he received from the outdoor community, his responses were blinded by a misplaced confidence. 'Just let me run!' he pleaded. Even if he were the most astounding athlete and ice-craft expert on Earth, which he was not, the most generous estimates would give him four or five days before perishing. It was another own goal by a British dreamer and scorn poured across onto our shores from other nations.

It is not just the British though, with an American team claiming in 2012 to have rowed across the Arctic Ocean – a physical impossibility at present. Their original plans involved a route across the North Atlantic, in no way an Arctic Ocean route, and after widespread criticism and a long phone conversation I had with their leader, they instead rowed along the Alaskan coast. Despite this equally non-Arctic Ocean crossing route, they again claimed to have 'rowed across the Arctic Ocean'.

I would endorse a voluntary policy of not announcing an expedition until it is funded and confirmed. In other theatres of life this is normal. It is unlikely a Hollywood movie would be launched and promoted until the backing has been secured. I got this wrong in my early youth, announcing my South Pole plans before we got a sponsor's signature and the result was both embarrassing and unhelpful for all. I think a new, common-sense approach might do something to temper the rise of baseless plans that are simply background noise and distracting for those inside and outside the trade.

Soon, if there is not a certain amount of self-restraint, expectation management and honesty injected into the community, we run the risk of losing what we love. The experiences that we are privileged to enjoy and learn from may be denied to us by those we rely on: the sources of funding, the media and public good will. Their patience is being tested.

•

The whale proceeded to travel along with us for some time. Wilki and I took the opportunity to take some photographs and record some footage, forever guessing where this majestic giant would surface next. Wilki exclaimed, 'I simply can't believe something that big can survive in such a bleak and freezing place! I'm blown away, totally blown away.'

At the very moment we were discussing whether we should start moving towards the glacier again, the clock was ticking after all and we wanted to make progress before the sun set and visibility reduced, the whale took its cue. In a sight made famous by nature documentaries and against the backdrop of the sea, icebergs, rocky cliffs and blue sky, the minke whale began its dive, bringing its entire fluke clear of the water. It seemed almost like slow motion, deliberate and with immense power. Our encounter was over.

Any trepidation that had built up over the past few hours had been instantly dissolved by the unexpected meeting and so, tension-free, we motored through the ice-free waters straight towards the Nagtivit Glacier. As we rounded the final corner, there it was. It was enormous in bulk and height, rising steeply from the ocean with twenty or thirty foot cliffs. The advantage of our drop off point at the south-eastern corner of the glacier was that a large 'beach' of moraine and loose rock was accessible by boat and a smooth ice slope then led onto the glacier. I had used this access point twice before, but both times in the spring when all was shrouded in deep snow.

With a bump, we touched the edge of the glacier with the bow of the boat and Wilki leapt ashore as I stood on the side of the boat. Lars began to pass our sledges, skis and rucksacks to us. I was taken aback by the sheer lack of bulk we had. I was so used to having to use three or four people to lift a sledge, but this journey was to be very different. We had only nine days of food each, totalling 8,600kcal per day each in freeze-dried packets, flapjack, cheese, chocolate, nuts and salami. This left us with nigh on no contingency over and above the record of sub-nine days we sought. We did, however, know that this vast daily intake could be made to spread across more days if need be. Instead of the target of one kilogram I had previously aimed for with a day's rations, we had well over double that per day. This was the price we were to pay for the mammoth daily distance targets and therefore, the energy required to stay fuelled.

Speed across the ice was critical and we had managed to keep our sledge weights around forty kilos per piece plus our light rucksacks. As ever, we needed everything from sleeping and cooking equipment to satellite phones and emergency beacons, except this time we took a little less spare than in times past. Failure of equipment would rely on our resourcefulness rather than on replacement.

Before we bade Lars farewell and let him commit himself to the vulnerable journey back through the sea ice to Kulusuk alone, we scoured the floor of the boat in case an item had fallen from a sledge. This reassuring double-check occurs before setting off anywhere and has long been known as the 'idiot check'. I have heard stories about less thorough expeditions forgetting crucial items, even skis – what an embarrassing end to an expedition that would be!

A quick 'team photo' of the three of us later and soon Lars was powering away towards the horizon with the wash from his large outboard engine creating waves that lapped against the shore. As is normal procedure on polar expeditions in polar bear territory, even if just for a few hours, we quickly test-fired our single-barrel shotgun and then loaded our sledges for the first push. We were only at risk until we were a few miles onto the ice, away from the coast, but the precaution was in place.

We were acutely aware of the fact that, unlike in the past, we were not against the clock only in terms of running out of supplies, but also against the target time of eight days and nine hours. Never before had I had to make an exact note of the time we set off and confirm this via satellite phone to mark the official start of our bid.

CHAPTER THREE

Hauling such a light sledge was a revelation. It is very hard to try and describe the sensation of hauling a sledge of various weights to a newcomer, largely because there are few 'real-world' equivalents. What is for sure is that talk of sledge hauling produces some of the most regularly exaggerated expedition facts and figures.

Just one example was the much-hyped *On Thin Ice* reality TV show with Ben Fogle, James Cracknell and relatively unknown, Ed Coats, who was shown to be the capable member of the team. The publicity blurb claimed, in Herculean language, that the team would have to haul seventy-kilo pulks for hundreds of gruelling miles. This accompanied wince-inducing claims about rewriting Antarctic history with regards to the British-Norwegian rivalry and 'conquering the Antarctic'. What they failed to mention was that pulling a sledge of that weight on a compacted Antarctic plateau requires only a moderate effort. It sounds a lot, the same as a small but fully-grown man, but does not take into account the energy-saving effect that a sledge offers. The weight is not taken through the back, hips and legs like a rucksack and so, to a certain extent, the body is saved.

In reality, the difficulty of sledge hauling is controlled by a whole number of factors; these include the amount of snow, the gradient of the slope, the amount of sastrugi (hard wind-formed ridges of snow), the type of sledge runners and of course, the weight of the load having to be hauled. Deep, soft snow will slow progress and sap the energy of a skier terribly. When temperatures dip towards thirty and forty degrees below, the sledge runners no longer melt the surface of the snow with friction and it feels like an anchor is being dragged behind. Sastrugi end any hope of building up a rhythm or any momentum as the sledge must be yanked up onto a ridge and then avoided as it careers, with a mind of its own, down the other side. Some sledges have tall, high profile runners that are brilliant on hard, consolidated surfaces but carve deep channels in soft snow. Some have shallow, almost non-existent runners which glide nicely after heavy snow but waste energy when cold temperatures have formed a hard crust on the ice.

Far less subtle than these factors though and more easy to describe, hence their inclusion on most polar 'sales pitches', is that of weight. As a rule of thumb, on a typical icecap surface with a quality sledge, some snow cover, some sastrugi and a little gradient, it would go like this: forty kilos is barely noticeable, only resisting a little when pulled over a major bump; eighty kilos provides a fairly constant but gentle resistance but still allows the hauler to develop a strong glide and move well. Only when a sledge heads above the one hundred and twenty kilo mark is the strength of the skier fully tested. Glide becomes a thing of the past except in exceptional conditions. Sastrugi become actual barriers and it is best to find routes around them, instead of boldly smashing a way straight over. A load of this weight is where most scales would end, containing enough common supplies and personal food and fuel for forty or fifty days on the ice, plenty for the longest, 'standard' journeys on Earth.

Committed and extended expeditions, which go that step beyond, will need more. Sledges, or when these are full to the brim, a pair of sledges hauled in tandem, can then reach daunting bulks. In 2008, George and I hauled nearly two hundred kilos to begin 'The Long Haul', sufficient for 110 days and a good raft of spare equipment to guarantee self-reliance. Testing which I have done has shown that, contrary to the opinion of many, a tandem of sledges can be hauled near-sustainably by a highly trained skier with loads of two hundred and fifty or even three hundred kilos.

And so, back to our modest forty-kilo, plastic sledges with their optional ski fittings. We were at the beginning and so far so good. The excitement of actually getting moving after four months since the first launch attempt spurred us on with full force. Soon though, the surface began to break up. The late summer, months since any meaningful snows had fallen, is not a time for easy glacier travel. The flat, smooth shroud of snow from the winter and spring is gone and what is left is a traveller's nightmare: bumpy, hard, unstable and heavily fissured ice. The Nagtivit is a relatively free-flowing glacier and so the crevasses, which litter its length and width, are extensive and some are truly enormous.

It was hardly a surprise. We would hopefully enjoy the benefits of the season we had chosen once above the snowline and on the flatter plateau in the stability of the polar high pressure, typical in summer. The price to be paid was the slow, laborious and technical glacier climb. Critical for us was the point of this snowline, the elevation at which we would find the crevasses and melt channels filled with snow and level enough for fast travel. Robert Peroni had warned us the snowline might be at a thousand or fifteen hundred metres, much higher than usual.

Each hundred metres of elevation equalled miles of horizontal hauling and so Robert's prediction was not good news. We had to clear that twenty or more miles of mangled ice fast, within a day or a day and a half, if we were to have a chance at the record. In spring, the same glacier could be cleared in less than eight hours of hard work, with twice the sledge load. We hauled on.

The surface was complicated. The ice itself was rotten in parts and scarred with moraine, crunching and subsiding unexpectedly underfoot. Every three or four feet there was a trough, cut earlier in the season by melt water; these troughs did not just run in one direction but were often perpendicular, giving the effect of a sea of ice islands. Needless to say, this made movement tricky. The edge of each trough had to be clambered onto, sledge in tow, and invariably the sledge would then slide off into a gap and sometimes get jammed, needing a sharp lift and tug to release. Then, after thirty or forty climbs, jumps and scrambles, there would be a large crevasse which we would need to scan to find a crossing point or which required a much simpler, blind jump of faith. Clearly this was no place for skis and so both of us had our long cross-country skis and smaller sledge ski setup strapped to our backs.

The light was starting to fade, which made distance judgement harder, and we began not to notice some of the subtleties of the surface. Our route selection began to suffer. Contrary to the repetitive boredom of a large icecap plateau, glaciers are mentally draining, requiring total and constant concentration. In order to keep our footing on impossibly difficult ice we were always scanning the middle ground for the best new route and then keeping an eye on the distant ice to make sure we were not heading for trouble.

We had travelled for around sixteen hours straight in order to move in the cooler part of the day and miss out the dehydrating hours around midday; our body clocks were soon in chaos. We could have carried on hauling and scrambling and yanking our sledges across this battlefield of ice forever, as the lack of real darkness in this late-summer polar night did not provide any visual cues. I was the first to suggest we stopped for a brief pit stop. Wilki had always been the sort simply to continue working and moving as long as he was well fed. This was a very useful attribute but I knew beforehand that on most occasions I would have to be the one to call breaks. My main drive was sustainability and I knew I must try and find a happy medium between the need for breaks and this fundamentally unsustainable expedition which would require us to overreach our limits of stamina without collapsing before we reached the West.

Like every proud athlete, stopping or being the first to blink is a bitter pill to swallow. Wilki was formidable in the hills and although I was confident our fitness levels were on a par, his strengths would undoubtedly be on the glacier climb section. A mutual respect and lack of insecurity made the atmosphere one of optimism and good spirits as we both searched our little block of ice for a human-sized spot to lay our foam mats and sleeping bags on.

It may seem extraordinary to forgo tents on such a mighty icecap, where the weather changes in the blink of an eye, but time was always going to be tight. We resolved only to use the tent when absolutely necessary. When we had only put aside two hours per 'night' to sleep, half an hour to set up camp seemed an awful waste. It was a liberating experience and strangely satisfying simply to stop, lay out our sleeping arrangement, slip inside and keep our boots from freezing by wedging them between the sleeping bag and our mats. Placing our sledges in a protective chevron at our heads would break any wind fairly effectively.

Soon, we were on the move again. Made even worse by the tough working hours we had chosen for ourselves and the brevity of our rest, the process of clambering out of our warm, soft bags and into the cold was as trying as ever. I like a warm, comfortable sleep as much as anyone.

Our second session on the Nagtivit did not give us any more luck than before. The nature of the terrain developed and became more crevassed, with some still-active melt streams causing momentary headaches. Our break came as we finally spied the edge of the most tortured ice and a snowfield running towards our intended heading. In a brilliant moment when we felt we could really crack this, one of the big polar prizes, our skis came into their own and three hundred yards an hour became two miles per hour.

The Nagtivit runs more or less south to north and our overall route to cross the icecap was more like an east-north-east heading. This meant that at some point, we would need to curve round to the left, leaving the glacier behind and joining the plateau, ready to put in the long, fast and hard days. The question was, 'When?' The entire coastline was lined with glaciers pushing their way down towards the sea between jagged mountains and headlands. Be too impatient and curve round too early and we would ski straight into the upper crevasse zone of the next glacier along. Be too conservative and ski miles to the north before turning to the west and we would travel unnecessary miles, wasting precious time and our chance of going sub-eight days and nine hours.

The choice was essentially mine. The concepts and strategy for my expeditions were planned long in advance and the responsibility sat with me. Wilki was clearly comfortable leaving this side of the expedition to me and we had discussed it previously. His work commitments were fierce and besides, the theory and nitty-gritty of research, ice charts and the strategy were my job to get right.

As a glacier extends up to merge with the stable icecap itself (Greenland is, strictly speaking, an ice sheet and glaciers are simply a feature of its edge, but icecap is a neater term), the crevasses become gradually less frequent and smaller, since the forces ripping the ice apart are fewer. This is true with the exception of the last few crevasses, including the final bergschrund crevasse, which always marks the head of a glacier; they can be real monsters, over three hundred feet deep.

I had to strike a balance, assessing where these crevasses would be easy to span and therefore worth cutting across; if I cut it too fine, they would be complex and wide, slowing us down and making a broader, circular route a wiser choice. There was, of course, one great unknown: the snowline. Melt, a few more degrees of warmth and greater movement made snow bridges, snow packed into the mouth of a crevasse, harder to find. Snow bridges are the lifelines of a glacier traveller and make them possible to cross. They are almost impossible to find on the lower slopes in summer. The flatter surface of a glacier in winter or spring is essentially a continuous series of snow-bridged crevasses that merge with the stable ice surface.

Around fifteen miles into our journey I called a gradual curve. We had been pleased with our progress having taken only an hour or so more than my ideal world estimate. We would not instantly change tack thirty or forty degrees to the west as it would send us straight into ice chaos. Instead, with five degrees here and five more degrees there, we would miss the adjacent glacier, clip the obvious and snow-bridged crevasses at the top and then march onwards towards our target.

This was not to be. After only five or six hours of quick hauling over reasonable surfaces of hard and soft snow and between the gentle ice slopes of the icecap edge, we spied trouble. As had been expected and hoped for, the summer weather was stable. There were clear skies, excellent visibility, chilly nights of minus ten to fifteen degrees and midday temperatures substantially above freezing when we took our few hours of rest. The dramatic elevation gain of climbing the steep glacier gave good vantage along the coastline.

I had a strange, uneasy feeling in the pit of my stomach for a while because our surface, although occasionally snowy, was still mostly dry. This meant that there was precious little snow cover on the base ice of the glacier itself. All was not well and there was nothing we could do about it except haul onwards. 'Where did

Robert say he thought the snow line was at the moment again?' Wilki asked quizzically.

'He said it was high; well over a thousand metres,' I replied, knowing that he was thinking exactly the same as me. If none of the crevasses were filled in here, they were not going to be anywhere along our initial phase. I had called it wrong. The extraordinary lack of snow that summer meant that I should have taken a super-conservative route and completely missed out the coastal zone, skiing twenty or more miles directly north before even thinking of curving west.

There was nothing to be done but forge on; we had come too far to backtrack and go the long way round. Before long, that feeling in the pit of my stomach became one of dread. We knew, from experience, what was to come. There had been relatively little danger on the initial crevasse field of the Nagtivit as the surface, whilst insanely bumpy, only contained small and frequent crevasses. We were now in a whole new ballpark.

Soon, we found ourselves in the crevasse field from hell. Incredibly, just a few hours before we had buoyantly been chatting about when we would decide to fit our 'sledge skis' and pick up the pace. There was a large crevasse, ten or fifteen feet wide, every twenty feet or so and they were all deep and black-bottomed. Most would have been between a hundred and two hundred feet deep, guaranteed death for anyone unfortunate enough to fall and there were no snow bridges in sight. For five minutes or so, we both stopped and looked at the ice around us, staring in disbelief. But what could be done?

There was no value in complaining, we just had to get on with it. Our tactics were the only option available to us; skiing along the edge of a crevasse until it naturally narrowed or merged with another crevasse and then jumping across the gap or stepping on a block of ice jammed into the fissure. Progress was down to yards per hour and we were hauling many more miles to the left and right for every mile made in the direction we wanted to achieve.

There are books dedicated to the dangerous art of glacier travel and as many opinions as to how it is best achieved. It is not an experience that most who travel to the Polar Regions will have to encounter, which is a lucky thing. Adventure tourist guides in the Antarctic tend to avoid crevasse zones like the plague and their equivalents in the North often skip them altogether by helicopter. Clients falling into large holes in the ice is simply not good business. Commercial clients are safeguarded from this and other hazards of the regions, like darkness, the stormy season, full-weight sledges and highly mobile sea ice and as a consequence, can easily come away with a false-perception of safety.

The problem is, of course, that the only way to avoid danger is to artificially shorten the route and manipulate aims, a luxury I would never allow for myself. For a real expedition it is not possible to pick and choose the bits you want, beautiful polar light and flat plateau surfaces, and then turn your nose up at the parts that you do not fancy: the dangers and trials, which make the Arctic the special place it is. Without them, you do not have a true expedition.

Some might call it fatalistic or even suicidal, but Wilki and I did not travel 'roped up' (connected to each other via harnesses and a rope) when hauling across crevasses. Logic suggests that it would be a no-brainer to have something that could arrest the fall of one or other teammate who made a mistake or got unlucky. It certainly makes sense for larger groups and those wearing only light rucksacks.

In our case though, I would assert that there was no more dangerous thing we could do than 'rope up'. If one of us were to lose our footing or break through loose ice and fall, there would be the initial jolt of our body in free-fall. Then, even if our partner had managed to maintain balance at first, the falling sledge would surely cause him to fall through as well. One person in a crevasse is better than two and allows for a slim chance of a rescue call if the injuries caused by the fall are not too severe. The point is that the emphasis is on personal skill and judgement. One mistake, misjudgement or moment of overconfidence can be a killer, especially when you consider the draining effect of having to cross so many.

I suppose that these endless mazes of crevasses in which we found ourselves sowed the first seeds of doubt about our chances for the record. Some might champion the 'it'll be okay if we keep pushing hard' mind-set, but it is a fairly deluded mentality and

49

one which can purposefully ignore the hard facts in order to stay positive. I have always felt that, whilst confidence and an optimistic 'can-do' attitude must be in the armoury of every successful person, it can lead to stupid decisions and only delay things until they get much worse.

We had two aims: firstly to cross the icecap and secondly to go sub-eight days and nine hours. Whilst we did not actually voice our feelings about the former, we had to have a quick team meeting about the future. Our going was so painfully slow that even clearing the crevasse field at all seemed like no certain thing. Our choices were few; helicopters were out and the ways were forwards or backwards. Forwards did not take too long to settle upon, largely because the idea of crossing those miles of crevasses, channels and chaotic ice again did not appeal one bit, to put it mildly. Surely, we reasoned, we were nearly at the end of this hell of ice and chasms.

The crevasses continued, larger and larger. We were essentially hopping from square to square of a giant chessboard, with crevasses on every side. Every few 'squares', we would encounter gaps to the next block that were simply impossible to reach and so back we would ski to try another sequence of routes. Patience was in short supply and Wilki and I had to call upon every scrap of resolve to keep smiles on our faces. To make life even harder, because the gradient was so gradual, we could only see perhaps one or two crevasses away. As a result, we could not spot dead ends in advance but only once we had made the effort of getting there.

Despite the elevation we were accumulating, there was still no sign of the snowline, which would mercifully provide snow bridges and even a flatter surface. Snow bridges alone would have been quite enough. We would not have been picky.

Each crevasse we crossed, jumped or went around posed a risk. We knew that the law of averages meant that, eventually, our luck would run out. One of us would, more likely than not, make a mistake and the consequences do not need describing. Some of the crossings were worse than others. With those where the gap was ten feet or more, making a jump impossible, Wilki and I would sometimes find the last remnants of a rotten snow bridge. At times this was after perhaps a dozen hours of hard work, when our eyes would be out on stalks and we had pushed ourselves to the very limit; we needed to use our every sense to notice signs that our bridge might collapse.

Our approaches to these genuinely menacing problems differed. Firstly, we had to choose a plan that did not destroy the bridge or weaken it too much as two of us needed to cross. I would usually walk along the edge of the crevasse to get a good look at the crossing point from the side, looking for the thickness of the snow and its firmness. The news was rarely good.

Clearly unable simply to walk or ski across the weak snow, Wilki decided to use his sledge as a tool. Gingerly, he would pull the blue plastic shell and its contents out onto the snow bridge and press down, to make sure that it did not give way instantly. Then, one foot at a time, Wilki would step down onto the bridge and push down with both hands on the sledge, transferring weight onto the wide shell base and lessening the chance of punching through with his boots. A final hop onto the opposite edge and he was safe, needing only to slide the sledge up after him.

My method was different. I would pull my sledge right up to the edge of the crevasse and push it as far as possible without causing it to topple onto the snow bridge and collapse it. With the rope traces, connecting me to the sledge, slack, I would then drop down onto my belly and slide like a snake onto the snow. My heart rate went through the roof every time as my face was up close and personal with the one thing between me and a long fall. In a curious sort of shuffle, I then spread my weight out across my arms and legs and moved across. When nearing the opposite side my traces would begin to go taut, threatening to bring the sledge crashing down after me. At that moment, I would need to slide my body into a position where I could get up, move quickly and then make my bid for the far edge. This singular movement would ensure I was at least partly on solid ice before the bungee elastic in the traces took up the slack and pulled the sledge, hopefully, straight onto the bridge. I could then, carefully, hand by hand, pull in the rope and reunite with my lifeline and supplies. I would then finally exhale, close my eyes and thank someone or other that I had made it. The relief never diminished. And so it would go on, again and again.

Only twice were we so unsure of the viability of a snow bridge that we decided to make the time-consuming effort of taking out our rope to set up a belay, ensuring both of us got across safely. Both bridges barely survived the experience.

Wilki, having calmly and modestly taken on multiple front-line tours of Afghanistan and independent climbs on Everest, K2 and alpine north faces, was clearly aware of the risks we had taken. There is no point in stating the blindingly obvious at the time, when the adrenaline is overriding fear, but he did concede some hours after we had covered the worst of the ice, 'That was pretty sketchy, fella. We took some very real risks then.' He had summed it up perfectly.

Our trials were not over however. Despite the constant battering the sledges had taken, they had survived, but one of the tent poles had bent and our anti-bear gun had punctured a hole in Wilki's sledge bag. This could, potentially, cause problems should we face large melt streams in the West. Our spare ski, too long to go inside the sledges and so strapped on top of a sledge, had parted company and was most likely at the bottom of a crevasse.

The good news was that on some areas of ice, there were now light layers of snow. There was not enough to fill crevasses reliably, but the number of snow bridges was growing and they were wider and stronger – most were, anyhow.

I had moved a crevasse ahead of Wilki in order to make sure I was clear of it before he arrived, trying to build our momentum and speed to minimise wasted time. This meant that although we were only twenty feet or so apart, sometimes our view of one another was interrupted by ice. I had reached a fairly complex set of crevasses, again in the chessboard structure we had contended with to that point. Longitudinal crevasses ran in one direction and transverse ones in the other. This meant there were 'crosses' where they intersected. I had used a number of these meeting points to cross as they meant killing two birds, or crevasses in this case, with one stone.

The particular one I had lined up next looked strong. I had checked the thickness of the snow from the side and I resolved to cross the bridge on foot, checking the snow with my ski poles every step. After three sharp taps, the rule of thumb was that the snow or ice should be safe. And so I made my move. At first, the surface seemed strong and I moved slowly and surely to the centre of the bridge, the only thing between a seemingly bottomless drop and me being a couple of feet of snow.

All of a sudden, I was falling. I flung my arms out in an instinctive attempt to break my drop and I came to a halt. Incredibly, my head was still above the surface, but only just. I had expected to see pitch black and sure enough, as I looked down, all I could see were my feet dangling helplessly in a vast black nothingness. Time began to move so slowly for me that I remember each moment. Now was the time to do the right thing. It was the moment we all muse and hypothesise about. Do the right thing and live; do the wrong thing and die.

Although I could feel my heart beat harder and faster than I felt it could possibly sustain, I was strangely calm and clear in my head. Panic had not set in. I knew what I had to do. Moving was not one of those things. Even the slightest movement made chunks of snow fall from the bridge and let my body slide gradually lower. Just a few inches further and it would give way, letting me fall to my end. My glance down had told me that there were no life-saving snow ledges below. Of course there would not be; it was the late summer. Wishful thinking, Alex.

My attention snapped back. I could not move back as I felt my sledge resting against the back of my head. It had clearly glided up behind me as I fell; thank goodness it had not fallen through itself. The only thing to do was rely on my teammate. 'Wilki! Crevasse fall! Rope please!' I called out as loudly as I could without breathing in too heavily. This was one of those 50/50 moments, when it could go either way, with my life in the balance.

Sure enough, moments later Wilki called back that he was grabbing the rope from his sledge and that a loop would come over my left shoulder. I would not be able to reach well enough to clip the rope onto a karabiner on my harness or anything as secure as that. Instead, as the rope flopped onto the snow by my left arm I slowly, with every ounce of hope in my world, slid first my hand and then my arm through the loop. I worked it up my arm until it reached my shoulder; it was the best I could do. Wilki was behind me and could not help, needing to keep his belay secure. It was time to make a move.

As alarmingly large lumps of snow continued to fall and bounce endlessly off the walls of the crevasse on their journey to the bottom, I lifted with my elbows. My legs and body were useless with nothing to push against. Relieved about my intensive training, I used my arms to lift my bodyweight upwards and to the left in an awkward, unnatural movement. After a few seconds, lying sideways on the snow bridge, I could finally lift my legs out of the body-sized hole and scramble back onto hard ice. At last I could breathe.

Wilki would say later that he had not initially reacted as he would in an emergency because my call for assistance sounded too calm; he only stepped up into top gear when he saw the situation. I suppose he thought I may have put a foot or a leg down a slot (a colloquial term for a small crevasse) awkwardly and needed a quick hand. I reminded myself to scream blue-murder in a future fall! There was a worrying point, however. The fall should not have happened. Yes, the bridge was otherwise strong and I followed accepted techniques but Wilki or I might not be so lucky next time.

There was no time for a committee meeting. Some might say that this close shave with death and the fact that it was a result of being somewhere willingly is foolish and irresponsible, especially given that many people living safer lives have their mortality thrust upon them involuntarily. I would argue that as long as reasonable actions are taken to minimise the hazard then the balance of risk and reward are worth it. Everything in life inherently comes with a certain level of risk. The question is whether that risk has a purpose that you are comfortable taking ownership of. I would go so far as to say that I cannot afford **not** to take risks; my life would lack much of its value without them. An existence of routine, habit and monotony sounds far more perilous.

We were still in the middle of a large crevasse field and were slipping further and further behind our schedule. All we could do was immediately tackle the next chasm and then the next until there were no more left. After a brief two-hour break, our only rest in that daily cycle, it took another six hours of mind-draining route-finding and physical effort for things to improve. I almost refused to let my mind contemplate that we had actually found the real snowline and the icecap itself, for fear of yet another crevasse maze over the next rise. Eventually though, Wilki and I were rewarded for our toil.

●

Moments of great strength do not occur without significant internal turmoil. It would be easy to gloss over the critical moment and claim some sort of unflinching mental strength, which falters not even once. The truth is, however, far from that. In fact, a person who is temporarily able to block out fear entirely and stubbornly pushes on at that crux – the moment upon which triumph or failure and death hinges – are the weak ones. A mind-set such as that is fragile and will inevitably crack, often spectacularly. For this reason, I think it is important for any honest recollection to include all the stages, the facts, and the battle that ensues within before a final coup. It is weak-sounding, self-critical and entirely open to being misconstrued, but authentic.

●

The sun had set, though it was never to dip far below the horizon; it was August and the Arctic Circle was only a few miles away. One of the amazing gifts the polar world has to offer is that the quality of light and the length of time sunsets and sunrises last have no equal anywhere else on Earth. The icescape was bathed in a warm, pinkish-red glow which graduated into a cool, pastel blue. We had gained nearly six thousand feet in elevation as well as dozens of miles as the crow flies. The sea, coastal mountains and glaciers ran the entire length of the horizon. For the first time on this brutal expedition, I was reminded of why I do what I do. I felt lucky.

Laid out in front of us was a flat, gradual slope punctuated by large, wide crevasses every hundred feet or so. These were old, slow moving sections of the glacier that lacked the turbulence of lower down. Magically, spanning these ten to twenty-foot-wide gaps were strong, compacted and safe snow bridges. There were weak areas best avoided but, for the first time in what seemed like forever, we could set a compass bearing and walk in an almost uninterrupted straight line. We even put on our skis – luxury indeed.

Before any of this, however, it was time to eat. We had become so involved with the glacial climb that we had neglected our strict calorie intake plan. We had sometimes gone three hours before properly refuelling and rehydrating, such was the stress of the physical work and concentration demanded.

Time moves at wildly varying rates on polar expeditions. On a flat icecap, it seems to proceed at a snail's pace and skiers will find themselves willing on that session end, when they can stop, chat, eat, drink and break the monotony. On jumbled, tortured or melting ice, the opposite is true and the endless concentration can allow two or three hours to pass without thinking about stopping for a rest. Discipline is needed, in both circumstances, to keep healthy and on target.

As we ticked off each consecutive 'good' crevasse, they became easier and easier, narrower and better bridged. We were in business. Our mind-sets had to change radically. It had taken us the larger part of two days to clear a glacial system which would have taken between six and eight hours in the springtime. Any way we looked at it, we were behind time and had to make up a lot of miles. Instead of the analytical and downright bullish attitude, which we had needed to clear one of the most dangerous crevasse fields in existence, efficiency was now all that mattered. We were back to thoughts of miles gained per hour, average mileages and the most direct line to the West.

We decided to ski through that first evening and night to regain our planned daily cycle of skiing in the coolness of the night, and then take a couple of hours to rest in the day. In the quest for the maximum skiing time and best chance of quick recuperation, we did not even count on using the tent each 'night'. Our first sleep on the icecap would be without shelter. We could only forget about using the tent in good conditions, for obvious reasons; although the polar summer is more stable than the other seasons, storms and snow can still rear their ugly heads.

I had become accustomed to a wonderfully relieving evening routine on most journeys. The hard work of the day was done and even if the wind was blowing, the procedure of getting the tent up, stabilising and protecting it and then piling inside with our tent bags full of equipment was always to be savoured. The trials of the day could be forgotten, the unknowns of tomorrow ignored and the best things looked forward to: calm from the wind, rest, food and best of all, my sleeping bag.

That day was to be different, with neither shelter nor six or seven hours of sleep to look forward to. It was no surprise; the whole premise of our speed attempt relied on a brutally tough system which we could just survive for the eight or nine days we needed. So instead of pitching the tent, we stopped skiing, removed our harnesses and skis and then pulled our sledges into their windbreak position.

I suppose the saving grace of our temporary 'bivi' camp on the icecap was that it took only seconds to set up. We did feel a little exposed though; the icecap seemed evermore intimidating. We rolled out our foam sleeping pads and then sleeping bags, weather-proofed against any drifting snow. All that was left to do was remove our boots and wedge them between our sleeping pads and lower half of the sleeping bag. This would give them a fighting chance of not freezing. Although we used vapour barrier liners in our boots (waterproof membranes between liner and outer socks) to keep them dry and warm, it was inevitable that some moisture would enter the leather and fabric from the outside, aided by the sun and snow.

CHAPTER FOUR

After just two hours of slightly restless sleep, my arch-nemesis, the alarm in my watch, began bleating. It was time to stir, eat a flapjack for a sugar and energy boost and then get going. Mercifully, our boots slid on without too much fuss and within ten minutes of waking, we had our harnesses on, ready to ski. I tend to fire on all cylinders late into the evening rather than the morning, so my ten-minute wake-up routine included an inevitable minute or two of coming to terms with the reality outside my sleeping bag. Unable to be robotic, I take my time to get going. Polar bear scares, moving ice or rude awakenings whilst training with the Royal Marines Officer Batch represent obvious exceptions to this rule!

It was another beautiful day in the making. Despite our harrowing experiences in the ice field below, we had at least been given low winds and clear skies thus far. Although only two o'clock in the morning, the glow of light in the sky remained from when we had stopped and so we could move with relative ease.

We had still not fixed our skis onto the bottoms of the two sledges and were hesitating to do so until we were one hundred per cent sure we were clear of the bad ice. Because they had to be highly resilient against the forces of hauling, the nut and bolt system we had devised would take an hour or so in a tent to complete. We decided on another day of normal hauling without them and besides, the shells were moving well over the thin layer of snow.

Wilki and I both had enormous confidence in our own athletic ability and that of each other. Wilki's quip to me was that as long as he has a good pair of boots and continuous supply of food, he can more or less work endlessly. Of this I had no doubt. What we did know, however, was that there would be variations between us in speed given the viciously demanding pace we had dictated for ourselves. Whilst both well built and suited to manhandling sledges across jumbled ice, Wilki was a walker, climber and a 'yomper' (a

Royal Marines term for someone capable of carrying large loads over long tracts of uneven terrain). In contrast, whilst I found tough 'yomping' perfectly doable, I was a road cyclist, rower, kayaker and runner by 'sporting trade' and so our strengths would not match perfectly. The glacier climb had fatigued my quads a great deal and we were not yet conditioned to the odd-action of cross-country skiing. I did not feel as strong as I would have liked a few days into a major expedition and hoped that my strengths of high cadence skiing and efficiency on dips and plateaus would come to the fore later.

The concern running through both of our minds was that we still had over three hundred miles to ski, including the notorious icefall on the West Coast, and less than seven days to do it in, if we were to surpass that tantalising record set nearly a decade before.

Of course, we had allowed for the slow climb on the east coast and descent on the west coast, but the lack of snow and my overenthusiastic curve to the left had pushed us behind. We had to average well over forty statute miles per day until reaching the Russell Glacier, a massive task. This meant, even with our lightweight sledges and optimised route over our icecap 'summit' at around eight thousand feet, we needed to ski at over three miles per hour for around twenty hours per day. But, we were managing it.

The gradient was still noticeable and so the big mileages would have to wait. Despite this, our first day free of poor ice netted us thirty-seven miles. I do not know how it was for Wilki, but I found the sudden blast of energy demanded by my muscles was both exhausting and liberating and the excitement of being free to stretch my legs was immense.

I suggested that we put the tent up for our rest time and that Wilki get the stove on whilst I fitted the ski brackets. With the sort of speed you would expect of two men who had put up an expedition tent hundreds of times before and who also fancied a sit down, we were soon under cover and setting about our tasks. The wonderful roar of the stove came first, sounding like a jet engine and beckoning all things 'good' on an expedition: food and warmth.

Sadly, as ever, it was not to be used to heat the tent, a luxury only a supported or more relaxed expedition enjoys.

As with the vast majority of polar or altitude expeditions, we used an MSR XGK stove on a custom built marine-ply stove board. It was simple, powerful, efficient and reliable. George and I had used one in 2008 for over a hundred days without ever having to unpack the spare. Luckily, this was a world away from the poor design and leaky, temperamental nature of the Primus stoves supplied the year before when I was guiding. From that day on, I vowed to be unflinching in my demands to use only the best equipment of my choice, whether with a teammate or paying clients. The MSR runs on many liquid fuels but by far the best, and cleanest, is the refined petrol called white gas or naphtha.

My reward for completing the fiddly task of securing all four skis to our two sledges was a piping hot meal in an orange packet handed back to my part of the tent. The calories were much needed but so was the experience of something approaching indulgence or comfort. Once Wilki had shut down the stove, having melted some snow for our Nalgene water bottles, he came back to inspect my work. There was a glint in Wilki's eyes that said he was as excited as I was to give them a try. Perhaps this eagerness was a hopeful manifestation of the worry simmering inside us both that we were losing the battle against time.

Sure enough, once the sledge bags containing our equipment and supplies were returned to their plastic shells, now sitting six inches off the snow surface, they moved with minimal effort. Almost like small boys playing with their new train-set around the Christmas tree, we dragged our sledges around the tent to get a feel for their glide and turning ability. Even though the sledges weighed only forty kilos or so and were losing two kilos per day as we ate food and burned fuel, we had to be careful. The aluminium and steel brackets were lightweight and were holding a heavy load aloft, so could break if mishandled. After a short rest, difficult in the middle of the day when the sun was high in the sky and heated the tent almost unbearably, we were away once again.

The next few days would be make or break. Aside from the stress, excitement and endlessly changing conditions of the coastal regions of the icecap and its halo of glaciers, we were now on the plateau. Granted, it was not a flat plateau, as any icecap is essentially a steep-sided dome. We still had around three thousand vertical feet to climb before 'summiting' just before the halfway mark and beginning the more gradual descent. Regardless, the ever-familiar three hundred and sixty degrees of white flatness surrounded me once more. The blue skies of the Arctic summer only added to this stark, otherworldly experience.

Being totally honest, the monotony was a godsend after the strain of the Nagtivit and upper reaches of the other glaciers. We had a job to do and this was to ski fast, very fast. With regular checks of the undercarriage of the sledges to check the skis were doing ok, we settled into our routine of sixty to seventy-five minute sessions with a five to ten minute break in between to 'refuel'. Some might consider the five hundred or so calories per hour excessive, but this was an all or nothing effort. There would be no chance to follow the age-old tactic of 'start slow and build up'. Water was more limited in supply now that we were miles from the glacial melt-streams (which must only be used with great care as some can be stagnant and algae-infected) and we had to melt everything we drank. This meant using up both time and fuel, neither of which we had in great supply.

Polar success is all about efficient routine, but ask half a dozen professional polar travellers what this is and you will receive half a dozen different answers. This is a result of there being no central forum for skills sharing and the very best in the world come from all its four corners, although most regularly the Canadian North, Scandinavia, Siberian Russia and Greenland. This means that, unsurprisingly, with the geographical isolation and 'lone wolf' mentality of those who harbour ambition, all their routines, systems and preferences evolve independently. Taking a metaphor from the natural world, there will always be differences in adaptations between animals, whose ancestry has never met, but if their habitats are alike then similarities will appear without knowledge of the other. This 'convergent evolution' is widespread in the natural world with the wing and camera eye, and so it is with polar practices.

I find it fascinating and sometimes alarming to catch a glimpse at the style of my contemporaries, often using them as inspiration to improve my own. Every single one of us will have areas for improvement. Point at every decision I make and each item I use and I could most likely tell you whether I came up with the idea or tell you who I learnt it from. Sometimes however, and far more commonly amongst the individuals who prioritise style over substance and commercial success over actual achievement, it is possible to see naïve decisions.

There is, for example, one Brit who has grown an impressive profit-making machine despite spending less time on the ice annually than an average family on a ski holiday. He used and apparently instructed his team to use full-length ski skins when hauling a light sledge on a low gradient with a good snowpack. Skins are mohair or nylon stick-ons to allow glide and grip when climbing or hauling. Usually short 'kicker' skins are more than enough and sometimes nothing more than some wax will do the job. Anything more is energy wasted. He and his hapless teammates must have struggled horribly on quite good surfaces.

Another example is of a self-appointed world authority on safe guiding practices who took a series of simply bizarre, infantile decisions with high-paying clients against the advice of a Russian polar legend. The result was never really in doubt: avoidable failure and a disappointed team.

Small, seemingly insignificant examples like the order in which the cooking and snow melting is done in the evening can have as much impact as a more obvious choice such as hard versus soft boots and geodesic versus tunnel tents. And so, in the polar routine I had developed over the years and fine-tuned for a short, high-speed expedition, incorporating the lessons Wilki had learned from his experiences, we watched the miles tick by.

The blue skies and non-existent winds were not to last, which was not a surprise since the summer is not immune from bearing bad news. A kind of 'clag', commonly experienced on the moors of England, closed in and soon we were skiing into the featureless white soup of a whiteout, where ice is indistinguishable from sky. This is actually not a major issue. Unpleasant yes, but it does not affect the progress of an experienced team.

Navigation by eye becomes the first victim of the whiteout. Instead of skiing using the reference point of the sun and our shadow or a little bump of snow on the horizon, the compass was our only friend. A frame held our standard, fixed-plate Silva compass out in front and we skied, taking turns each hour, on a predetermined bearing.

It is in the very nature of a pressured expedition that equipment is at the same time heavily relied upon and most prone to breakage. We had to keep a close eye on the more irreplaceable items. We noticed fairly early on that the vertical steel stems which supported the load running through the ski brackets were bowing slightly, letting the aluminium cross beam bend a little. This would most likely worsen with time. Our hope was that their lifespan would exceed seven days.

Wilki was also having an irritation with his ski bindings. Although I have found them great in the past and championed the use of soft boots with flexible plastic bindings for all types of polar travel, there was one mismatch. Wilki's bindings, newer than mine that had lasted thousands of miles, were designed for the oversize Baffin mukluk boots we had planned to use in April. The summer, with temperatures unlikely to drop below minus ten Celsius, did not call for such insulation and so lightweight Sorel boots were swapped in. This left some space to the left and right of the boot in the binding and with each step, Wilki's feet slipped. A well-placed piece of rolled gaffer tape wedged in the gap solved this minor but potentially very annoying problem.

I have no doubt that in both of our minds, as we glided across the compacted snow surface, only to be slowed by the occasional snow build-up, the same mental arithmetic was going on: average speeds, distance completed, distance to go and that all-important deadline. Projecting the expected progress over the coming days could not be done with maths alone but with the gut instinct of someone who has a feel for what is and is not possible. This comes only through experience.

I could not make the numbers add up. Even if the glaciers had initially only taken us the projected day to clear, we still had to crack the forty mile mark on each day until reaching the disturbed ice in the West. Although our performance was strong, we were only maintaining a pace at or just below forty miles per day. To put this in perspective, it took a whole month to break the ten miles per day barrier on the 2008 'Long Haul' and on another icecap crossing, I considered around twenty miles to be a strong day.

I was finding that my leg speed and endurance were starting to flag after around fifteen or sixteen hours of hauling, making the final few hours before each rest period less valuable. Wilki and I had, for obvious reasons, treated every opportunity to exchange ideas as a cup half-full exercise, but we had to have a heart-to-heart.

Our purpose on the icecap was two-fold: to cross from east to west and to break the speed record. If we had, through a combination of terrible quality ice and an early decision to curve west, made it mathematically out of the question to take the prize, we could still cross very quickly indeed. The record and the quality of those who hold it is evidenced by the fact that so few other expeditions have got anywhere near it. If a team finished days shy of the eight day and nine hours then it would still be one in the handful of fastest ever crossings. Personally, one of my biggest motivations was to show myself that my polar skills were diverse and for that, I needed a high-speed journey under my belt. After all, a professional cannot call himself or herself so unless their breadth of experience is wide and complete. After all, I was untested at speed and an ultimately good life is nothing if not a series of rewarding tests.

A couple of other Scandinavian teams had skied within a couple of days of the record and there was a fairly hopeless British attempt a few years back. That bid finished in sixteen days, but not without summoning out Greenlandic authorities to deal with unconfirmed, 'menacing' polar bears and then shooting at the Australian photographer from Tasiilaq, who I met earlier in the year, whom the team had mistaken for a bear. The pair's previous go at the icecap had resulted in frostbite in challenging but entirely predictable conditions and was one of the many rescues that have led to the post-2009 clamp down on Greenlandic expedition insurance.

I was very angry with myself. The snow condition could not have been helped, but I could have saved us at least something by holding my nerve a little longer and then changing our bearing later. I had taken the lead on the route choice; I had climbed the glacier twice in the past after all, and had let the side down. We would still be behind our knife-edge schedule without it, but I had compounded our problems.

Wilki and I had known each other since I was sixteen and he was twenty-seven and I knew he was an observant friend and colleague. 'You really are incredibly hard on yourself, aren't you?' he said with a grin. 'It is what it is.' That final phrase had become our mutual catchphrase since the trials of April and we had a good laugh together on our murky icecap where the wind was starting to grow a little. It was true, though. One of my strongest traits, apart from my impatience, was the stratospheric standard I set for myself. Anything less needed a serious self-debrief. Like my impatience, I see it as, at once, the strength and drive behind me and also as a necessary flaw.

What we had to accept, though, even though only four days or so into the crossing, was that we had to forget the record. Our daily totals would have to knock on the door of fifty miles; that was beyond anyone's sustainable ability. Instead we resolved and were reinvigorated by a decision to cross the ice in a fast time and one we would be proud of. It would be Wilki's first crossing of the ice sheet and so that was one major motivator, plus I still wanted to fine-tune my style on a high-speed journey and add that new string to my bow. It would be one step further towards a kind of professional completeness and on a personal, perhaps masochistic level, fun.

We passed the highest elevation of our route, a little short of the halfway point and looked forward to a subtle increase in pace, courtesy of the gradient. It is unnoticeable minute-by-minute but makes its presence well known on the progress charts.

The weather had continued to be somewhat unhelpful, with plenty of cloud and a rising wind, but snowfall was not a problem. I hoped we would soon see the sun again, but at least the surface was fast. There were very little sastrugi, largely due to the lack of snow and wind in the summer, and only small patches of dunes, which were soft snow. Our skis relied on hard surfaces to avoid getting bogged down with added friction.

Our daily rests, I cannot really call them night-times or sleeps due to their brevity, were allowing us just enough recuperation time to keep going. With the record out of the question and the need to navigate by compass, we had averaged thirty to thirty-five miles per day. Sometimes we used the tent; sometimes we just stopped and slept where we were. Somewhat used to icecaps taking much, much longer to cross, I found the idea of starting to mentally plan our descent and finish quite bizarre. It just seemed too soon and we had barely settled into our new home.

The ski brackets were beginning to cause a problem or two as the steel uprights began to bow further and I made running repairs to both mine and Wilki's using spare parts and strong duct tape. Even on a super-lightweight expedition, vital spares are needed – I had learned this over the past years.

Others had fared much worse and paid the price for inadequate preparation; on one occasion a solo skier wasted tens of thousands of sponsor's pounds and the chance of the North Pole by failing to take spare ski bindings, which weigh grams. Bindings, like satellite phone batteries and stove pumps, are on the list of critical, 'always, always take' spares on any kit list. There is no point having a sledge ten kilos lighter than that of a competitor if you cannot keep going after a couple of predictable breakages.

CHAPTER FIVE

Finally, eight days since we had stepped off the boat at Nagtivit, the sun returned. Wilki was the first to notice after glancing behind when leading a particularly monotonous hauling session. 'Blue sky!' he exclaimed. 'There's a break in the cloud. I was getting a little bored of white!'

This was great news and it came not a moment too soon. Although irritating, whiteout or cloud whilst on the plateau is workable. Fast approaching, though, was the great icefall of the Russell Glacier and for that we would need to be able to see. I had last descended the Russell the year before, as a guide, and it had been a trying experience for the clients and also for me, having to route-find for twenty-six hours straight through a maze of ice. That was in May, and by August the months of additional melt and no snow would make it so much worse. What we would have done for an ice road! In all seriousness, I would not have considered the use of one to be 'fair game'. If you take shortcuts where does it end? The logical answer is that you might as well skip all the hard bits, like most Pole attempts these days, or just fly there, as many rich tourists do.

•

Polar goals or destinations, unlike mountain summits, are, by and large, arbitrary points and indistinguishable from the ice to the left or the right. This makes their attainment symbolic. I simply do not understand the mentality behind a tourist flight to a Pole or polar 'prize location', or similar 'ski the last few miles' trips. A person with a desire to really experience the place, rather than tick something off a bucket list, would spend half the cash and visit far more beautiful cold places of the world: Lapland, South Georgia, Melville Bay, the list goes on.

'Focus on the journey, not the destination. Joy is found not in finishing an activity but in doing It.' – Greg Anderson, author.

•

Within a half-hour, the sky had cleared fully from the east and once again, we could see the perfect straight line of the horizon and the subtleties of the snow ahead. The wind that cleared the cloud had picked up and was now well over thirty knots. We had exchanged one annoyance for another but were happy it was this way round. With face protectors to stop the wind-chill damaging our skin, we were ready to go again. For the first time on the expedition, we found ourselves wind-milling our arms to force warm blood to our fingers. I have not yet found a wind-chill factor chart which I would fully subscribe to, but it felt at least twenty degrees colder than the minus five or ten degrees we were measuring.

My soft leather boots were working well; they were less intensively padded than my normal, extreme cold-weather mukluks but they had caused very little rubbing or soreness to my feet. This was despite the fact we had covered well over two hundred miles, including an elevation gain of around eight thousand feet in only eight days.

Wilki was having slightly less luck. During an elongated mid-'day' break of twenty minutes, he stopped to dry out and see to his heels. I took the opportunity to do a little filming and wander around the immediate area, which was spectacular. The icescape was the perfect stereotype of an ice sheet in summer; it was featureless blue sky from horizon to horizon, with the sun high in the sky and the surface glistening like a million crystals.

As I watched the scene through the viewfinder, I noticed some small marks on the otherwise pristine snow surface. A few yards further on I saw the same. We were still thirty miles or so from where I expected the icefall to begin in earnest for the final, gruelling twenty miles. It then dawned on me that the snow layer was again disappearing, as it had in the East. The more gradual slope on this side of the icecap, as it flowed slowly towards the coast, meant that a snowline at a given height was further inland.

Not knowing quite how to break the news to Wilki, I carried on filming for a little longer and confided in the film, before walking back to our sledges. We had expected to see good, flat icecap surfaces for fifteen or twenty miles yet. Wilki and I were pragmatic. It was what it was, after all.

The marks on the ground ran in a perfect line to the north and south. They were, in fact, the tops of tiny little cracks or slots at the very top of the mobile ice. In thousands of years they will grow into crevasses and eventually break off into the sea or into melt rivers. These cracks actually continue all the way across the icecap. There are sometimes even reports from expeditions of crevasses in the middle of the plateau – it reminds you that the icecap is forever in motion. The difference is that the snow is so perennially significant above the snowline that they are never exposed. Although a hauler would not even notice a bump as he or she skied over these cracks, they would only get larger from now on. They were the omen of bad ice to come.

As these ground undulations and marks became more and more frequent as the miles passed, we also spotted a black object a long way in the distance to the south. At first we hoped, unlikely though it was, that it could have been an old marker flag from the upper reaches of the fabled ice road from years past. Although long since destroyed, the road would have followed the best contours of the glacier and icefall and could have been a help. Alas, it was a long-abandoned automated weather recorder and some old marker posts. It took us quite some time to ski over to it as distances are masked by the lack of reference points in the featureless wilderness. Man-made objects stick out easily – something that was a great help to George and I locating our self-laid depots in 2008.

The next day, as the sun was rising into the sky, turning it from a warm orangey-purple into a vibrant blue, large marks appeared a mile or so ahead. We had been making good progress, feeling strong and our equipment was holding together. We both knew what the marks were: melt pools. The question, we mused helplessly, was whether they had begun to refreeze yet as the summer ebbed away through August. We certainly hoped so. Open water obstacles this high up would be a disaster. It is amazing how just a few detours and surface undulations can destroy a good pace. Three or more miles per hour can drop to one mile per hour or below in a matter of yards.

Soon these menacing marks across the surface were approaching as we picked up our pace once again. We had, at some point during one of these sessions, passed the eight day and nine hour mark since we started the clock with Lars, over three hundred miles away. Still with a few dozen miles to negotiate, I sent a message to our Twitter account and blog via satellite to salute the prowess of the record-holders.

I knew we could have been in with a chance of getting within striking distance of that time, but sometimes in life you cannot have it all. Besides, we had bigger problems of a more immediate nature to deal with. With a sigh of relief, we found the melt pools were indeed refrozen; we were still above four thousand feet elevation after all and the summer zenith was long since past.

The pools were recessed a foot or two into the ice and snow surface, with a bowl-like shape. Clearly visible was the azure blue which was the tell-tale sign of frozen standing water, rather than the whiter ice and snowpack which is a consequence of snow being compacted under extreme pressure over many years. On top of this slippery ice, which would be akin to an ice rink, ice crystals had formed, making the surface crunchy and giving it more grip. Thankfully, we did not have to lose much time as they were wide apart and avoiding them only caused the odd deviation. An uneasy relief ran through my body, as if I knew we were not out of the woods yet but was delighted that a potential threat had proved surmountable.

In an instant, something leeched every drop of optimism from me. The year before, I had led my team through ten miles of crevassed and melting ice, with perhaps five more miles before that of slightly bumpy terrain as ice blocks poked through the snow. We were four or five times further out than that from 'Point 660', our target. It was not something I saw which filled me full of dread; it was a sound: water, rushing water. It was powerful and fast-flowing water, not the trickling sound of a foot-wide brook on Dartmoor.

It took another ten minutes or so of skiing before we found the source of the noise. Stretching directly across our path, from south to north, was a thirty-foot-wide melt river. Melt rivers usually flow from melt lakes in dips further up the icecap slope and will terminate in one of three ways. Firstly, if on the lower slopes, they can find their way directly to the sea next to a glacier or onto the permafrosted land if the icecap ends inland. Alternatively, they can flow into a large crevasse and make their way down through the icecap. Recent research and scientific expeditions in the relatively benign summer months suggest that tunnels and channels like wormholes form a network thousands of feet below the ice surface. Some of these hidden tunnels can be three hundred feet in diameter: plumbing on a gigantic scale. Finally, and most disturbingly for an expedition, they can spontaneously drop down a vertical sinkhole, a moulin, carved out by the torrents of water. These are inescapable and monstrously powerful. This water is likely to contribute towards the subsurface 'plumbing' and also lubricates the entire icecap's snail-like advance over the bedrock towards the oceans.

Our own personal river was complex. Beautifully crystal clear and a fresh shade of blue, it was thirty feet or more wide and was, in parts, made of two or three smaller rivers. Crossing would be no easy task. Sure to be the first of many, there was no time to go walking up and down to find the source or the end; it could be ten miles or more.

We had to come up with a quick, effective and if possible, safe way across. Whilst most of the riverbanks were steep and perhaps four feet high above the water, there was a thin ledge of ice that extended a few feet out into the flow. Experiences which we had both had crossing rivers in the past, in military and civilian scenarios, made us wary.

We estimated the water to be around waist height and decided to avoid the multi-channel areas. The water was flowing faster in rapids there but still had the depth to be dangerous. Instead, we decided to take on only one bank on each side, rather than four or six, and cross the wider part. It was time to get on with

71

it. I volunteered to be the guinea pig and go first, with Wilki waiting behind on the other end of the rope which would be round my waist. If I were to slip and fall without it, I would die at the bottom of a crevasse or moulin, or drown on the way there. The water was hovering around zero degrees Celsius.

Knowing that we had the most technically demanding part of the expedition ahead, I was worried about my boots. Without feet in good working order, we would both be useless. Thousands of miles in the hills and on the ice had taught us that. Although we could keep the water away from our torsos and the sledges would float to a certain extent, our legs and feet could not be saved. I was not keen on the idea of saturated boots for dozens of miles, so decided to remove them. The riverbed would be smooth ice, after all.

Wilki could see the logic but was unconvinced; so with my socks off and boots hanging round my neck, I inched towards the edge. I knew the ice ledge would only tolerate my weight for a step or two and would then plunge me a few feet down into the water. It was vital I retained my balance at that critical moment. In a worst-case scenario, I could be dragged under the ice layer and drowned.

I looked behind to see that the rope to Wilki was fairly tight; we exchanged a grin, and then I placed a foot on the ice. It held. Just as I lifted my second foot to take the next step, with ski poles steadying me, the ice cracked and sent me crashing down into the freezing water with a massive splash. Anticipating the shock of cold-water immersion and not wanting to stop and check if my rucksack or arms were wet, I focused straight on the opposite side. I had stayed upright and that was the main thing, and my bare feet were gripping well on the glassy ice river bottom, although I could feel nothing.

In a series of long strides I made the other side. Adrenaline surging through my body, I looked for a reasonable exit point. We had identified a few possible spots from the other bank but it was hard to tell white against white until closer up.

Finally, I stepped up from the river onto a reasonable gradient of softer snow and ice. I was suddenly aware of the fate of my sledge, floating behind. Although a roughly boat-like shape, it had low sides and was not designed for floating, unlike its larger North Pole cousins. I had felt its drag behind me as I strode across. My main fight, though, had been trying to stay upright against the powerful flow of water.

The main job of the ski brackets under the sledges was done. They had reduced our sledging friction brilliantly but would now become a hindrance over the bumpy ice descent. It being a major job to unscrew and stow them only to reattach them, I had decided to keep them on and let them break when they broke. The break came sooner than I had anticipated. A few bow waves had crashed over the water-resistant sledge bag but, critically, it had stayed upright and I pulled the traces towards me to retrieve my precious supplies. With two long skis running the full length of the sledge, they became caught on ice protrusions and ledges very easily. My ability to manoeuvre the sledge was limited to balancing tugs on the ropes with the flow of the melt water. My luck ran out as one ski became lodged and I could do nothing but apply enough pressure to allow them to part company. This was no great loss; the skis were now a dead weight and the ice thereafter would not suit a sledge in 'racing' mode.

Before I was able to swap roles and help Wilki cross the river using the path I had forged, I had to secure the sledge and look after my feet. Although I had not felt my feet for a few minutes due to the numbness, I knew they would not be in danger of frost damage as long as they were cared for rapidly. The sun was out, the wind was slight and I was otherwise mostly dry; not a high risk recipe for frostbite. First though, I had to climb the bank onto the flat.

Only a few moments after I had done so, Wilki yelled across the deafening noise of the water, signalling to me to look down. Completely unaware, I had been walking bright red footsteps up the snowy ice bank. Instantly, I stopped and inspected the soles of my feet to find countless, razor-blade cuts across the skin. Made to look worse by the dampness, blood was pouring from them. The gamble had not quite paid off, to say the least. I had dry boots and that was a real bonus, but although I had chosen safe, smooth ice to walk on for ninety per cent of the crossing, I had failed to notice that the far bank was of a different composition to the other. The action of the sun had made the ice sharp as droplets melted down through the surface, and I had paid the price.

Once I had dried them and replaced my warm woollen socks, the benefit of dry boots was obvious. Then the feeling returned. Usually a proud owner of two blisterless feet throughout expeditions, largely due to my unwavering belief in soft boots, I was not used to painful feet. Hundreds of miles of travel will surely cause a little soreness, but I had always avoided the agonising experience of bleeding blisters and skinless heels which some seem to advocate as the 'proper' way. As the numbness ebbed away, shooting pains surged through my feet and up my legs and I could think only to call over to Wilki, 'I recommend you keep your boots on!'

Thoughts of my feet put to the back of my mind, it was time to get Wilki across. His life was in my control and so I fed the wet rope through my hands to ready it for his own soaking. I did not particularly envy him, knowing what was to come. I had removed my gloves to do this belay job, as the hundred feet of climbing half-rope was sodden. No gloves are really waterproof and so it was best to keep them out of the way and dry.

Soon after, Wilki leapt into the gap in the thin ice which I had created and began striding his way across, eyes fixed on the exit point. Short of one slight slip, he met me on the bank without drama and we set about repacking the rope, wringing out Wilki's socks and getting ready to move on. I do not know who had ended up better off – me with sliced soles or he with sodden boots and socks. What was for sure, though, was that I could not repeat my tactic; soon I would have both cut and wet feet. For the future, having 'sacrificial', river-crossing boots would be the way forward.

Of course, we knew that one river, especially at that elevation, meant many more to come. We braced ourselves for a torrid final few days, even though one saving grace was a clear and calm weather forecast. We had been on the icecap for nearly ten days and were exhausted both through ruthless lack of sleep and the sheer physical battering we were subjecting ourselves to.

The terrain rapidly deteriorated as the next few hours came and went. Before the ground required so much attention that we could not think of anything else, I hurriedly did new sums in my head to account for the situation we found ourselves in. I needed to let our UK support team know roughly when we planned to finish so that a Danish group, based at Kangerlussuaq, could arrange our pickup.

Kangerlussuaq is an important hub in Greenland as it is the only place a large, wheeled aircraft can land outside the Far North. Even in the capital Nuuk, passengers from the outside world must fly into Kangerlussuaq and then connect to Nuuk on a smaller Dash 8 aircraft. The US Air Force also uses the runway as a base for their cold-weather aircraft in order to train their Antarctic pilots on the icecap. The rest of the narrow Greenlandic coastal halo of ice-free land is so mountainous and inhospitable that Kangerlussuaq's value appears secure for the future, the entire settlement being reliant on the airport for employment. Only the Thule Airbase, hundreds of miles north, can also land cargo aircraft but it is for government and military use only. In 1968, at the height of the Cold War, a USAF B-52 bomber crash-landed in the dark winter on the sea ice near Thule, killing one of the crew. Part of one of the four nuclear weapons it was carrying was never recovered and the area had to be decontaminated by the US and Denmark.

Not only was the ice now covered in bumps, snowdrifts and channels previously caused by melt, but the terrain was developing on a macro scale too. Instead of a dead flat plateau, we now entered rolling 'hills' of ice, which indicated the start of increased ice flow downhill. Although not particularly fiercely steep, these had the unfortunate side effect of blocking our view of the ice ahead.

As opposed to the freedom of simply walking in a straight line on a fixed bearing, like the majority of expeditions on permanent icecaps, glacial systems (or sea ice) are dynamic and require route-finding skills. The subtlety of the signs that might lead to the difference between a reasonable path and a dead-end and also the mortal consequences of a bad decision make this skill very hard-won. It is also the reason why the handful of novice teams who attempt these routes often choose to overfly glaciers by helicopter and why the same helicopters are often called back to rescue the injured, or worse.

If the slope was smooth and uniform, like one or two glaciers on the east coast which I have climbed and descended, the ice 'falling away' can allow visibility of ten miles or more. This is clearly a godsend for making choices and can reduce travel time by a factor of ten. The Russell Glacier, like most others, cannot be counted amongst these.

We both now faced the prospect of making major route choices every half-hour or so with often, no more than a couple of hundred yards of view. The distance was obscured by another hill of ice. Behind it could be melt channels, a river, a crystal-clear blue melt lake or flat surface. We simply had no idea.

Our 8,600kcal per day had allowed us to stretch our nine days of food out relatively easily. This was always the intention but even so, the sheer quantities of flapjack we had to eat were hard to stomach. Wilki, in particular, was less than enthusiastic about the monotonous diet, conceding though that its effect was like rocket-fuel. I joked that the dozen or so flavours we had was a massive step-up from the three George and I had on 'The Long Haul'.

Soon, the two of us picked up speed on a decline into a bowl between higher areas of ice. The ice had now deteriorated to the point where it was a constant series of dips and furrows, some with melt water and some dry. It became impossible to walk more than three or four steps in a straight line and skis had to come off. At least the sun was shining.

My sledge had been moving with total ease on the flat, even when the winds picked up on the plateau crossing, but I was now reminded of the Nagtivit. The blue plastic shell snagged on every ridge and bump, and careered off course given the slightest opportunity. It felt twice its weight as the surface was becoming snowless. The action of the sun melting the surface allows droplets of water to form and they, warmer than the surrounding ice, burrow downwards. What results is a high friction, broken and uneven surface with a crunchy, ankle-twisting feel.

Again and again we hauled up and over the rises, then down the other side, barely breaking a mile per hour and only roughly being able to stay on course. As the elevation continues to drop, the nature of the ice changes; snow gives way to ice poking through the surface, then additional evidence of melting as the temperature creeps up.

After crossing a narrower melt-river with steep, ten foot high sides, we had a small respite. A mile-long zone of the icefall was criss-crossed with melt channels a foot or so recessed into the surface and a couple of feet wide. With our skis back on, I took the lead and shot off over the flat and smooth ice, tripling our speed. We were slaves to where the meandering ice motorways took us but on balance, the plan was working. These routes must have only refrozen a few days previously as, every ten steps or so, the ice would crack alarmingly and we had to scamper forward to avoid a dunking.

The routine of seventy minutes skiing, stopping, handing over the compass holder, eating and drinking, quickly exchanging thoughts and then skiing another seventy minutes had given way to more fluidity. Wilki and I were constantly talking things through, considering each other's gut feelings and checking on each other when out in front. It was a welcome change; the whole point of working as a team is to combine past experiences, make better decisions and to share the journey. Wilki was typically upbeat, although I noticed his pace had tempered and his boots were not comfortable. Bizarrely, as long as my feet were being used and were not left to settle too long, the pain of my cuts was almost forgotten.

Our magic ice channels came to an end at the base of a large ice hill which we had picked out to climb. The surface appeared, from a distance, to be flatter there. Almost taking us by surprise, an unusually quiet and very wide melt river appeared. Many smaller streams flowed into it but it did not seem deep and some parts were even frozen over. Step by step, we both chose our ice carefully, hoping that it would not give way. With more than one breath of relief, our sledges were hauled onto the far bank and we looked forward to reasonable going, just for a while at least.

First though, a broken slab of ice revealed fast flowing water, from which we filled our water bottles. Every litre of free water meant minutes saved melting snow, fuel saved and added hydration for our hurting bodies.

Up we hauled along the hill, eventually choosing a contour to follow. The ice, for some reason, perhaps due to the angle it presented to the sun, had suffered less than elsewhere and we gained a mile rapidly. This gave us a rare viewpoint over the icecap to our rear and the glacier all around us. To the east, I could even make out the flat icecap plateau. It was as if those hours of work since leaving the flat surfaces had gained us just a few steps. It was such hard work for so little return, but they were the yards that mattered: the difficult ones.

To the north was the ground close to that which we had just hauled across and the network of melt streams. Finally, we saw something not entirely unexpected, but we were thankful it was not in our path: a vast, dazzling and pure-blue melt lake.

Onwards we travelled, bouncing from peak to peak and across trough after trough of ice. There was a pattern that had been formed and each hummock of brittle ice was the same six feet wide and each trough the same foot or two deep. The obstacles were not too massive yet, but disabling nonetheless.

Inevitably, that melt lake which had captured our gazes for what seemed like an eternity, had to have consequences. The water could not be contained in that single area (although having said that, there is some evidence now that crevasses or sinkholes can spontaneously open on the bed of a lake and allow millions of litres of water to drain in just hours).

Although it is impossible year on year to predict how each zone of the glacier will look – the upper slopes, the melting zone, the crevasses fields and so on – we were hoping for a change. According to my GPS unit, which I checked every couple of hours or so, we should have been only three or four miles from a former dog camp named as such on our maps/charts. Nothing existed there, just a GPS location, but it was where the handful of dog teams who had ever crossed the icecap with Inuit drivers would have stopped to let skiers continue on foot. The reason was crevasses, something dogs cannot tackle. Where the ice speed increases, so does crevassing and it is harder for water to collect for obvious reasons.

Before the predicted crevasses, Wilki and I wanted to know where the lake was draining to and where the now ever-growing and ominous sound of water was coming from. Hoping upon hope that it would be the last major crossing, I inched my way forwards, half dreading what we would find. The news was not good. There lay a twenty-foot-wide river that had carved down another twenty feet, leaving almost sheer walls. It was so far cut into the ice that we could not see it until almost falling over the edge. To the left it became even deeper and wider, so we tried our luck in the other direction for a glimmer of a crossing opportunity. A wide and previously substantial snow bridge had recently collapsed, so that option was off the cards. Down we would have to go. The problem we had, as we took turns to peer over the edge to look, was that there were no 'beaches' to set up on with our sledges and ropes before leaping into the torrent.

Eventually, we found a partially crumpled side of the ice gorge that had formed a makeshift ramp down to the water. Each moment spent walking up and down the river was time wasted in our quest for the West and I leapt at the opportunity to make our way across. For sure, the crossing was not ideal but it was all we had. On the opposite bank the way back up was a far less inviting prospect with a very steep gradient and unstable looking ice.

Tempting though it is, it is always hard to use terms such as 'ground level' and 'gorge' when talking about snow and ice travel. Unlike when walking on earth and rock, everything is relative and the surface level might be ten or twenty feet different just months before or after. Conditions are always dependent on the amount of ice uncovered by the quantity of snow which happens to exist and then the action that the annual melt has on that dynamic system.

Wilki volunteered to go first this time and, after I had once again unpacked the rope and secured it, he rolled up his trousers to save them a soaking. Placing both ski poles out into the flow to judge the speed and the depth, he went for it. Despite having boots with deep treads on, his first foot placement slipped alarmingly. After a quick recovery, and a few more sure steps, he was across. With a quick look back, I saw Wilki slightly wide-eyed in a way I had not seen since our crevasse-crossing escapades in the East. He was not in danger of his life since the rope would have caught a fall but the prospect of full immersion in the near-frozen water with a rucksack full of equipment was enough to focus any mind.

We ferried across both sledges in a sort of pulley system and then it was my turn. Wilki said he had spied a way up his side of the bank and learning from his foot placements, I made my way across with little fuss. Of course, my boots had been saturated since the second river crossing and so we both climbed up the crumbling ice wall and went through the routine of wringing out socks and pouring out the water. The surface was a far better place for hanging around since the sun provided a semblance of warmth. Down in the river gorges the sun was excluded and cold air collected, making them a grim and uninviting place.

Onwards we went, praying (Wilki, unlike myself, at least knew who he was praying to) for an end to the water and in fact, almost hoping for crevasses. Water finds it difficult to collect where there is crevassing and my hunch was that, from experience guiding this same icefall in May 2010, the crevasses would be plentiful but narrow enough to walk over.

After cresting a particularly tough ice hill, the sun was dropping towards the horizon, lengthening our shadows. I was momentarily reminded of the beauty of the barren ice wilderness in the face of an unrelentingly demanding test we had set ourselves.

CHAPTER SIX

According to my GPS, we were at Dog Camp. In these summer and post-summer months, dog teams and sledges would not have had a hope of getting within ten or twenty miles, but even in the springtime when the label is relevant, I had my doubts. Times are changing and what was reasonable only ten years ago is often not today. Dog teams, one of the most efficient, historic and aesthetic forms of polar transportation, will always come second to the humble man-hauler when presented with open water or violently complicated ice.

Almost on cue, the crevasses began. They were narrow, well-filled and easily navigable. We even saw a near straight line of flattened ice, which we mused may have been the end of the mythical ice road. Life was looking up, for a time at least, and we began to build up a pace, the sledges bouncing enthusiastically over the surface as we yanked them along. We were helped by a downward gradient, but this only meant one thing: there would be a bottom to this dip and where there is a bowl, water collects. We had a little over twenty miles to travel to our planned end point, and were just into our eleventh day.

Our despair when we heard water, yet again, was a horrible, sinking moment. This was not a rushing sound or splashing which had announced the presence of rivers past. This is was a roar. The aggression was obvious before we had even worked out exactly where it was. By now, the ice was so devoid of snow that it was an energy sapping and ever undulating, crunching surface. It felt almost like I was walking on a vertical foot of crisps. Instead of holding our weight, the sharp and brittle shards crushed under every footstep, making each one a frustrating exertion.

Then we saw the water. My jaw dropped and we simply looked at each other without a word. The river was a raging torrent, which I would have thought twice about tackling even in my white-water kayaking days. The din was hard to be heard over, but we had to come up with a plan. Our experience told us that going upstream would, most likely, only cause us more problems. A river of this size could only come from multiple sources and so upstream we would probably have to cross three, four or more tributaries. Crossing here would be instant suicide. Downstream then was the only option left. With luck and being this far from the coast, it would either disappear into a gigantic moulin sinkhole or dissipate out onto ice too hard to carve a river into, leaving an area of shallow 'arctic wetlands'. The question was when and where. Keeping a nervous eye on our watches and the time being lost walking perpendicular to our ideal route, we set off, keeping the river to our right.

I had felt a sneaking suspicion for the previous couple of days that Wilki was in pain, ever since the half-hour foot 'administration' he had near the first glacier cracks. His usually fluid ski stride and walking gait had changed but, characteristically, he had pushed on without a word of complaint. After a couple of – I hoped – tactful questions, it was obvious that one foot and both lower shins were causing problems; it was an insidious injury to have and one that rarely responds well to painkillers.

Wilki was dropping back a little. I am not sure whether it was due to a sudden loss of motivation to meet our self-inflicted deadline or because he was feeling the pain. Conversely, I felt a wave of energy and desire to get along this river as fast as possible. The time spent going in the wrong direction was horrid and I wanted it to end.

I looked back every five minutes or so and would hold a little until Wilki caught up. Pacing amongst teams on expeditions is an historic source of tension and the root cause of most arguments. The psychological effect of seeing a teammate shoot off into the distance can snowball out of proportion and can even make people feel abandoned. In at least one desperately sad episode in the High Arctic in the nineteenth century, an Inuit guide was shot and killed by his employer because he moved off ahead.

As such, every expeditioner with maturity and experience must temper his enthusiasm and match the pace of the other. This can be hard to do without constantly looking behind and back up on the icecap, Wilki had done just that for me. Realising he was outpacing me a little, he took a few sessions to get a feel for my pace and then more or less matched it. I did the same here and soon reined myself in.

I was worried about Wilki, largely because complaining was not in his nature, and so I wondered how badly he was suffering. Most importantly, I could not see anything I could do to help him. It could well have been that the massive river had been a 'what will be will be' moment for him and speed was no longer a priority.

Regardless of this, the light was still dim by the standards we were accustomed to, and making out changes in the ice was tricky. The river was widening quite dramatically but was still not crossable due to the body-blowing force of the water and our rope being barely long enough to stretch halfway across.

Persistence paid off, however, and a mile or so later what was previously a death trap had become what resembled a sort of ice marsh. Snow and ice poked through the surface like giant lily pads and although the water was still flowing, it was rarely more than ten inches deep. We knew that this terrain still needed a great deal of caution. We could not rope up effectively over the four or five hundred yards of wet ice and without warning, what we thought to be an innocuous slab could become a quicksand-like slush.

Tentatively but it has to be said, enthusiastically, we forged across the mire and had a mini-celebratory hug on the other side. Comparatively at least, what we found beyond was pretty good surface; it was bumpy and hard on our ankles, but we could walk directly on our bearing.

As we moved from mile to mile and zone to zone, without any reference from above of where we were heading relative to the twists and turns of the icefall, we simply had to contend with what we found. I daydreamed about the luxury of exorbitant funding and being able to fly the entire route by helicopter before even setting off. We would be able to GPS-mark the flatter ice, avoid the worst rivers and sidestep the more aggressive areas. In hindsight, of course, this would remove most of the skill and challenge from the journey, but you cannot blame a tired man for dreaming.

The bumps grew larger yet again and the old melt channels grew deeper. Crevasses were curiously absent yet again and we could not see above the peaks of the ice blocks as we walked along the labyrinthine succession of passages. Wilki climbed up onto a series of blocks that he thought might allow a more direct route than lower down. I clambered up onto a slightly different section, planning to meet his path a little further on.

Looking to the left and right, constantly scouring the white surface with my bleary eyes for a good way forward, I suddenly saw something massive and dark straight in front of me. Completely dried up and almost perfectly circular, a ten-foot-wide black hole in the ice was a matter of four or five paces in front of me. This, a moulin from the summer, was seemingly bottomless and most likely dropped thousands of feet vertically to the bottom of the icecap or into one of the trans-glacial tubes. Intimidating is not a strong enough word to describe the sight.

Having cautiously, and ever-conscious of my sledge which as usual had a mind of its own, walked around the moulin, I caught up with Wilki as he approached a hillcrest. Sledges will, unsurprisingly, follow the path of least resistance and a skier whose concentration lapses for just a moment can be caught out. Aside from the ever-frustrating ankle bashing we receive when a heavy sledge is tugged over a sastruga and shoots down after its owner, I saw a near miss just the year before in 2011.

I was guiding five people across the icecap and we had reached DYE II, a surreal American Cold War relic in the middle of the ice. Over a hundred feet high, it contains a radar dome and until it was abandoned in the late 1980s, was manned year-round and scanned the skies for Soviet missiles. The persistent katabatic winds had, when hitting such a prominent object in their path, created dramatic formations. Behind the vast, white, spherical dome, spindrift had built up fifty feet or even higher. The enormous structures were actually built on support legs to help protect against the violent drifting snow. Today, over fifty years since they were first constructed, they have the appearance of sinking into the icecap. In reality, the actual height of the icecap is rising and building up around them. Due to the complex nature of the wind, however, there is a cavernous bowl, thirty feet deep or more, carved out below the building's mass, exposing the metal legs. The sides of the bowl are steep and the fall most likely fatal to a skier.

Although an absolute joy to guide, the five in my team were human after all and one decided he wanted to have a look over the edge. Forgetting he was attached to an eighty-kilo sledge with low friction runners, he peered in. The sledge clearly decided it wanted a closer look too. Seeing the sledge picking up speed towards his legs and being too far away to get there in time, I yelled for his teammate to 'ski across his traces now!' Quick-minded, his friend immediately complied and stopped the sledge's motion just a couple of feet before it would have toppled its owner face first to his death.

Wilki and I had estimated that we should be able to clear the remaining ice, given that there were no extra bad surprises along the way, and finish, with another full twenty-hour day of skiing. Exhausted, we decided to take advantage of some large ice protrusions and have a last rest before the final push.

Although not too windy, there was a breeze from the east from which we needed shelter if we were to get any meaningful sleep. The conditions were clear and we did not expect any snow in the following few hours at least. Again then, a tent would be a waste of time and effort. Instead, we chose to shelter behind a large ice boulder and set up camp. We were generous to ourselves and decided on four hours of sleep instead of the normal two or three.

Out of the wind and with our roll mats and sleeping bags laid out, we were both eager for a lie down, but not before a quick supper of salami and flapjack washed down with a hot chocolate. With the sun below the horizon but leaving the sky full of colour, from red and orange to a cold blue, Wilki was last to take his boots off and get inside his sleeping bag. Turning around to look at the way ahead, he caught a glimpse of something. He jumped up onto our wind-break ice and exclaimed, 'Mountains!' Although still miles from our destination, the motivation of seeing something that was not ice and which represented the finish line was indescribable. On every journey I undertake, these moments are often amongst the most special.

Looking up from my bag, watching the wind-vane ribbon flapping in the breeze, I suddenly realised how tired I was. I could not have been awake for long before drifting off. When pumped with adrenaline or focused on a job in hand, it is amazing how both body and mind can ignore exhaustion. In fact, the progression of our fatigue could be catalogued by the amount of photography and film we made through each part of the crossing. Taking the time to record our experiences and thoughts tends to be most enthusiastic when full of energy, obviously. Since we had entered the icefall a couple of days before, our enthusiasm had ebbed away and in this final, open-air bivi, the last of our video clips and photographs en route were taken.

After those few hours of reinvigorating deep sleep, I awoke to that intolerable beeping which was my alarm clock and noticed Wilki had already started to stir. It was our final push. I am sure that you would have been able to see the sheer tiredness in our eyes but the mood was buoyant. The sky was clear and the additional sleep had paid dividends. It had been just over eleven days since the clock started. Although not able to break the speed record set all those years before, we were moving considerably faster than the next best British effort.

Our first hour of hauling led us down a noticeable decline and with that, the mountains and glacier ahead uncovered themselves to a certain extent. We decided to aim for an area that seemed least 'crumpled' and set a good pace of around a mile per hour. Our sledges, lightened by food and fuel consumed, were down around thirty-five kilos and could be yanked and pulled over all but the worst of the bumps with a healthy tug on our harnesses.

Then, from behind, our luck began to change. A bank of grey cloud moved in quickly from the icecap and soon the contrast dropped, but not enough for us to lose sight of the mountains or icescape ahead.

As the glacier rolled and flowed over the ground thousands of feet below, its contortions made the nature of the surface ice vary with each wave and compression. At first we encountered small crevasses, barely more than slots, which were easy to hop across. Then, the ice morphed into a complex patchwork. It was almost

86

like a miniaturised sequence of steep hills, around five to ten feet high and set twenty feet apart, endless hills set amongst valleys. Roughly a quarter of those valleys had small four or five-foot-wide rivers flowing directly downhill. The advantage of this was that, unusually, the valleys were pointing in the direction we were going and we only occasionally needed to sidestep to another when the river became too large or it pulled us off-course.

Like this we continued, our spirits rising and rising as, counter-intuitively, the ice seemed to be helping us a little, rather than getting worse. The only drawbacks were the occasional river jumps and making sure we did not fall through the ice on either side. How long could this last? Even the ice itself had improved and was no longer that infuriating, energy-sapping, crunchy consistency as before.

Before long though, and only just over ten miles from where our GPS told us the end was, the rivers were becoming ominously larger, the result of many smaller ones joining up. There was a large dip ahead, perhaps a mile in length and we could see the tell-tale blue of lakes nestled in this low area. A large detour was necessary, as well as an unexpected major river crossing. We had both been enjoying boots that had mostly dried out, although this had allowed my wounds to start to scab and hurt even more.

We leapt back into the water; it was a river of surprising ferocity and we both only just made it across whilst keeping our footing. Thank goodness we had both prepared our sledges properly, sliding across the double zips of the cover. The only real entry point for water, therefore, was at the back. This meant that the waves crashing over the bow of the sledge could not pour in and soak our equipment. I thought the times of having to stop, empty out boots and vapour barrier liners of water and then wring everything out with freezing bare hands were over. No, not quite yet.

Over the remaining crest, following our unexpected 'dip', the melt seemed to be absent and the ice blocks, plus the severity of the gradients and number of dead-ends, were getting larger. Every hour seemed to bring with it a fresh set of obstacles and we could never get into any sort of rhythm. Wilki's pace was again a little slower and he did begin to mention that his lower shins were in agony. We tried re-lacing his boots and altering his sock combination but it was one of those helpless moments when not much could be done. It did not seem the right time to discuss the issue, but I was never quite sure whether the pain was holding him back or whether I was naturally picking up the pace with a combination of anxiety about the ice ahead and keenness to get us to the finish. Regardless, it did not seem to matter a great deal as we still worked together as before and even managed a smile or an attempt at a joke when stopping for food and water.

Just when the pair of us thought we had it under control, travelling at a reasonable pace on the right bearing and having the measure of the giant ice blocks and mini-dips in between, our first big blow arrived. The ice had turned a dirty grey colour and was totally dry; the last speck of snow was miles back. Every small undulation jarred, not so much through our boots, but more in the way the sledges bounced around behind. My feet were really feeling the sharp pain of dozens of razor slices but I felt more for Wilki, who was occasionally biting his tongue in obvious discomfort, never once whinging or shirking his duties. Then came a large crevasse. It was around four feet across, with vertical glassy blue walls and had that look about it that said, 'I'm going to be like this for hundreds of yards in each direction.' The only noise was of water dripping off icicles down into its pitch-black depths.

Our mind-sets had to instantly flick back to Nagtivit-mode; crevasse fields were, again, the order of the day. Time was short and our extra few days on the ice had made things yet tighter. Although flexible, our return flights from Kangerlussuaq to Copenhagen were looming and Wilki had an unavoidable family commitment on the horizon. The pressure was on and so we set about getting our teeth into the crossing with renewed vigour.

Once we had walked along the edge of the crevasse for a distance, careful not to let our ever-twitchy sledges career into the chasm a couple of feet to the side, we found a part of the ice which had collapsed and bridged the crevasse. It was our chance and we took it, hauling ourselves onto the next area of ice.

Expecting to haul for a little further, given the subtle characteristics of the glacier we had compared against our past experiences, shock was visible across both our faces when an identical crevasse appeared not even twenty feet beyond. We could also see another exactly the same distance beyond that one. My heart sank. It was simply not feasible to walk endlessly the length of crevasses to find a safe crossing spot for each one; our criteria for when to cross had to change.

The widths of the gaps varied between four and ten feet, with a foot or so of ice on the other side too steep to gain a foothold. Out came our microspike attachments for our boots for added purchase on the dangerous ice. Occasionally, the crevasses would be only two to four feet wide and we took the decision to use these as opportunities. Besides, it could take ten, twenty, thirty minutes or even longer to chance upon collapsed sections to use as a bridge. There is no doubt that the human mind has a remarkable ability to control fear. We began to leap, one at a time, from the lip of one side of the crevasse to the other. This required a run-up to pick up enough speed, then a spring of faith and then a desperate moment of relief when our boots found solid ice beneath them. Not able to relax then, we would have to continue trying to run up the other side in anticipation of our sledge clattering along behind. In most cases, the sledges would fall straight down the crevasse, vertically against the side and yank us backwards. It would be our job to keep enough forward momentum not to be pulled back into the crevasse and to our deaths, or at least, a major injury.

And so we jumped, crevasse after crevasse, but fear never really came into it. We were too fixated on the task and the time for reflection would come later. Even with this bullish approach to progress, we were down to mere yards per hour, perhaps a couple of hundred. At this rate and with no idea of when it might improve, or even get worse, we were running out of opinions.

Again it was time for mental arithmetic and calculations about pace and projected completion. The last time I descended the icefall, and from studying satellite images, the general tendency was for the ice to become increasingly chaotic and tortured as it picked up speed (a relative term of course) towards the terminus. Based on this grim fact, I worked out it could take us three or four days at best, or up to two weeks at worst to negotiate nothing more than these final few miles. Given the fact that we had crossed over three hundred miles in little over eleven days, the thought was appalling – realistic, but appalling.

Eventually, Wilki and I came up against a particularly aggressive-looking crevasse with an unstable lip and no evidence that it was narrowing to either the left or the right. We both lined up a section we had a smidgen of confidence in and went for it. My first boot hit the opposite ledge, knocking off some loose ice which I heard echoing down the chasm beneath me. My second boot gained better purchase and I was over. All of my effort had been used up getting my body to the other side and there was no impetus left. Stationary, my heart skipped a beat as I realised that the sledge was most likely in mid-air behind me and on its way down. I had to move forward.

Using my ski poles and every ounce of effort I had, I lurched forward and felt the ropes connected to my harness pull tight and yank back. Relieved not to be hurtling backwards into the abyss, I was, nonetheless, going nowhere. My sledge was hanging off the two rope traces and had become caught on an ice outcrop. Through all of this, I had not had the chance to check on Wilki. To my horror, he was in exactly the same situation as me. Exchanging sheepish glances, we had to come up with a plan, and fast.

Neither of us could extricate ourselves from this fragile equilibrium and so we needed to help each other. Sidestepping cautiously towards each other, the ropes reached the full extent of their length and the shock bungees. One false move and one of us could topple over. Slowly and carefully we worked at each other's ropes from the side until they were free and we could inch our way forward. Finally, with combined heaves on one sledge at a time, they bashed their way over the lip and to safety. One-nil to teamwork over going solo.

We had to think very carefully. Mindlessly attacking each crevasse without thought to the quantity of them remaining to our ideal finish point would only lead to problems. On the one hand, we could end up getting further and further into an impenetrable icefall zone and eventually reach an absolute dead-end, forcing us to lose more days backtracking.

Alternatively, with each crevasse leap we were playing a game of averages. Sooner or later, one of us would run out of luck. Crossing a crevasse field is usually controllable and with someone with plenty of experience, there is no reason why it should not be cleared without incident. Perhaps we are talking about an average icefall or a partially snowed-over glacier. Dozens of crevasses may pass unnoticed or are small enough to step over. Perhaps ten might need close attention. This was not an average icefall. Wilki and I were staring into a totally dry and 'fast-moving' ice stream which continued for many miles. The state of the ice was also getting worse, not better. There could be five or six hundred of these monsters to survive.

What was for sure was that we needed more information: a better view. Both Wilki and I left our sledges and rucksacks on a safe block of ice and he went right as I walked left along a crevasse. Finding a particularly turbulent area of ice that had thrown up some truly gigantic blocks, we climbed up to look at the way ahead.

Walking back towards each other, we both shook our heads whilst still out of earshot. There was nothing to the front but the same, with our target of rolling mountains in the distance. Looking behind, it was incredible to see up that last slope and grasp the sheer quantity of desperately bad ice we had crossed.

Faced with a decision such as ours, it could be said that this was the big moment. How should we behave? Should we stubbornly forge on with questionable survival? Should we try and go back and try another route? Should we change our target finish point? To say the least, neither of us were the sort to enjoy the idea of not finishing what we started. We had to assess our priorities. Firstly, we wanted to see the next day, and the next. Secondly, I wanted Wilki to cross the icecap as it was not a first for me but it would be for him. Finally, and although it was always on a knife-edge, we wanted a real shot at one of the major polar records. Failing that, I, personally, wanted a real showcase of Wilki's and of my high-speed credentials. This, without doubt and with the addition of a truly satisfying technical effort through horrendous crevassing, we had achieved.

After a long discussion, considering every option available to us, we were agreed. We would continue and locate an alternative finish point on the glacier and then cancel our vehicle pickup from 'Point 660'. Instead, we would charter a helicopter to meet us at this backup location. Undeniably, it was disappointing given that 'Point 660' was almost visible those few miles away. We knew that, on paper, our journey would not count as a crossing since it did not finish at 'Point 660'; it would not sit amongst those fastest times set previously. Instead, we would have to be satisfied with our own performance.

Our reflections would have to wait, though, as our scheduled flight from Kangerlussuaq was looming a couple of days later. Chartering helicopters in the Arctic is never a simple task and Kangerlussuaq was not a main charter base for Air Greenland's fleet. To describe Greenland's air coverage as sparse would be an understatement. Often, a single machine serviced entire coastlines and these were frequently grounded for mechanical reasons. Also, we knew we would be at the back of the priority queue even if a helicopter were available in the rough area. As expected, at the top of the list were medical emergencies and rescues, since these privately owned aircraft serve as Greenland's air ambulances too. Then came scheduled settlement flights, mainly to allow local Inuit Greenlanders to move between villages too far away to access by boat or dog sledge. Then these settlements needed basic supplies delivered, such as perishable foods and so freight came next. Finally, if the weather was acceptable and there were no other demands on its time, a helicopter could be used for private charters.

All we could do was contact our UK support team via satellite and ask them to speak to the special charters department in Nuuk. Amazingly, ten minutes after my initial call to request the pickup and communicate our expected GPS coordinates, I received a message. A helicopter would arrive at the pre-designated position in a little less than three hours. We were seriously contemplating a wait of at least a day, if not longer, so this was wonderful news. As it happened, one of the newer Eurocopters used by Air Greenland to service the growing resource-exploitation industry in the rocky halo of West Greenland was in the area. It had just finished dropping two hunters back at their village before flying back to Kangerlussuaq to refuel and then continue northwards. Our phone call had been at the perfect time and the pilot could just alter his bearing to fly over the ice and meet us.

In the short time between receiving confirmation and our pickup arriving, we had a lot to do. Our equipment had to be repacked and strapped down for loading into the heli, we needed to contact the Danes on the coast to cancel our land pickup and also record a video diary to illustrate the situation.

Walking up to the edge of a crevasse, peering over the edge and feeling the sometimes unstable and sometimes slippery ice under my feet, the primal fear of large holes in the ground returned. I had not thought twice about taking leaps over these giants just moments before. I marvelled at the resources of the human mind.

We decided to complete the final satellite transmissions from the shelter of our tent as it had just begun to snow; it was a wet, unpleasant snow, typical at lower elevations in the warmer Arctic months. This was to be our last camp on a truly brutal skiing holiday.

So as to make the charter as quick as possible – we were paying by the minute after all – we took the tent down fifteen minutes before the agreed time, removing each ice screw that anchored it down. This was also for safety reasons. The downdraft of even a small single-engine helicopter can be fierce and cause loss of or damage to equipment.

Looking to the west, I saw a speck in the grey sky and then that familiar engine noise. The pilot came directly for us and then made a wide loop to position himself for landing. There was no landing spot worth speaking of although we had done our best to avoid the worst ice. Devoid of snow and scarred with crevasses every few metres, a landing would take every bit of his skill. Hovering twenty feet off the ground, the helicopter held position and I could see the white helmet of the pilot looking around outside the windows at the area we had indicated on the ground.

On his first try, the skids touched the ice and wobbled around on the hard surface before he rose back up a few feet, unconvinced. Moving a few feet to the side, on the edge of a large crevasse, the decision was made and the pilot touched down and signalled to us to load up. Wisely, he did not reduce the downward thrust from the rotors and so, although in contact with the ice, the helicopter was still, in essence, hovering. This made for a particularly windy minute or so ferrying the sledges and skis to the rear doors and getting Wilki on board. I collected the final items and a loose sledge strap caused the only delay. A couple of forceful bangs on the door latch were unsuccessful and after finding the offending strap, all was secured.

Moments later, we lifted off. Our pilot was a former Swedish military pilot barely out of his twenties and he was intrigued by our journey. Keen to show us as much of the ice as he could, we overflew the route we planned to use to 'Point 660'. Well, I knew it would be bad, but what we saw from a thousand feet or so in the air was indescribable. The quality of the ice did not just deteriorate, it fell off the proverbial cliff. The scale of the crevasses grew and grew beyond the point of being navigable. To the north and south it was no better. Some areas also contained vast melt lakes and raging torrents of water. In a way, I was relieved that we had not simply chosen the worst route and it was all as bad as the rest.

Finally, we flew over the tongues of ice which reached onto the snow-free barren rock and hills of Greenland. It was to be our last view of the icecap for a while at least. Within half an hour, the airstrip of Kangerlussuaq came into view and in a curious manoeuvre, mirroring the landing route I imagined a fixed-wing aircraft would use, we flew the length of the runway. The surrealism of, one moment, considering our route through a killer glacier system in true wilderness and only hours later stepping down onto tarmac was not lost on me.

The shock to the system was physical as well. It was as if my body had flicked a switch. Gone was the adrenaline, the cold and the stress of our self-inflicted predicament and instead, I had warmth, comfort and a completely flat ground to walk on. Somehow this allowed all the soreness, pain and fatigue to manifest itself in a way I had not noticed whilst on the ice. My feet were in abject agony and the rest of my body weak and in serious need of a lie down.

Deciding to stay in the guesthouse adjoining the airstrip terminal, our gear needed to be moved the few hundred yards along a few corridors. Sorting the 'keep' from the 'throw away' pile could wait, but just this basic operation took us the best part of an hour. Wilki's feet were sore but seemed far more capable of walking than mine. My gait involved a pathetic hobble on the outsides of both feet and even that took time to achieve.

Wilki and I sat down on our beds to assess the damage. Those eleven and a bit days of our journey had taken their toll. Completely unlike long expeditions like 'The Long Haul', sustainability was not a possibility. We did not need to survive for months, look after our body weight or get plenty of sleep. Now, after it was all over, the debt, which our minds had suppressed for days, had to be repaid. We had both lost around a stone in bodyweight, alarming given our six to eight-thousand-calorie-a-day diets and the brevity of the expedition. We had ulcers, rashes, chafed skin and my feet were sliced to pieces with the remaining skin hard and agonising to touch. We were certainly not pretty sights, but we did not need to be and we did not care one bit.

Beyond the temporary physical effects, the journey had taught me something. This was something that does not often come easily to young people and especially, ambitious young people. There are varying shades of success. In a completely unapologetic way, we had failed and that hurt. We did not hold the record, which we knew full well was within our capability, both in terms of skills and fitness. I am the last person, even now, to try and dilute the consequences of failure by either moving the goalposts to dress it up as success, or consider failure to be acceptable. However, I saw the speed crossing as a part of a long-term plan. It was not a one-off, box-ticking exercise. I knew we were where I wanted us to be, record or not. That could wait for another year.

CHAPTER SEVEN

I had been filming with a young, indie film crew in the Ammassalik region in the winter of 2012. Feeling that there was a major gap in filmmakers' productions of the cold regions, we took matters into our own hands. I grew up watching the genius of David Attenborough and the BBC Natural History Film Unit. This partly inspired me to follow my own path in life and certainly prompted my choice to study zoology at university. Despite this, I could not help feeling that a few things were wrong.

Firstly, historical documentaries seemed to rely heavily on the same old archive footage and a smattering of cutaways from low-budget reconstructions. Secondly, in spite of the available technology being revolutionised between the 1970s and 2010s, I felt that the progression in terms of creativity was far less significant. The clips and sequences seemed eerily similar to before in their content. The changes seemed to be the clarity of the 1080p high definition, the sharpness of the stunning modern optics, the smoothness of the gyro-stabilised heli-cams and the cinema-like colour grading. The style had evolved but there was no revolution. Glancing back to the landmark series of my youth, like *The Blue Planet* and *The Life of Mammals*, the footage now appears dated, yet the style is consistent with that of the present day.

It all just felt a bit safe, not in terms of the incredible lengths the film crews went to in order to capture the wonders of the natural world – that is never in doubt– rather, in terms of the ambition of the story telling. I am sure these production companies, the masters of their industries worldwide, know their audience and their work certainly sells, but I always feel pangs of regret for style risks which are never taken.

A quick glance across the most-viewed adventure and nature films on online sharing networks like Vimeo, shows that the talent is there but it seems locked away into niches, rather than being unleashed into the mainstream. Car pioneer, Henry Ford is alleged to have said, 'If I had asked people what they wanted, they would have said faster horses.' Doubtless many people, myself included, would still be riveted to Attenborough's gems even if they had not progressed one iota since the 1970s. The revolution is yet to take place.

Opinions are merely opinions and the only way to justify one's own view of things is to meet the challenge by turning a vision into something real. How was I going to do this? As a natural world stills photographer from my late-teens, I was not a filmmaker but I had a feel for what works, a love of cinema and a good understanding of the mechanics. I decided to recruit young filmmakers into a team; I wanted those who seemed to have vision and originality, unjaded by thirty years in the industry. I did not want copies of what had always been the norm.

Within weeks of forming the idea, I had scoured the show reels of dozens of talented twenty-somethings and found a group I thought would have everything covered and would get on well. Social media proved invaluable. Two filmmakers/cameramen, Adrian and Matt, had spoken at length via Twitter previously. I hoped to serve as the catalyst to get us all around a table. The thread that stitched us all together was an affinity for using the internet to its full potential: for communication, feedback on edits, inspiration and distribution.

•

The internet can be seen as a threat to authority and to the status quo and also as a way for unpleasant people to gain an audience. It can also be argued to have contributed to the demise of some traditional professions by allowing market saturation and 'crowd sourcing' for unsustainable fees. It is, however, the ultimate forum for meritocracy; those with talent, skill and determination can compete on equal terms with those who have the backing of a big and often complacent corporate machine. The web has also given a voice to those who want to consign myths and plain hot air to history; something which is of particular relevance to the exploration world. 'Brilliant!' I think. 'Vive la Revolution!' Maybe I would not go quite that far, but it has to be a positive force.

It was this instant fast track to the people I wanted to work with that was so wonderful and enabled a project to be born in no more than a matter of days. In an invigoratingly pure process, I put together a team, we decided what we wanted to create and then set about it.

•

The third thing I really wanted to pick up on and change for the better was the filming season. One thing always seemed to remain the same, whether for Bruce Parry's *Arctic*, Chris Packham's *Operation Iceberg*, David Attenborough's *The Frozen Planet* or Gordon Buchanan's *The Polar Bear Family and Me*. Filming almost always took place in the easiest times of the year, late spring and summer, which are essentially the tourist months. I would understand this if all the magic moments of the frozen North or South fell within these four or five months, but that is not the case. The storms of the pre-winter and the extreme stresses caused by the polar darkness can be the backdrop to some of the best wildlife drama, vistas and human stories of all. The reason for the bias is actually very simple. April to July is the time of year with the most reliable blue skies and offers the best chance of reliable and more frequent flights.

So, my plan was to produce and present the story of the remote polar world of Eastern Greenland in winter, integrating with local Inuit hunters. This, instead of descending on a tiny village like the proverbial sledgehammer with a massive production team and crew, might just perhaps allow for an insight they could miss.

The outcome is still to be released but suffice to say, the few sequences and time-lapses of aurora (the Northern Lights) dancing across the entire sky I have seen are testament to the talent of these young filmmakers. The slightly wayward approach towards deadlines, perhaps unsurprising given the crew are not long out of student-life and increasingly in demand as niche adventure cameramen, seems a price worth paying.

The experience allowed me the opportunity to learn the art of presenting to a camera, rather than a theatre full of faces, and I found myself feeling more and more comfortable each day. Ideas circled my mind about the potential of this new way of expressing my thoughts and passion for the frozen world that so enchants me.

Filming varied from day to day. Making concerted efforts to communicate with villagers on their terms, being invited into their homes and conversing in their own language as much as possible, we captured some genuinely moving moments on film, unlike anything I had ever seen before. The next day would be all change and would involve showing the effect on the body when falling through thin ice into the sea and the best way of getting out again. The next, we would travel with dogs with an old Greenlandic Inuit friend, Georg Utuaq, to a glacier and shoot sequences with both Adrian and me dangling on the end of a rope in a large crevasse.

In spite of the adage of never working or filming with animals, one daylong hunt we were filming with three locals and their dog teams went in search of our quarry, seals. Seals provide food for both people and dogs through the dark, long winter and save cash-strapped Greenlanders from having to shell out on imported dog kibble.

Two years before, Georg had proudly shown off the head of a vast, four-metre-long Greenland shark he had caught on a long fishing line and was feeding to his dogs. It was a truly ugly creature; its skin was almost jet-black, teeth disordered and jaggedly emerging from the enormous jaw and its near-blind eyes were set deep into its head. It was just as well it was for the dogs, since the urea content of the flesh is so high that it has to be boiled many times over before it is edible to humans and even then, it tastes revolting.

Just before the hunters struck gold and one humanely dispatched a small seal with a single gunshot, the dogs that were dozing on the sea ice suddenly became excited about something. It was usual practice to avoid having a runaway dog sledge by either flipping the wooden sledge on its side, sticking a harpoon though the runners or lifting a front paw of the lead dogs through their harness to stop them running. On this occasion, a harpoon secured each sledge.

In the moment of excitement, one whole team of dogs jumped to their feet and set off. The harpoon pinged into the air like a matchstick and the sledge shot along after them without a driver. Thinking quickly, the two men nearest to the other sledges jumped on their foot brakes to stop the now frenzied dogs in the other teams from giving chase. Urged on by Georg and his friend in Greenlandic, I gave chase on foot.

I was never going to catch up with a lightly laden dog team at full stride, especially since I was dressed for a cold and slow day by the ice edge. What I did, though, was to settle into a sustainable pace aiming to intercept them when they eventually got bored. In spite of the steady pace, the cold weather gear had me sweltering in seconds.

Opportunistic almost by nature, the film crew back at the hunting point filmed the whole comical sequence. I looked ahead and noticed the dogs were slowing. A dog, one of the lead females, had taken a tumble, fallen underneath the sledge and was being dragged along behind as the other dogs continued unperturbed. Eventually, they reached their goal and spontaneously stopped. By the time I caught up, the entire team stood there facing me, tails wagging and barking endlessly, clearly happy with their bid for freedom.

Grabbing each dog in turn by his or her harness and lifting them in the air, I untangled the web of hauling ropes. I turned the dogs and sledge around in anticipation of their return. I was always struck by how patient and well-behaved sledge dogs are when being harnessed or reorganised for a journey, getting into a scrap with their neighbour only when my back was turned, almost like a mischievous child at the age when they realise they can get away with things.

Looking up, I saw that another sledge was heading towards me, thankfully with a driver at the helm. Once he reached me and turned around, we set about getting the dogs back. Only having a passing grasp of the Inuit commands and thoroughly aware of how tricky driving native dog teams can be, I set off using the other team as my lead. These were not near-domestic huskies driving tourists around in Minnesota; these were some of the most primitive and authentic 'Eskimo dogs' in existence. Their breed had worked unchanged for thousands of years.

Comforted by the fact the dogs more or less knew the route and also that my commands, some of which might have been correct, seemed to be having the right effect, we re-joined the others and I handed the team back to an unfazed Georg. I pointed out that the fallen female had a bleeding paw. He responded with a grin and a shrug; these were tough dogs.

Our final, unexpected taste of the ways of a traditional Inuit settlement in winter came back in the village. Heading in amongst the brightly painted wooden houses, we noticed a commotion by the frozen-over harbour and hurried down. It was as if the whole village had turned out for a great event. Surely enough, emerging from the north on a large sledge from behind the pressured sea ice, our boatman from the year before, Lars, was driving at breakneck speed towards the crowd. From hundreds of yards away, I could almost make out his ear-to-ear grin and wide-eyed excitement.

Like a film star, Lars slowed his dogs as the crowd, many of them children, engulfed him. The source of the excitement? A polar bear. Polar bears are protected and unless in self-defence, native people of the Arctic are only allowed to hunt a quota each year. Masters of their art, the bear would quickly be skinned by the women of the village and then every part of the carcass would be used for anything from food to tools and ornaments.

The sight of this unfortunate, mid-size male bear contorted and strapped to the sledge brought out mixed emotions in me. As a naturalist, it seemed sad but I understood why it happened. The whole story is far more complex than some might believe and the local people of the Far North have been able to hunt sustainably for thousands of years without upsetting populations of wildlife and the natural balance. As outsiders, we stood back and watched. It was not our moment; it was theirs and a major cause for celebration. I did feel privileged, nonetheless, to witness a special and rare occurrence at the tail end of our time with this community before flying back out.

After the new experiences of filming, my own story that winter really developed – not on location, but on the way home. Iceland is a regular stopping-off point, at roughly sixty-six degrees north, for many travels to the Far North. It was our stepping-stone for filming and Reykjavik, the capital, had become a place for which I had a real fondness. As a twenty-one year old about to set off into the cold wilderness for nearly four months, my final and nervous preparations had been played out in this small city, as had the elation upon our successful return. Whether guiding or training in Greenland, to Reykjavik we would come.

It had not escaped my notice that Iceland itself had a fine collection of icecaps – small and with unpronounceable names but intriguing nonetheless. The year before, I had arrived in the country a few days early for a solo explore before meeting clients. In my little, yellow hire car, I had set off across the volcanic wastelands and got a real feel for a truly spectacular country. The seeds were sown and it seemed crazy not to take advantage of already being there.

This, I suppose, leads us neatly to the question of what is polar. Labels are just labels but as I loosely describe myself as a polar expedition leader, surely my quarry should be polar and the term should be unravelled? My speciality is to travel on ice, whether it is floating on the sea or moving slowly over rock in the form of glaciers or icecaps. There are, however, glaciers near the equator and they do not solely reside next to the two Poles.

I once had it posed to me that surely a polar explorer or a polar expedition must go to either North or South Pole. Taking into account, of course, that other Poles (the Magnetic for example) exist this would be overly restrictive. Also, given that some of the greatest polar explorers of all time never reached a Pole, Otto Sverdrup and Fridtjof Nansen to name just two, it simply cannot be the case.

I think that much of the reasoning behind thinking the Poles are the only legitimate targets for exploration is a product of our time. Due to the commercialisation and risk-diluted trophy-hunting going on around our Earth's Poles, the other staggeringly demanding parts of the Polar Regions are neglected. Funding, book deals and media attention certainly favour lesser ventures over those with vastly more inherent significance simply because of an end-point at a Pole. As an example, Jerry Kobalenko's *The Horizontal Everest* about Ellesmere Island deserves to be a polar classic but is outsold by repetitive authors with a fraction of his insight or experience simply because their journeys reached a Pole. I am certain that the early pioneers would be shocked and saddened by this. The Poles are symbols, but offer only a tiny proportion of the opportunities for polar endeavour and achievement.

So, what is polar? The common-sense answer would include areas within the Arctic and Antarctic Circles. This, however, cuts out significant parts of Greenland and even parts of the Antarctic mainland. Other definitions of the Arctic include the 60th parallel – perhaps a little too inclusive – the timberline or the 10-degree isotherm. The Antarctic Treaty of 1959 considers that the southern 60th parallel defines the Antarctic and others say that the continent defines its extent. As such, there is no hard and fast answer.

What is for sure in most people's minds, though, is that Iceland is not polar. The climate there, contrary to its name, is unexpectedly mild and stormy due to ocean currents and weather systems from the Atlantic. Regardless, the largest of the icecaps, at barely a hundred miles across, the Vatnajökull, captured my imagination. During the summer, the 4x4-crazy Icelanders drive their super jeeps all over it and reasonably benign ski-tours can be enjoyed on the less-crevassed areas. At that time, it would hold little attraction for me.

The winter, however, was a different matter. Few icecaps of any size or location on Earth have the same fearsome notoriety as the Vatnajökull in winter. Essentially, it is considered to be one constant storm with the occasional lull. The approaches to the icecap are also formidable with steep valleys, melt rivers (this time over land, unlike the Greenlandic ones from my speed crossing), and tumultuous lava fields flowing across the land from countless volcanoes.

As part of my unrelenting desire to be the complete traveller on ice, I knew I could handle the longest of journeys. I also knew I could ski at speed in a lightning attempt at a crossing. I had experienced big storms before but the stories of the merciless Icelandic winter, like being in a freezing washing machine, had me hooked.

The planning was actually fairly straightforward. We would need no sponsors; I had a large supply of equipment and was already in Iceland. As a real shoestring journey, my plan was to catch a lift with a friend along the No.1 ring road, which loops the Icelandic coast, and jump out at a spot nearest to the western extent of the ice. We would then ski and walk across the rugged landscape to the edge, climb up and ski the full width of the Vatnajökull and then walk out to a tiny fishing town, Höfn. It looked easy enough on paper. But who was 'we'?

I had known Niall McCann, a zoologist and now a television presenter, for some time before meeting Finn, his brother, in Tasiilaq in 2011. A tree surgeon by trade but rock climber by lifestyle, Finn is one of those people who just exudes ability. This could be said of his brothers too and indeed, the entire McCann clan. They are true originals; there has never been a moment since getting to know the family that I have not been struck by their collective vision and energy, or impromptu ukulele sessions.

As such, and given that Niall and Wilki were tied up with work, I called Finn some weeks before whilst I was on the train. He, Niall and brother Rory were en route to Skye in Western Scotland for some wilderness time and climbing. In five minutes I had persuaded Finn to accompany me and was satisfied we would make a really effective pairing for an Icelandic winter trip.

Finn flew into Keflavik, the airport near Reykjavik, a day after I had returned to Iceland with the film crew. Our 'wrap party' was delayed by a day because of a snowed-in flight from Greenland but the long and short was that I do not think anyone had much recollection past 8pm that night. The Icelandics do wilderness, volcanoes and whales very well but my goodness they can do parties too... Not envying the guys their flight back to the UK, post-party, I set off on foot around the city in search of my one errand: stove fuel. Having exhausted the possibility of finding sufficient naphtha, 'white gas', I settled on kerosene from an Olis petrol station. Although smellier and dirtier than 'white gas', it would do fine for a projected eight to ten-day expedition.

Finn arrived at our rented apartment and after typically efficient equipment sorting, we set off for a burger and a pint on the main street in town. I was dying to get my teeth into this expedition. We had the right team, thorough research, a novel plan and the southeast of Iceland had experienced a lot of snow that winter. This was good news for us as skiing over snow is easier than walking over rough lava fields on the approach.

Due to the wonders of social networks, it had taken me barely a day to find a friendly local who agreed to drive our small sledges and us out of Reykjavik in the southwest, across the island and along the south coast, past Vik and to a place called Kirkjubæjarklaustur. Yes… we thought the same thing and called it Kirk thereafter.

For ninety per cent of our road journey there was torrential rain, not unknown even in winter in low-lying and coastal areas of Iceland. This was clearly not great news for us, as, even though it was most likely to be falling as snow further inland, it would be warm, wet snow and would lead to melting. The many waterfalls from the cliffs to the lowland were being so buffeted by the wind that precious little of the water reached the pools below intact; most was blown into the air as a mist. It seemed like something from Tolkien's Mordor.

Protected and with a false sense of security, we dozed in the warm truck, only stopping to fill up the tank and refuel ourselves with Danish pastries. Without exception, each Icelander who asked about our plans expressed wide-eyed surprise that we intended to cross the ice the long way (west to east) at that time of year.

Our luck was in as the rain had reduced to a very light splatter by the time the church and small, elegant, red-roofed buildings of Kirk appeared and our turning off point came into view; we planned to start on the closed, summer-only F206 road. Jon, our driver, wondered how far the track would be passable to a vehicle, snow-covered gravel as it was. We were only too happy to agree to let him shave a few miles off our approach. If anything, it was the cross-country trek to the icecap that concerned me more than the icecap, where I expected to feel more at home.

Sledges laid out on the snow, buckles done up and zips closed, we bade farewell to Jon and watched as he struggled to turn around and make progress back towards the main road over uneven ground. We were standing next to a slightly sorry-looking, half-buried fence, something that would become a regular feature of our first phase before the ice. Microspikes attached to our boots and skis stowed, off we went up the first steep hill.

Needless to say, this was not the way a crossing of the Vatnajökull would classically be undertaken. It is not exactly a regular expedition but, those who have crossed it, mostly Icelanders, do so across the much shorter North-South span and do so in the late spring or summer. Also, they get dropped off and picked up either by super jeep or helicopter to avoid the laborious extra fifty or sixty miles.

Within an hour or so it was sleeting. We had eVent (a breathable fabric I consider superior to Gore-Tex in the wet) clothing and water-resistant rucksacks and sledge covers. The significance of this cannot be underestimated. In the consistently cold conditions of the Arctic or Antarctic, outside of the brief summer temperature peak, there is no need to wear waterproofs. This is great news for two reasons: firstly, it means more breathable fabrics can be used, my favourite being Pertex, so body moisture can be wicked away and can evaporate quickly; secondly, nothing save a rubber suit or wax-coated jacket is actually waterproof and so there is no need to wear a flawed garment. Nothing is ever going to fall on or get blown at the clothing except for snow or drift, which just bounces off without any lasting harm or discomfort.

Unfortunately, Iceland in winter has a truly malevolent side to it. Temperatures can bounce around daily, dependent on cloud, elevation and weather systems, between plus ten degrees and minus twenty degrees. That range, even if less extreme than that, straddles the freezing point and therein lies the problem. Rain can fall, get everything wet and then hours later be frozen by cold temperatures, dangerously cooling the poor occupant. A strong wind will just make this ten times worse.

Our eVent was doing its best but before long, it was saturated, as was our merino wool underwear and everything else for that matter. It was not a quandary we had overlooked, just a discomfort we had accepted we would put up with.

Unsurprisingly, the wind picked up as well as we settled into our routine of keeping an eye on our map but following the rocky, side-markings of the road. The hills were steep and rolling and the murk descended so that we could only see a few hundred yards ahead. Regardless, spirits were high as we set a fast pace; our light sledges, which were set up for little over a week on the trail, bounced along happily behind. We only expected a half a day or so of travel before first camp. It took a while to sink in that as long as we did not run out of food or fuel and we made our pick up in Höfn, the clock was not ticking, so this was fine.

Just as the light was starting to fail and soon after we had lost exactly where the buried road was, I spotted a couple of structures. In the distance, with no point of reference, they looked like a large farmhouse and outbuilding. We approached and on closer inspection, found two very ramshackle hiking huts for use in the more favourable summer months. The door unlatched and having wiped down the filthy interior, Finn and I looked forward to a first night under a roof. The wind was ever-worsening and as I got the stove fired up, Finn stuffed anything he could find into the numerous gaps in the walls that let in drift snow and a loud whistling sound.

The mind-set of someone resigned to a tough life in a tent is very different to that of the same person at home. Your expectations of comfort are wildly different and once you have switched from one to the other, it is hard to readjust. I had not expected a hut on the first night and was worried that we would not want to leave. Getting out of a tent in miserable conditions is vastly easier mentally than leaving behind four walls and a roof.

However, the next morning, after a restless night's sleep, we found that our wet clothing and the equipment we had hung up had not dried and so the only option was to get out there and dry them manually– that is, the old-fashioned way with our body heat. The rain had stopped and we had a chance to locate the track and get back on our journey. We expected three or four days of hard work to clear the prologue of miles before getting on the ice – I could not wait.

I would achieve little by detailing the endless repetition of ravines, hilltops, valleys, lava fields and rivers we encountered, but the combination was draining. Navigation was always a struggle due to the regular loss of signs of the road, poor visibility and the constant wet and windy weather. Our tactics with the rivers were bullish – not hesitating so as not to waste time and effort. Instead, we picked a spot that looked a little better than the rest and leapt in. Our sledges coped admirably, floating along behind and only letting in some of the more determined splashes.

The wind had built, even in these relative lowlands, into a buffeting sidewind and the light was failing once again. We had travelled over ten miles as the crow flies and given the terrain, were more than satisfied. As a pair, we were working really well together. Behind the soaking clothes and dripping facemasks we were confident – the miles were ticking by.

We had the tent up in very little time at all, impressive given the fact we were a new duo, but as we unpacked, I did make one sad discovery. The rivers had taken their toll on our sledges and I found my camera pouch waterlogged; my camera was dead as a dodo. Luckily my electronics box containing communications equipment and the 'Oh Shit' box (a phrase I coined on 'The Long Haul') were both sealed and safe. The latter contained vital spares and backups, without which any expedition could easily fail. I jumped into the tent; the snow surface was not the cold, dry snow I was used to and was prone to melting given the slightest opportunity.

Once in the tent, we cooked a hurried supper of rehydrated food in packets, melted some snow and updated the outside world about our progress via satellite, then closed the inner partition to our sanctuary. This left us in a neat and comfortable section for sleeping whilst our boots, stove and other equipment stayed in the porch area. The wind was pounding the tent all the while.

It was unsurprisingly difficult to sleep, but it must have been midway through the night when I felt Finn vigorously shaking me in my sleeping bag. Something was wrong so I shot out of my warm cocoon and we unzipped the partition. The tent was being thrown around violently. In the darkness of the middle of the night we had just enough torchlight to try and see what was going on. The entire porch area of the tent was flying freely in the air, aggressively flapping with each gust of wind. The only way to describe the surprise would be to liken it to a nightmare when you get out of bed in the middle of the night, open your bedroom door and are confronted not with a landing but with a cliff edge, a swirling bedlam of a storm and nothing ahead but thin air.

Instantly we set to work to fix our new-found disaster, me holding the tent fabric down under control whilst Finn attached new corner loops and slid the ski corner posts back through them. With the tent finally under control, we assessed the damage and found that, incredibly, nothing had been lost. Even the near-empty rubbish bag was found flapping, half-buried in drift snow. With a sigh of relief, we mused on the cause, which became increasingly obvious after the commotion ended. Each corner of our tunnel tent was anchored to the surface by a ski dug into the snow and attached by a loop of super-resilient Dyneema cord. This wonder-product boasted far better strength and properties than normal nylon cord. Both of the leeward cords had snapped, or rather, been sawn through.

As a side effect of the snow being barely below freezing and seemingly very keen to melt, all of the snow I had piled onto the valance 'skirt' around the tent had disappeared. This is usually the main tactic for stabilising a tent and stopping any air flow beneath it; packed valances can often do a good job even without the tent being anchored – not this time. Presumably the tent fabric had insulated the snow piles and allowed them to melt or blow away, leaving the tent like a kite. The violent gusts had caused enough movement and friction against the cords to make the ski edges gradually saw through them.

Having checked that, in our tired states, we had not made a novice error and placed the skis 'skins out' rather than 'skins in', a sure-fire route to snapped cords, we put it down to unavoidable back luck. Beyond that, our fortune had held and the only thing we ended up losing was an hour's sleep.

The next day our target was Laki, a vast extinct volcanic system, which can be visited in the summer months yet remains totally cut off otherwise. In the eighteenth century Laki (or strictly Lakagígar) erupted, killing over six million people globally through famine caused by gas releases. Making our way round the northern side of the mammoth volcano rising into the cloud and gloom, we hoped to use its bulk as a form of windbreak. This meant a slightly longer route but our progress out of the worst of the blasts of wind was more than worth it.

As we had found on parts of the journey so far, wetland areas and small lakes were frozen over and sometimes barely recognisable beneath the snow. Often, the only tell-tale signs were the lack of volcanic lava debris sticking up through the white blanket and a suspicious flatness.

Considering a section of frozen lake to be safe, withstanding multiple ski pole jabs, Finn led the way out across a route that would eventually leave Laki in our rear-view mirror. At first all was well and we skied along at a healthy pace, enjoying the experience of relative ease.

Almost in unison, our skis broke through the ice as we had moved from a safe to a, presumably, deeper area of water where the ice had not formed as thickly. The colour of the ice is usually the safety indicator in these situations but it was mostly obscured by light snow. Dark/black ice would mean thin ice over deep water like the sea and blue/green ice can suggest the same over shallower waters. Only once the ice is a few inches thick and strengthened will it usually appear white. In sea ice travel this graduation of new ice 'nilas' are graded from dark to grey to white and correctly interpreting their hidden message can mean the difference between life and death.

Our situation was less perilous, though, since we knew the ice covered a snowy slush, which could hold our weight in spite of its syrup-like consistency. We were unlikely to drown. Our recently dried-out boots and trousers were soaked through and we cantankerously stomped our way to the shore, right next to the rocky face of Laki. My first reaction to seeing cracks suddenly circle our skis was to go back the way we came onto ice we knew was safe. Finn had spotted what he thought was thicker ice to our side and so we gave it a go. Although we broke through the ice layer occasionally, it was workable and saved us having to go back and then around.

We expected just one more sleep before reaching the icecap edge and the final major river marked on our map was in our sights. It is always much nicer to start a day having already overcome an obstacle rather than being lazy and leaving it to the morning. Although the light was again starting to dim over the gloomy, overcast and windy skies, coming over a crest and down a steep hill the river appeared in front of us.

It was much larger than those we had encountered previously and the snow coverage made it impossible to work out where the banks were. In fact it appeared to be one gigantic, two-hundred-foot-wide flow of freezing slush puppy. The fastest flow was evidently towards the centre and we knew that once committed to a crossing and even if we were fatigued by the first section, we would have to make it across the most dangerous main flow. A retreat to the first bank would achieve nothing and only leave us to go through it all again.

There is no magic formula for crossing a large, part-frozen river of this scale. It is hard, tiring and dangerous work and the lack of light made it even trickier. From ground level the other side was nigh on impossible to make out, indistinct though it was due to the burst banks. If one of us reached a dead end or broke up the ice too badly it would seriously affect the other, so we chose separate starting points about ten feet apart and set off, sledges in tow. At first the ice layer was just supporting our weight, visibly flexing beneath our feet. It would only be a matter of time before it gave way. Then, looking to the side to see how Finn was doing we broke through, almost in unison. As our boots broke the ice they shot downwards and then slowed as the flowing water and snow mixture was compressed. It was energy sapping at its best and although our sledges were neatly staying on the surface, soon we were moving one step at a time, pausing between each one.

It had taken only ten seconds or so for the water to permeate our boots, socks and lower halves up to just below our waists. Neither of us were strangers to cold-water immersion or discomfort in general but it is hard not to take a sharp breath as you feel the icy cold spread across your skin. There were so few points of reference it seemed like we were making no progress at all and dusk was truly upon us. For some inexplicable reason, but perhaps it was for the best, we both found the whole situation quite funny and starting spontaneously laughing at each other.

Some areas were deeper than others but it was impossible to tell where; one moment I would think the slush was taking my weight and the next I would half stumble and nearly end up face down. After what must have been ten or fifteen minutes, Finn called across that it was getting shallower where he was and the ice layer was almost holding his weight. I began to notice the same and my thoughts turned towards the opposite, slowly rising hill. This barren, rocky and characterless rise would be our comfort for the night. A long day had taken its toll and the wind and wet had left us battered.

As we settled into the normal tent routine following the aberration in the hut on night number one, the freeze-thaw nature of Iceland really sank its teeth in. It is one thing wearing damp clothes when kept warm by hauling and climbing, but moisture in the tent is bad news.

Moisture management is the primary skill in the portfolio of any cold weather traveller. In truly cold, polar conditions this is actually reasonably simple: do not wear too much whilst hauling, keep perspiration away from insulation layers using vapour barriers and keep out snow and hoarfrost (ice forming on surfaces within a humid tent) from things it might melt into.

There is a point, though, when it becomes nigh on impossible. We had the horrible combination of weather that would saturate you with water in minutes and then freeze you hours later; in addition, the cloudy cover never allowed us to dry out in the sun. Even if the weather was clear, it was winter and the sun would appear for only a few hours and be weak and low in the sky. The only positive was the wind, which could sometimes help speed up the drying process for breathable fabrics.

In the tent we created the customary amount of unavoidable humidity from the stove and our body heat produced clouds of vapour from our wet clothes. As is the familiar norm amongst those working in the field in the cold and wet, the clammy, clinging clothes had to stay on. Contrary to the 'wet and dry routine' that the infantry (in particular, from my experience, the Royal Marines) champion, the best way to keep a garment in service is to dry it on your body. Anything else I deem to be counterproductive and out-dated. If we had left garments off overnight we would have zero chance of using the resultant rock-hard, frozen block by the morning.

Then came our next quandary. Our sleeping bags were goose-down filled. These are much lighter and easier to pack for a given temperature rating than their synthetic counterparts. The disadvantage is that, if water or ice gets into the insulation, the puffy loft is lost and they become about as effective as a damp paper bag. A fully waterproof vapour barrier liner (VBL) can help from the inside but hoarfrost and drips from the roof will soon soak the outer shell. Some advocate a bivi bag to cover the sleeping bag but my experience is that moisture tends to pass through this bivi bag as well, leaving ice or water to form in between the sleeping bag and bivi which, in turn, soaks straight into the bag.

If on an icecap in the twenty-four-hour sun and if weather is reasonable, these problems are temporary as sleeping bags can be strapped to the outside of a sledge whilst hauling. This will evaporate any water and directly sublime any ice. Loft can be returned to even the worst affected bag in a few hours. We did not have that luxury.

Our system was never destined to be sustainable in these conditions and we simply needed a way of getting across the icecap whilst getting enough sleep and not succumbing to hypothermia. This we were managing through a combination of experience, discipline and a good dose of stiff upper lip. I am the first to condemn suffering for suffering's sake, a sad British stereotype and one that is, at times, avoidable. We knew, though, that we had our hands tied to a certain extent – we knew it and accepted it.

Once the tent was up, a process which took no more than ninety seconds with practice, the main discipline was not to jump straight into a sleeping bag. The VBL would stop a lot of the dampness from us getting into the bags, but our clothes would never dry if we were lying down in what was essentially a plastic bag. Additionally, the stove used to boil water would, even with the most careful technique, let some steam out which would form condensation or hoarfrost on the tent, depending on which side of freezing the temperature was.

So, we sat in the tent in our working clothes, shivering slightly, and barely being able to see through the clouds of steam-like vapour pouring off every part of us. Our body heat was drying the clothes and we needed to get this drying-out mostly completed by the time we got cold. It was a tough balance and undeniably, on the miserable end of the comfort scale. We were out of the wind, though and after a hot meal, morale was sky-high again. I had various tricks picked up from months on expeditions and one was to pull a wet sock over a plastic Nalgene bottle filled with boiling water. Placing the steaming sock and Nalgene near a tent vent to let most of the vapour out, the sock could be dry in a few minutes. This beats sleeping with a wet sock over your shoulder any day! It does, however, need the expedition to have a little extra stove fuel since the water in the Nalgene needs to be re-boiled after in order not to cool to the point of freezing later on. For a shorter, high-speed expedition it was an ideal trick.

Once the steaming effect had died away from our bodies we took out our sleeping bags from their drybag protection and slipped inside. It was a wonderful moment, as ever, but undeniably ruined by the overwhelming feeling of damp. Nothing was immune from it and we were sentenced to prune-like fingers throughout.

Hopes of keeping the bags dry, even with these precautions, were slim but we had to do our best. In hindsight, I do believe my confidence in relying on technique to keep the sleeping system dry was overoptimistic. I vowed to move to a synthetic system thereafter for these shorter minus twenty to plus ten degrees freeze-thaw expeditions. We learn something new every day.

Like this we travelled on the next day, constantly damp but performing well. The terrain was changing gradually and we remembered, somewhat glumly, that we were still only on the approach and were yet to see the icecap, our actual goal. The lava fields were becoming less pronounced; vast mangled lumps of lava now stood two or three feet high instead of the six to eight feet of the day before.

Finn had some blistering forming on his heels. He used the same Alfa hard leather boot and NNN-BC system I saw so many times and simply could not understand. It is one of the few areas where my opinion differs with the Scandinavian polar skiers and allies more with the traditional Canadian and Russian viewpoints.

I use soft boots and flexible bindings that are loosely based on the Inuit kamiks or Yupik mukluks, used for thousands of years. I have never had a single blister or 'hot-spot' in thousands of miles of cold weather expedition skiing yet see dozens of them on the feet of those using 'Alfas' or similar. The latter do seem to have a fan base, though and it seems impossible to reason with some users. The sadness is that often those going through the learning process can be given only one side of the story and never know soft boots are available. Do not get me wrong, for hut-to-hut day tours or track ski racing, hard-sole boots and three-pin bindings are the only choice for efficient speed and ski control.

Finn, being a climber for ninety per cent of his time 'in the field' and with less polar experience, had the hard boot system. I felt bad for the pain he was clearly feeling but never complained about. I was fast realising Finn was a class act.

CHAPTER EIGHT

As if someone had been listening to our quiet pleas to the weather gods the clouds cleared a little, even enough to expose the sun. The wind dropped and we could actually see the landscape. It was incredible. For a few hours, the tiredness we were feeling after just a few days and the sogginess of everything we owned could be forgotten. The lava was smooth enough to allow us to ski a fairly straight path across the snow. Only small clumps of the black rock stuck through the surface.

We had left the end of the 'summer road' track quite some miles back and now relied fully on compass and map for navigation. I had a collection of maps and satellite images that indicated the critical features we had to know. These were the contours and gradients, the major melt river locations and the up-to-date crevassing maps for the icecap. These were usefully updated every year by the Icelandic authorities, mainly to aid the safety of tourist trips in the summer in those super jeeps the locals are so keen on.

As the instigator of the expedition and therefore the researcher, I was carefully picking our route through all the hazards and taking a gamble on the glacier slope I hoped would be most crevasse-free. I was seeking out slow-moving ice which was not calving into the sea or a lake; I hoped this would translate into relatively safe ice and allow us to avoid the crevasse drama of 2011.

I wanted a view of the ground, between the icecap and us, to add to the mental picture I had and our newfound ability to see the horizon did not come a moment too soon. A gentle snow ramp took us into a sort of col between a couple of rocky outcrops. It was as if a giant map had just been laid out before me. We could now clearly see the white icecap spreading all the way across the background and in the middle ground, a myriad of melt streams and dark blue patches which indicated standing water.

Blind map work could never overrule such an immediate and accurate source of information and so we stood on our observation point for twenty minutes, taking the chance for a lunch break too. I had a few things I wanted to get done and had previously put off due to the wretched weather conditions. I could now, for the time being at least, give my sleeping bag an air and open up my sledge bag properly to empty out some drift snow and pour out pockets of water.

Most importantly, however, Finn and I stood with outstretched arms and worked from the left (north) to right (south) along the field of view pointing out ideas and potential routes to each other. Often one path which looked promising resulted in an apparent dead end; it was hardly a situation I was unfamiliar with. Having chosen the best of what was available to us, we set off once again.

That six or seven hour period of clear weather was to be, unbeknown to us, the only significant block of good conditions we would experience and what good timing! The view was breathtaking. To our left was a string of enormous volcanoes projecting surreally from a snow and lava rock surface. They were your stereotypical cartoon volcanoes: perfect cones with a neat, flat-topped crater. The slopes were still covered in a blanket of snow. This boded well for us since the angled snow would be amongst the first to thaw away as winter turned to spring. Snow was our lifeline and our key to safe and fast travel.

We skied at a ferocious rate, reinvigorated. I suppose we might have moved at three or maybe four miles an hour, seizing our opportunity over flat snow and in a lull instead of being half knocked over by the wind. We took the chance for a few photographs as well. As often seems to be the way, the photographic record of an expedition tends to be skewed in favour of the less dramatic and 'blue sky' moments, something I always make a mental note to try and balance out. We were down to Finn's compact camera given the watery demise of my own.

One thing we noticed and marvelled at was the optical illusion of the fore, mid and background in front of us. With various gradients and no points of reference for our eyes to use, we could not easily deduce what was flat, what was a decline and what was a rise. It appeared, bizarrely, that we were on a decline and the icecap was like some kind of otherworldly, white ocean extending flat out into the distance. Of course, this was nonsense. We were on the flat and the icecap was a slope leading up onto the dome.

The appearance of this glacier was like nothing I had ever seen before. Unlike the scarred and chaotic glaciers of Greenland or even the glaciers flowing fast and crevassed between mountains on the Vatnajökull's southern border, this western extent was smooth and calm. It was not unlike a steady flow of candle wax spilling out onto a table. This was, of course, what I had hoped and why I had chosen it from maps, even in preference to some of the more accepted glacier access points.

After an hour or so, we reached the first of the wet areas. It was inevitable, no matter how kind and gentle the glacier might be, that some melt would occur in the relatively mild Icelandic winters. We found that only a couple of the rivers were actually cut into the ground below them and most were running on top of the snow layer. This made life fairly straightforward and accepting that we would need to dry out and re-wax our skins, we skied straight across all but the worst.

Occasionally, we would have to move one behind the other almost using 'stepping-stones' out of the better ice so as not to break through. We were somewhat surprised by how non-dramatic it had become; even finding a flow of water in our way was not a disaster. We simply had a look for the shallowest part and then skipped across with full commitment. The only things likely to result in a dunking would be hesitation or poor judgement of the surface.

Finally, the icecap was at our feet and we were ready to take it on. It had been over three days of real discomfort and serious hard graft, but I was proud that we had forged our own path and not been dropped off by an airlift, though a vehicle insertion would have been highly unlikely in these conditions.

With barely a step up, we started the climb and took a bearing for my first waypoint along the spine of the icecap. The only objects to break the flat, hard-packed snow were glassy-blue ice boulders, easily avoided, and the occasional dip with waterlogged snow. What a change from the past! We gained elevation very quickly as we tracked a diagonal route from the leading edge of the ice stream. Stopping for a food and water break, I looked back to see an ominous bank of white cloud approaching from the south.

Our respite was never destined to last long but for the next hour or two it was hard not to look over our shoulders whilst skiing. I am lucky enough to have seen some of the most special Arctic vistas imaginable, but this was so unique. We could see the mountains, snowfields and lava flows for dozens of miles and so, so many volcanoes. The entirety was covered in a blanket of snow still and we thought we could even make out Laki and much of our route back to the coastal lowlands.

With not one crevasse in sight nor detected underfoot, Finn and I could really stretch out and develop a ski rhythm on the slope. Not unlike the vastly larger Greenland icecap, the rises were gradual and stepped.

We made our camp on the ice, the first of the crossing to be made in classic 'polar' style rather than backcountry style. Having been moving for around eleven hours, we were not pushing to the barely sustainable extent of Wilki and myself the year before, for there was no need. It was wonderful not to be against the clock once again and simply to have completion as the goal. Polar travel, or any long-distance travel for that matter, has few peers in the sense that it is the journey not the destination which counts for everything, the survival and not the arrival.

By the next day, the weather had deteriorated and we braced ourselves for a continuous trial until descending off the ice towards Höfn. The visibility had dropped and the wind picked up a little. Having reached the mid-way point of the icecap (from north to south) and therefore being on the central, horizontal spine, we could ski fast and straight until near our exit glacier.

My maps of the crevasse zones seemed to be overly-conservative for our purposes at least. I expected them to be more accurate in the summer when the snow has subsided, leaving the ice behind. Also, the definition of 'hazardous crevasses' to a 4x4 vehicle is very different to hazardous for a skier. As such, we scooted happily, if still a little cold and damp, across the areas marked 'to avoid'.

The only feature on the Vatnajökull itself, apart from the halo of mountains around the edge, is Grímsvötn. It is a volcanic caldera and sub-glacial lake which can produce explosive eruptions and to a traveller, can be deadly. There are many stories of disorientated skiers in the spring and summer seasons not noticing its presence in the low cloud and whiteout. Some have fallen hundreds of feet down the steep sides and suffered injuries.

I had to keep an eye on our position relative to this stark bowl in the otherwise smooth icecap and as the pair of us skied within a mile or so, the clouds once again parted briefly. It was a good thing, since the exact boundaries and drops are not accurate on the maps and the ice to the left and right from our perspective was never described on paper.

My original plan was to leave the exposed part of Grímsvötn to our right (to the south) but our short snap of visibility made it clear that this was not the best plan. Even though we were free of the actual feature, the ice and snow for a mile or two to the north was disturbed and had formed into steep, crevassed ice hills. The south offered by far the best route, the higher 'ground' being much smoother and faster.

Once past, we had spectacular views down the Öræfajökull to the south. It was a new experience to be able to see the edge of an icecap when standing on its spine; my sense of scale was confused for some time! Encouragingly, it appeared that the crevasses down this more dramatic ice tongue were not too intimidating. Instead, they seemed regular and small in size; it was a good omen for our eventual descent of a sister glacier on the eastern side.

In a complication to our otherwise steady travel along the plateau, these topographies had resulted in a large but gradual bowl in the ice and we needed to get beyond it. Rejecting the option to skirt around for miles, we decided a straight route would be the best. At least we might then get out of the area that needed a view and minute-by-minute decision-making. This would leave the simpler eastern half of the icecap for when the weather was to attack yet again.

The slope was steep and in a peculiar experience so rare for a cross-country skier, we actually got some downhill glide. There was no need to remove our grippy ski skins since they were waxed and the only limitations were our somewhat unruly sledges, which seemed determined to overtake us by whatever means possible. Enjoying ourselves a great deal, we must have covered the mile's width in just ten or fifteen minutes before facing the long slog up the other side.

The temperature was dropping as the night drew closer, barely into late afternoon, as is the nature of the winter at the higher latitudes. Our windproof shells and base layers still held a certain amount of water, as did our socks and boots. Light cloud had limited the insulation of the surface and given our elevation at just under three thousand feet, the thermometer dropped to twenty below zero.

It was time to camp. A beautiful blue and purple hue glowed across the sky and ice, leaving us to erect the tent. Luckily, the wind did not bring snow with it. Unlike down in the lowlands and around Laki where the temperatures were not cold enough, we actually managed to load the valances well with snow to stabilise our little red home.

Once again, going through the drying-out routine, shivering in the tent and with our sleeping bags barely lofted at all with the damp, we tucked into a big meal of spaghetti bolognese amidst the unavoidable odour of our kerosene fuel. Later that night and not having been able to sleep due to a growing nausea, I lay awake, huddled in my damp sleeping bag.

After the first couple of days it had been impossible not to shiver at least a little whilst trying to fall asleep and our rest was suffering at the best of times. Again, as a strong opponent of the idea that suffering is necessary, this troubled me a great deal, but there really is a point at which discomfort must just be dealt with mentally.

I had become so nauseous that I had to shuffle partially free from my sleeping bag and hang my head into the 'cold sink' we always dug into one side of the snow-floored porch area. Lying there, the feeling grew and grew until I knew there was no hope of getting away scot free. With only soft-bottomed down boots on my feet that were, you guessed it, not dry, I did not have time to get my boots on. Instead, I beckoned over to Finn urgently, having heard him toss and turn, to lend me his tent boots, which had soles.

Without further delay, I shot out of the sleeping area, opened the tent door and sprinted outside. I only made it around four or five feet when my insides violently made their feelings known in both ways. Instantly relieved and having checked that no item of clothing had suffered as a result, I got back in the tent and soon fell asleep, regardless of the ineffective state of my sleeping bag.

Finn, concerned at first and then amused, asked what the problem was in that jibing tone of a friendly teammate. Having had a good laugh about the situation in only a way two men with 'toilet humour' can do when in the wild, I made my apologies for being so objective when demanding his boots. There had been no time for niceties but at least they were returned in pristine condition.

An outdoors-person, or even the casual observer, might comment on the fact that, within a few days, Finn and I had become accustomed to working with a complete set of either wet or damp equipment and also that a stomach upset had occurred. It is absolutely true that a major killer on expeditions and in fact, the first thing a professional should avoid is key equipment becoming wet. This is absolutely reasonable on a classic polar expedition, high-altitude climb or another given discipline.

In Iceland in winter, we were dealing with these hybrid sets of conditions. The usual procedure of keeping sleeping gear bone dry at the cost of all else and a dozen other unwritten rules simply becomes impossible given the nature of the conditions. Instead, what a serious expedition must do is accept the limitations and realities. At the cost of trying to attempt perfection in vain, we had to make an arrangement that would allow us to survive and tolerate the problems. We were experiencing exactly what we expected and were actually very chipper about our progress, sending optimistic satellite updates to our website and social networks.

The stomach upset was more of a mystery. Our food was in date and our discipline of keeping fuel and drinking snow and water separate had not faltered. Usually, I have only heard of an inexperienced guided client with limited awareness getting their food laced with fuel – an instant recipe for bad news. I was absolutely sure it was not the case here. The kerosene was obvious by its smell everywhere it went, even once it had vapourised slowly, and so I knew my thin contact gloves were not the culprit. Unresolved, I put it behind me.

The next morning invaded my senses long before I had even opened my eyes. The noise of the wind had grown from 'very noticeable' on my arbitrary scale to 'bloody noisy'. I could also feel the floor of the tent, connected to the tunnel flysheets themselves, moving and tugging away with each gust and it must have been this that woke me.

Having had a hot breakfast and moved from our damp, clammy sleeping bags into our even damper outer clothes and frozen boots, we both grimaced as we assessed the state of the world outside the tent. Unsurprisingly, the view was that of a classic whiteout; everything was milky white with no features, horizon or contrast. Not only would we have to haul blind, we had a strong wind that would be half in our faces as we got going. Still, we had been gifted the half day or so of good weather previously, so were not really due any more.

Moving past the halfway point of our icecap crossing and in this manner, with a stubborn headwind, we made as much progress as we could in eight to ten-hour days. Snow was falling heavily, which made the sledges drag more than normal. Also, the heavy cloud had infuriatingly raised the temperature so that the snow instantly melted as I watched flakes blow against my sleeve. What I would have given for it to be twenty or thirty degrees colder, even with the wind and snow.

A side effect was that my flexi bindings were showing a rare Achilles' heel. Snow had accumulated around the straps and become compacted. When warmed slightly and then refrozen overnight, they had iced up. To get them to tighten properly around my boots they needed constant tweaks and often needed taking off for a proper seeing to with the back of a knife blade. Ironically, apart from the odd bit of ice caught in the mechanism, Finn's rigid pin bindings were faring better. His feet continued to deteriorate, however, but in his pragmatic way, he just got on with it.

Navigating from our chest-mounted compass, the path we skied was a pretty reasonable straight line and after a couple of days, we had just twenty or so miles till we would face our descent glacier. With a choice of two long, narrow ice tongues to choose from, the Hoffellsjökull and Lambatungnajökull, we hoped to have some sort of view from the top of the icecap in order to make an informed decision. The former would be a shorter route and not be too far from another summer track which could help lead us to the main ring road, but we heard that the step-off area could be waterlogged with melt.

The wind was growing and growing. Our UK support team and Niall, Finn's brother, were sending us through the best forecasts they could but the conditions on high icecaps are so hard to predict. The speed was certainly now in excess of fifty miles per hour with much stronger gusts.

Both of us were finding it a struggle to stay upright and on course, but the truth of high winds on expeditions may be surprising. It is, in fact, safer to be up and skiing when it is particularly bad than to sit it out in camp. Yes, progress may be slowed and it might be stressful and physically arduous, but very little damage can be done and there is nothing dangerous to be blown around like falling rock. Putting up a tent and keeping it stable is a completely different matter. For this reason, it is not always just stubbornness and a desire to push on which leads polar skiers to stay out in the mêlée.

There does come a point, however, when enough is enough and it is necessary to build up defences and camp. The real skill and something that requires judgement from seeing various previous situations, is to know when to stop. Too early and you risk feeling a little daft and losing precious time which could have given you extra miles. Too late and it might be impossible to get the tent up at all, leaving you without warmth and shelter in a place which is hardly suitable for a rescue aircraft to come and pay a visit. The likely result, if unable to construct a satisfactory snow cave, would be death from hypothermia and exposure.

It is taking this decision, a very hard one to make amongst those with eyes set on a prize and for whom stopping can feel like a sort of weakness, which separates the professional from the amateur and ultimately, the living from the dead.

I signalled to Finn that I was stopping, crossed poles above my head, and beckoned him forward so we could talk. We had to stand just a foot or so apart to be heard. I told him I felt that the wind was getting progressively worse and so we must choose a point when we thought we could still get the tent up. I told him I thought that moment was now. With only a split second of thought it was clear that Finn was happy with the call and we set about making camp.

One bonus was that, unlike down in the lowland lava fields, the snow was thick and of a reasonable consistency which would allow us to build a snow wall and pile it onto the tent valances. Some form of windbreak had to be constructed before even considering getting the tent involved. Less promising was that, as we started shovelling snow into a long pile perpendicular to the wind, it shifted direction more than once and its power was stripping each shovel-load of half its contents.

It is a sort of art form to make a neat, strong and quick snow wall using cubic blocks of cold snow. It can be done on polar icecaps and in places like Norway in winter, but blocks were not possible here. The wall ended up only four feet high due to its unwillingness to stay put but it was something. I used the two sledge shells angled in the air and then supported with snow to add another layer of protection.

Now it was time for the tent. With incredible care and doing away with our sodden Primaloft (synthetic down which insulates when wet) mitts, we took the 'tent sausage' from the sledge and instantly put two windward skis through the new corner loops. Making sure not to let the wind get underneath it and cause an impromptu take-off, we unrolled it, poles already gaffered into the sleeves, and then tensioned it.

Whilst Finn dived inside to try and create some semblance of order in the living section with our tent bags and rucksacks, I did my best to load snow onto the valances, much of which became drift, and secured any loose items with karabiners.

Inside and somewhat relieved, the wind howled and I got on the satellite phone, to try and see if there was any chance of a let up, whilst Finn worked on the stove. We could not descend any glacier, no matter how clear of crevasses, when we could see nothing and could barely stay on our feet. As the loud beeps signalled each message that arrived into the handset, I read them with increasing dismay.

Wondering how to break the news to Finn, I double-checked the date and time against when the forecasts were time-stamped to. The wind was due to build and build further with even the more conservative estimate predicting seventy mile an hour maintained wind speeds. The worst estimate was nearly ninety miles an hour with potential to grow faster and with gusts well in excess of a hundred miles an hour.

Our tent was the best in the business and we had as good a snow defence as we could manage, but this storm, which showed no sign of abating for at least forty-eight hours, would most likely be too much for it. We were also nervous about the direction of the wind. As a tunnel tent, it is stable with winds running along its length but a side wind can cause havoc. One change of approach and we would be flattened.

Trying to concentrate on the tasks in hand – drying ourselves out as well as possible, melting snow for drinking water and eating – I sat behind Finn in the main sleeping area as he sat forward with legs in the porch. We both froze instantly as we heard a loud crack behind me. I flung myself back quickly to see that a tent pole had been snapped clean in half and was threatening to rip the tent fabric with its two sharp ends. If this happened, the gusts would make short work of the ripstop fabric and we would have no tent left.

I grabbed the two ends and held them in place and then raised my feet up in the air to try and stabilise the next set of poles, attempting to halt a chain reaction. Fixed in my somewhat ungainly pose in the tent, I called to Finn that he needed to go outside to try and build up the wall of snow and maybe move a couple of the guy lines.

Within a minute Finn had geared up and jumped outside, calling back in with a description of what he saw. The wind had shifted almost ninety degrees to the side, exactly the worst-case scenario. This meant that all our work previously to build defences was rendered useless and the tent was being attacked from its weakest side.

As I heard Finn's efforts from outside, the almost uncontrollable jerks on the tent tempered slightly and I could look around to assess the damage, still holding on with both hands and feet. It would later turn out that our tent had suffered over a dozen separate 'injuries' but our focus for now was on saving our shelter in whatever form possible. Our survival depended on it.

Dripping with melting snow and with drift forced into every crevice, a rather battered-looking Finn emerged back into the tent from the maelstrom outside. He had done a great job of stopping its state getting any worse and so I swapped places to get a better look at the situation myself.

Armed with the shovel and adding to the new wall – well, more a heap than a wall – I checked the sledges and our equipment stored outside to make sure nothing was lost. A combination of good discipline, clipping everything onto everything else, and perhaps a little luck had ensured it was all still there, if a little bedraggled.

The tent was still, evidently, very unstable and the force of the wind made it impossible to make a repair or replace broken parts. I decided that I had to secure our shelter for the medium term as all reports suggested the storm was here to stay. I had to let survival overtake a successful expedition at the front of my mind.

I decided that the broken windward end of the tent was unusable and so the only way to keep it from getting worse was to bury it. Having called inside to Finn to let him know why half of our living quarters was about to disappear, I spent about twenty minutes, kept warm only by the effort, piling a couple of feet of snow onto the canvas of the first quarter of the tent.

Having clambered back inside and got into our sleeping bags, which were ever deteriorating to the point of being useless, we needed a council of war. The previous estimates of progress based on past performance and expected conditions had to go out of the window and hopes of making our pickup on the Friday from Höfn were gone. It was late on Monday night.

A push for the edge of the icecap, the glacier and the lowland walk-out totalled approximately fifty miles and would, even in perfect conditions, be a massive ask in one march. In the present storm, though, we had to assume that if we took the tent down, we would not be able to put it back up. A decision to try and ski out would be a massive gamble. An attempt to use snow caves for shelter and rest would be futile as the snow surface was nigh on impossible to work with a shovel. The chance of a collapse and death by suffocation would be almost certain.

We had only a couple of other options. Either we choose to wait out the current storm and hope for respite afterwards for a two-day dash to the end via a glacier we could actually see, or we end the attempt. Which one of these we were to choose depended, pride aside, on the weather. We needed a weather window that would let us ski fast and accurately until out of danger. Knowing full well the brutal nature of the Vatnajökull in winter, the entire reason behind the attempt, that chance was slim.

DYE II radar dome in Greenland, 2010

Robert Peary in 1909

Practising contact drills in the Brecon Beacons, 2009

Robert Peroni's base
in Tasiilaq, April 2011

Wilki as we approached the Nagtivit,
August 2011

Wilki in good spirits in our open air
bivi on the Greenland icecap

Hauling my sledge over the ice on
the first day of the speed crossing

Alex showing the vast
scale of crevassing on
the Nagtivit Glacier with
no snow cover

Soon after fixing skis to our sledges
on the Greenlandic plateau

Continuous obstacles on the Russell Glacier; melt river (above) and crevasses (below)

Our helicopter pickup from the end of the speed crossing

Driving dogs on the sea ice near Kulusuk, January 2012

Climbing the Vatnajökull,
February 2012

Our wrecked camp after the storm

Dave, our dog

Hauling 270kg on the 'Dark Ice Project',
December 2012

Qaanaaq in
the polar
winter at
midday

CHAPTER NINE

I used the satellite phone to call in the latest forecasts and to talk in person to someone from our support team, who happened at that time of day to be my father. Having served for forty years as a Royal Naval Officer, I could always expect a succinct, calm response from him and indeed all the members of my family.

We discussed the latest images on our private, weather advisory service satellite feed and it confirmed the new text forecasts arriving into the phone's inbox. The storm was to get worse and there would only be one lull of six or seven hours when the wind would drop to thirty miles an hour or so, which is hardly a light breeze.

After a long discussion and a real battle against the emasculating prospect of having to ask for a premature pickup on an expedition that, whilst uncomfortable, had been entirely in hand, we decided we had little choice. Wind speeds over a hundred miles an hour would have untold effects on the crippled tent, half buried though it was and survival in such a hell, without shelter, would be near impossible. Even the most eternal optimist could not make that short lull, most likely still with whiteout conditions, a real opportunity to ski out.

Saddened but with little choice, we decided, during the evening, we would have to seek assistance. We had to move fairly rapidly as that predicted lull would be the only chance of a safe pickup. Calling back to the UK, I handed over our GPS coordinates and asked for a dialogue to begin with our insurers, who should then arrange with Icelandic companies for either a helicopter or overland pickup.

In what became a drawn out saga with Mapfre Assistance UK, who underwrite dozens of UK insurers, the issue would eventually have to be played out via ombudsmen and courts, who took the underwriters to task for a series of failures to follow procedure correctly and a systemic 'error' – it must be said with them kicking and screaming at every opportunity and without a hint of remorse.

My own view on insurance is strongly driven by an ethical viewpoint that promotes responsibility but common sense. Skill and experience can avoid the need for the vast majority of claims but when bad fortune overrides this, sometimes action has to be taken. Expeditions can, in many situations, choose to insure themselves and when permits are involved, are usually compelled to do so. As a matter of basic professionalism, I always insure. Whether I then choose to use that insurance is a matter for circumstance and ethics.

If it is not possible to finish an expedition at the exact time or planned location, there are a series of options that should be attempted in a very particular order:

1. Try and travel out to another finish point, without external assistance.
2. If there is time to negotiate and plan, take personal responsibility and charter an aircraft or vehicle.
3. If time is short, use your insurance for which you have paid a (usually substantial) premium and use the option provided by them.
4. As a last resort, call on the pickup ability of a government or non-profit service.

Of course, number one is the best option by a country mile. It is worth noting that option two, one that would have prevented much of the post-millennium expedition insurance crisis, is barely ever used by expeditions for purely financial reasons.

A common reaction amongst casual onlookers, whether referring to the pickup of a team on a foreign icecap, rescue of a mariner in international waters or the rescue of a hiker wearing jeans and t-shirt on a wintery UK mountainside, is one of disapproval. 'That selfish fool put himself and the rescue pilots in grave danger – shame on him. He should stay at home in future,' are repeated ad nauseum. I think that there should be some temperance and balance brought to bear.

I, as I think most people would, condemn thoughtless, reckless and downright insane actions in the wilder areas of our world as it wastes the time of those sent to help. When in the context of a challenging but well planned venture, though, it is more complex. Rescue teams are, by and large, whether in the Alps, moorlands near to large cities or in remote international territories, either government-backed or private 'charters' acting in place of official vehicles. For example, in the Canadian Far North, private Kenn Borek Air provides Twin Otter rescues due to the lack of Canadian Air Force or Coast Guard capabilities in that specialist area. In the UK, it is mostly the Royal Air Force and Royal Navy who provide search and rescue.

Two points need to be made. Firstly, nothing should ever be done to endanger the life of a rescue pilot or other SAR team pointlessly or unnecessarily; it is a case of basic respect for the efforts of fellow outdoors-people. Secondly, and inextricably linked, is the fact that rescue professionals do what they do for a living for a reason. They may find it rewarding, enjoy the wonderful lifestyle and experiences but also, they are paid for it. Some are volunteers but of these most are climbers, sailors or similar themselves – quite simply, they share the passion and the motivation of the rescued and understand the potential misfortunes. Support teams, search and rescue and other outdoors-people (some are just bystanders who join in the effort) should forever receive the gratitude of those they assist, but they make a choice and the armchair vitriol should stop.

Having initially confirmed that Mapfre were checking helicopter companies for quotes and having recorded our location and the weather window, our UK team found out by chance that our insurers had decided to cease all action and had made no attempt to communicate this to us. Just twelve hours from the predicted lull which still appeared on the forecasts, action had to be taken. Unaware until late in the day of Mapfre's decision to cease any action on their part and with the pickup window fast approaching, our UK team had to work through the night to secure the help of ICE-SAR, the volunteer-led Icelandic service, via the UK relay at Falmouth.

Finn and I started preparing our equipment physically to make a pickup as smooth as possible and I saved the battery power in the satellite phone. My normal procedure is to transmit vitally important information to the UK via satellite and then let our support team undertake protracted discussions at leisure and without lost signal or other problems.

Speaking later to an Icelandic official on the sat phone, I confirmed our position and assured them that an emergency rescue was not necessary during the night. We were healthy, had secured the camp for now, identified a good time the next day, Wednesday, and were only in the situation of needing ICE-SAR due to a betrayal by our underwriters. We were keen to keep the pickup as calm and procedural as we could.

All we could do then was to wait. This provided unwanted time to dwell on how unhappy we were, to say the least, with the unexpected demise of an expedition that was a couple of days from putting smiles on our faces. Needless to say, as a professional I was dismayed at the need to ask for vehicular assistance. Whilst there were relatively few positives to take from the situation, we could at least outline tweaks that could be made for a future reattempt. The route was ideal and I was particularly happy to have spotted it with just maps for reference when there was little precedent.

Of all the changes we could make, the only expedition-saving one would be in the choice of tent. A shelter with all-round wind protection rather than bi-directional protection would be essential. All other substitutions would be purely for comfort and related to the freeze-thaw cycle we had suffered. Goose-down sleeping bags should certainly be swapped for those with synthetic filling and all other down insulation should be exchanged similarly for kit that performed better when waterlogged. The sleeping bag issue was, of course, something we had considered prior to the off but we deduced wrongly, that placing them in drybags whilst not in use would keep a reasonable loft in the bags themselves.

Waterproofing is nigh on impossible and so no clothing, from outer shell to underwear, could ever be safe from a soaking. For this reason, and only because of the short duration of such a crossing, a future attempt would probably use daily sets of fully protected clothing to be swapped in once the previous day's had saturated. The used sets could be allowed to freeze and be stored at the back of a sledge. It would not be an elegant or low-weight solution but one that had few real drawbacks for a hundred or so-mile expedition where speed and comfort come above a slightly lighter sledge.

A final tweak would be to save our boots from a dunking in rivers and the subsequent freezing they suffered at night. Skiing in squelching boots is not fun. Instead they would be stowed in our rucksacks when submersion was inevitable and replaced with grippy-soled neoprene boots.

All of these new ideas would have to wait for another day. With only the occasional task of taking turns to gear up and go outside to bolster the defences, we shared some damp chocolate bars and tried to doze a little.

Wednesday came and as forecast, the wind noise did seem to lessen, becoming just a stiff breeze. Looking outside, I even saw a tiny speck of blue in the sky. Our lull had come and the agreed arrival time from ICE-SAR was perfectly positioned. Half an hour before we expected them, Finn and I began to break camp and unbury our sledges and most of the tent. Looking back in, the usually palatial living quarters of the tent had been reduced to a size just big enough for us to lie side by side with our legs squeezed under the load of snow.

A few minutes early, through the gloomy, grey snowscape, Finn heard the noise of engines first and we looked to the southeast to see three snowmobiles appear. One of them had a trailer attached for our sledges and equipment. Having pulled up in a horseshoe around where our camp had been, the three friendly and relaxed Icelanders introduced themselves and asked how our expedition had been up until that point. We chatted with them as we strapped everything down to the trailer and leapt aboard the snowmobiles.

What was immediately obvious was that there was no urgency or concern on their part and we hoped that we had, in some way, contributed to this by providing them with real-time weather reports, accurate locations and an optimum pickup time when the light was good. Secondarily, it was obvious that they were having a lot of fun. Their machines were top of the range with heated elements and satellite navigation maps. For most of the next half hour, the snowmobiles raced each other. Whilst the trailered vehicle lagged a little, the other two made easy work of fifty or sixty miles an hour. With everyone well insulated to protect against the wind-chill, we felt a buzz of adrenaline that differed from that of the past few days.

We rendezvoused with three super jeeps, which we jumped into, and the snowmobiles then led the way off the icecap through the whiteout. We had an opportunity to speak to and thank everyone who had come up. Despite the total ease with which the whole pickup went and the jovial atmosphere amongst the Icelanders, Finn and I kept exchanging glances which said it all. We were disappointed by the fact we had not made the crossing but that is part and parcel of difficult travel; sometimes you win and sometimes you lose. What was very difficult to stomach was reliance on a thirty party. We had to swallow our pride and that is particularly galling when I was confident in my ability – a confidence that is vital for success.

Snow was falling heavily and even these monster trucks with oversized wheels became stranded every ten minutes or so and had to be towed by one another. Our driver, in between chatting with his passenger and us, smoked possibly the most fragrant cigarette I had ever come across. Perhaps the scent was heightened by the contrast to the odourless and barren place we had emerged from, but my normal revulsion towards these death-sticks tempered for a few moments.

Eventually, as the light was fading, the sight of rocks next to the route showed that we had descended off the glacier and were joining a very rough track. This developed into a reasonably well-defined F-track, similar to the one we had followed on the first few days. Snaking its way down towards the lowlands, we forded rivers and were treated to spectacular views of the forbidding winter landscape as we dropped below the low cloud.

The first stop would be to offload gear at the ICE-SAR base in Höfn. This gave us an opportunity to speak with the guys who had given up a good part of their day to meet us on the icecap.

Thanks all round were in order and we were given a large area in a warehouse to lay out our gear to let it dry before quickly giving a few more details about what happened for their records.

At that moment, the weather forecaster came hurrying down from the elevated office section and said grimly to Finn, myself and the others, 'It was an excellent judgement to come down off the glacier today. Tonight, all hell is going to break loose up there.'

The thoughts running through my mind were put to rest after speaking with the ICE-SAR commander, Brando. He commiserated with our bad luck and reinforced that the team who went onto the icecap were very relaxed about the whole thing. He put the following in writing: 'your preparation and management of the expedition were of the highest standards.' Brando and Oskar, one of the snowmobile riders, then signed off by saying we must come back the next winter and finish the job, offering us local knowledge about the state of our descent glaciers.

My momentarily dented confidence was restored as ICE-SAR continued to issue statements about how they supported our actions and handling. Regardless of this though, our gratitude for their assistance and positivity will never lessen.

It turned out that a week or so later, a pair of globally recognised Belgian mountaineers climbing virgin winter routes on the edge of the icecap had to activate their EPLB beacon and have an emergency helicopter rescue in marginal conditions. The Belgians had the misfortune of having their dramatic rescue using the helicopter winch filmed and shown globally online, bringing with it the customary angry responses from embittered and ignorant, anonymous web critics.

My own experiences with the public and the media had always been so positive, largely due to the success of my first few years professionally. Life is easy when you are winning, no matter how hard-fought that win is. I soon realised, before we had even settled into the only hotel in Höfn, that this was not to last. On switching on my iPhone, it beeped and buzzed furiously for a minute as no less than forty voicemails and texts arrived from national media, mostly British and otherwise Icelandic. The media attention my public relations colleagues and I worked so hard to generate when stories were positive and expeditions were being announced was now beating a path to my door. It was unsurprising but I had to think about how I was going to handle it.

Like any other professional in the expedition world, media and coverage was vital to create profile and deliver value to sponsors, but this was different. I knew deep down that damage was going to be done. I could give them the silent treatment but this could come across as petulance and they would most likely be less kind as a result. I decided that I would cooperate to a certain extent to try and gain some form of control over what was published in an attempt to encourage the media to stick to the facts.

What interested me was that the British media went straight for sensationalism and focused heavily on the fact that I was young and had used my father as a relay point in the UK. *The Daily Mail* was the most inventive and even began putting bizarre things in quotation marks which I would never have said, claiming, for example, that we had wrapped ourselves in a tent flysheet to stay warm. In the aftermath, and given the dozens of comments generated by the inaccurate reporting, a request had to be sent to the online part of the newspaper to have edits made.

On the flipside, the Icelandic media showed none of the ignorance or probing attitude of those back home; instead they wanted to hear stories of my time in the Arctic and asked when I was to come back to reattempt. I was so relieved. To be honest, I could not care less about the British response; it was the attitude of the locals I valued. Like Greenlanders, the Icelanders will always be some of my favourite people in the world.

There was one exception. An Icelander apparently, but I could never be sure, began bombarding my Twitter account and email with hate mail. At first I responded with as much humility as I could to a stranger and actually accepted his first few comments. As they became more and more offensive and more frenzied, I simply stopped responding and put it down to experience, physically shaking a little at the onslaught I had received. After all the moments of danger and uncertain survival I had overcome on my journeys with barely a backward glance, this cut deeper.

As we flew home, following a beautiful sunny drive along the entire South Coast with the outlet glaciers in full glow, I reflected on Finn. I have had the privilege of working with some truly remarkable human beings during my professional life – from Rich Smith and Adam Griffiths in my formative years to George Bullard and Wilki on later journeys. I had been truly lucky. Finn represented a continuation of a true pleasure I enjoy, that of working with truly capable friends who exude professionalism. As Finn's brother Niall told me, he has an almost bottomless pool of talent to draw upon, combined with an unflappable confidence and ease. He is a star and someone, like Niall, I am proud to call a friend.

I think the Vatnajökull icecap highlighted a real maturation in my expedition life, but not in the way that might be expected. In 2008 on 'The Long Haul', there was little doubt that I was mature beyond my twenty-one years, but the 'grit-your-teeth and get on with it' which got us to the finish line on day one hundred and thirteen would, most likely, have killed us in Iceland.

Different circumstances demand a different response if the real goal is long-term success, not short-term glory. Expeditions that push boundaries or operate in the high-risk category sometimes fall short for no reason other than chance. It is in their nature. The onus is therefore on the team to make the right, and often heartbreakingly difficult, decisions.

I often draw parallels between polar travel and mountaineering. This is not because they are the same, because they are not really. They vary regarding their location, the skills required and often, the personalities needed to reach the highest levels of performance. There is, regardless, an overlap and some professionals and amateurs alike move from one to the other. Two immediate examples are Wilki and Finn, who having been my teammates, have also worked together to climb the infamous north faces of the both the Eiger and Matterhorn in a single season. It could be argued that mountaineering demands more raw technical expertise with regard to placing protection and with subtle body movement. Polar travel, conversely, rewards those with impeccable camp-craft and an ability to focus a stressed and tired mind after weeks or months of severe discomfort. Both draw on the need to control fear and exercise judgement when the right path is not at all obvious.

There is another difference, however, and its effects are most often seen far from the ice but in the eyes of those looking on. There is a difference in the common perception of how success is defined and until the Vatnajökull attempt, it was not something I had pondered. Putting aside the fact that climbing and mountaineering are accessible to the masses in a way that polar travel can never be, with clubs, national teams and dedicated magazines, expectations also differ. If you are to discount recreational climbers and look at the most talented amateurs and the professionals, there are observations to be made.

As a quick tangent, note here that my fervently held view as a meritocrat is that talent is not defined by someone's status as a professional or amateur but by the talent itself. Professionals in any field are defined simply by the fact they make a living from it, not by their automatic superiority over an amateur.

If you look at mountaineering feats: new routes on Everest or Nanga Parbat or E8/E9 rock routes, they require a lot of attempts. It is considered totally normal and reasonable to make an attempt, retreat and then go back a day or even a year later for another go. Systems and tactics need tweaking for the big prizes to be won and sometimes, pure luck is the decider. No-one batted an eyelid when Andy Kirkpatrick retreated from the Troll Wall in Norway during his winter attempt. He simply went back and whilst I was writing this manuscript, succeeded in incredible style and with characteristic dry humour. In fact, he did so in the company of polar skier Aleks Gamme, who relieved George and myself of our unsupported polar distance record in 2012.

Now look at polar expeditions. There are fewer to choose from, as is the nature of the discipline, but consider Thomas Ulrich's 2006 dramatic rescue from his North Pole attempt or Rune Gjeldnes and Cecilie Skog's 2011 summer Arctic Ocean retreat. Instead of being seen as a natural stepping-stone to eventual success they were considered failures as single entities. The response was very black and white without a hint of the grey which mountaineers and their commentators seem happy to embrace.

I suppose there might be a few reasons for this. Firstly, because polar expeditions are rare and usually accompany high budgets and hype, it is more noticeable when they fail. Secondly, because of the incredibly remote locations inherent to polar journeys, there is an added chance of expense and drama to recover an abandoned expedition, whether a retreat or a rescue. Only mountaineering false-starts with a particularly high profile or news-worthy content seem to be noticed, one example being the rescue of Tomaž Humar on Nanga Parbat's Rupal Face in 2005. A dramatic helicopter rescue involving great danger to the pilots and slinging Humar underneath on a rope made headlines. Another Himalayan peak, Langtang Lirung, would tragically claim Humar's life in 2009.

I think that for expeditions where the chance of success is not at all certain, the only ones with value in my view, there should be a more pragmatic and realistic response, whether it involves mountains, icecaps or jungles for that matter. Sometimes these things take a couple of tries or even more. There is one way to guarantee success and only one – to attempt only that which is easy. They are hardly worth considering if you ask me. I must qualify this by saying that expeditions which are badly planned or undertaken flippantly are not really relevant to this – they simply should not occur at all if those people involved are expecting the support or help of others.

Given this, any person who wishes to be part of this unusual and niche world of expeditions must make a decision. They either play along with the status quo and accept the pitfalls, publicly reject and fight against misleading actions or finally, simply ignore that the problems exist and pretend – head in the sand and blissfully unaware of the way we are represented.

The second of these options is by far the hardest. It is difficult to justify, open to criticism, frustrating and not the making of a quiet life; but you have to ask yourself what the purpose is. If you want to make money as an end in itself and be called an explorer, choose option one. If you care little about others' thoughts and are happy that you are content with your own travels, choose three. There is similarly nothing dishonourable about a music enthusiast playing guitar in their room for nobody's benefit except their own. Expressing our passions to an audience is not compulsory. But on the other hand, if you have a craving for reality, honesty and things being done properly, then the second way is the only one.

Most importantly, once you have decided what you think, which side of the fence you have sat yourself on, what do you do about it? This is relevant to almost every decision we make in life and the answer differs on each occasion. Let us consider style in a polar context. It may seem of no interest or significance whatsoever to someone not familiar with polar travel, but the way in which we haul, ski, scramble or swim across the ice, our 'style', is of paramount importance. This is not to patronise those looking on from outside the community, as the differences can initially appear to be very subtle or abstract. Indeed, you may feel that there is no purpose whatsoever in any polar expedition and this is important not to dismiss. We do, after all, travel to places that we know exist, burning aviation fuel on our entry and exit and often returning to the place where we began. Words borrowed from climbing to describe a style can be siege-like, solo, pure, alpine-style or one of many other adjectives.

Typically, British siege expeditions, involving dozens of men, women, animals and machines are expensive, time-consuming and not necessarily more effective. They fell out of favour as the twentieth century went on as the militaristic style was replaced by a more thoughtful and immersive set of tactics, driven by a handful from Northern Europe and North America. Attitudes change quickly. Just looking back on the clothing and philosophies of the 1990s harks back to an altogether more innocent era of wilderness travel, when the true value of things was known and the cost often half-forgotten in a wave of charming bravado. Standards are higher now, for sure, but the current day is just different and perhaps not necessarily better.

Mountaineering, again seen as a sister-sport to polar travel for our purposes due to the overlap in participants and technical skills, has always had an active, sometimes healthy and sometimes bitter debate regarding style. Due to the fact that there are thousands of times more mountaineers in existence, it is not surprising that polar travel's own debate has been less widely reported but can be just as hard-fought. There are, for example, dozens of climbing magazines published around the world but barely a mention of polar travel amongst the columns of mainstream or outdoor media.

I do not like cheating or cutting corners, like most people, and so my views on style and more importantly, the way that style is broadcast to the public, are fairly straightforward. I believe that there is no such thing as an unworthy expedition – there can, however, certainly be a dishonourably promoted or reported expedition. As long as a team honestly and proportionately claims to be doing what it is they are, in fact, doing, there cannot be a problem. Unfortunately, an honesty about this can be less widespread than we would hope due to a combination of media pressure and personal egotism. It is no secret that highly physical and challenging endeavours attract their fair share of competitive, ambitious and macho individuals. These personalities can sometimes be tempted to exaggerate or knowingly let a poorly briefed media overstate the facts or statistics.

I think that the best way to explain something as subjective and potentially explosive as polar expedition style and difficulty is to liken it to the better understood competitive diving, which is scored as a combination of difficulty and execution. A low difficulty of 2.0 for a dive is no match for a dive of high difficulty, perhaps 4.0 or more. And so it is for polar expeditions.

This is not meant to discredit or abuse the entry-level trips or novices, as no polar travel is remotely easy. It is supposed to accurately represent the risks taken by and efforts made by those who dream bigger, work harder and wish to push boundaries. There is a risk that this debate could distract attention from the journeys themselves and so it serves to say that I have interest only in expeditions which involve very high levels of uncertainty, risk, uniqueness, danger, mental pressure and that also demand much technical skill. It is these journeys that excite and motivate me.

CHAPTER TEN

The winter of 2011/12 heralded a lot of activity for the less icy, London-based side of my life. Making a living from expeditions full-time is never an easy task – which is perhaps no bad thing. It is not like a classic business where you sell a service or a product, gradually building that service or creating products that you then market. It is a far more complicated mixture of things, amongst them recounting stories and lessons learned during my polar travel and writing for books and newspapers, which had grown to resemble a career – or rather, a lifestyle that had the good fortune to pay. The principle was the same, though: to create value first; the rest could be nurtured over time. Nothing has changed. Sir Ernest Shackleton and his contemporaries spent much of their time on lecture tours and attracting wealthy patrons.

As I am sure most self-employed would attest to, even those far more mainstream than in my chosen vocation, life becomes a rollercoaster ride of freedom, disappointments, frustration, elation and pressure to make good decisions. My sponsorship agents, based in London, had made real efforts for me on a personal level as my career grew. After months of negotiations, pitching and discussions, a three-year funding deal to develop expeditions to open unsupported new routes to both Poles fell through due to, from what I gathered, an internal mistake by the sponsors. A great deal of my medium and long-term planning had been based around the expeditions, not to mention thousands of hours of research and preparation with suppliers.

The news had come through on Christmas Eve that it was dead in the water and it hit hard. Funding has forever been the scourge of professional expedition leaders but I did feel I had already had my fair share of bad luck. I felt that this time it would be different – the package was good, my agents the best in the business and the potential sponsors really engaged. What followed was a couple of really dark days. I could not summon my usual irrepressible conviction that it would work out if the plan was good and the people involved worked hard enough.

Like the troopers they are, the directors at the agency vowed to push on with a new sponsorship package with new brands which needed to be partnered with sports teams or people like myself. I was fortunate, in any case, since I was the only person outside of mainstream sport being matched with their potential sponsors. However, knowing full well that sponsorship is a long game to play and results can take months or years with little information to go on in the meantime, I needed a plan.

It had not escaped my notice that 'The Long Haul', my career-making journey, had occurred nearly four years previously and I could fall into a trap. I had seen a few others with expedition ambitions let years and even a decade slide by whilst stubbornly holding out for the funding they desired. Often they would not compromise, think laterally or even wonder whether there was a reason why it was not working. High-budget sponsorship is a truly cruel business and you either commit, or you must walk away for an easier life. As in every area of life, we do not have all the answers from the word go, regardless of our drive and ambition – rather, flexibility is the key.

As I have always tried to do, I decided to have multiple strategies running at once. The team at the agency would continue to put the long-term deals in front of those I did not have direct access to. I would build my career at my level and hopefully open doors via the corporate speaking bookings I was enjoying, and get on the ice regardless. This final part was crucial. My criticism of one or two is that they will not go and do what it is they claim to be a professional at, polar travel, unless the perfect, 'ideal world' funding appears on their laps. In actuality, they cease to be polar 'explorers' or whatever label they claim for themselves and become professional marketers, writers and speakers who used to do expeditions. It does seem to suit some, as style overtakes substance in an altogether more comfortable existence – the originating foundation of their success becoming overshadowed by the alternative path of least resistance that follows.

No matter what, I decided I would continue to use my earnings to fund a 'moderate budget' expedition, or part of one anyhow, no matter how difficult or scary it might be financially. As an aside, I strongly advocate the use of personal contributions or purpose-made travel grants to fund expeditions not commercially suited for corporate backing. After all, why should a company fund someone's personal quest if it holds little value for them and others? I receive dozens of emails a month from novices with dreams of seven-figure funding yet with zero technical knowledge of their chosen goal and no answer as to what they would offer their backer. Avoiding an automatic hunt for sponsors leaves the corporate deals open for ventures for which this 'secondary funding' is not sufficient and could solve the currently saturated marketplace – differentiation at multiple levels.

This, I reasoned with myself, would be the way I would keep my skills sharp, progress and not become the 'also-ran' or perhaps worse, the embittered 'all talk and no walk' type. No-one is destined to be an 'also-ran' – they simply decide not to fight and are overtaken by the passage of time. I had my focus, positivity and energy back. I had to get out on the ice every year to be a true professional.

I often champion, as I have previously in this book, the wonders of the Polar Regions as opposed to the Poles themselves. There is undeniably, however, a primal draw to these symbols of polar achievement. As amongst the most financially costly of goals, they dominated my large, agency-driven sponsorship packages but I wondered about what I could do to get myself to the Pole.

Necessity makes us inventive and my inclination was simply to forge a brand new path. Financially, this meant stripping away an expedition budget to the raw, bare bones and replacing the expensive bits with the only thing I had in abundance at my disposal, hard work.

Looking at my 'North 08' North Pole plans, which were shelved due to 'The Long Haul', nearly half of the £110,000 budget was the single insertion flight by Twin Otter ski plane to the Arctic Ocean coast. Original budgets always include brand new equipment and everything planned with the knowledge that the optimum funding is in place. Without this allowance, I had to be more compromising. Still, this postulation and notes on the back of an envelope whilst still at my family's home for Christmas were just thinking aloud. How could I do this? Surely I could rekindle the pioneering innovation and lateral thought of the early explorers, lost by all but a few modern travellers in deference to buying off the shelf?

I eventually calculated the North Pole could be attained, unsupported, by a team of two, for less than £40,000. With a couple of small sponsors and personal contributions, it could happen. We would have none of these lazy, modern aeroplane rides, though. Given the opportunity, of course, I would take the insertion flight, but it was not going to be an option. It could take a year or many more to raise the 'ideal world' funding.

The more eagle-eyed would observe that it is possible to fly to the North Pole as a tourist or for a short 'polar experience' for less than £15,000. This is essentially pocket-change compared to any budgets I was seriously entertaining. Why not take that option? I would be almost certain to stand at the Pole – job done. There is no need to reiterate the value of the journey over the cheap thrill of standing at the finish line in neatly ironed clothing still smelling of washing powder. The idea never even crossed my mind.

How could so much happen for comparatively so little? All luxuries would be replaced with what was available. Serviceable equipment from past expeditions would be reconditioned and brought back into use. Expensive custom and specialist clothing would be sought from manufacturers and instead of those all-important flights, we would ski, walk, swim or crawl if that is what it took. To get within striking distance of our goal, we would use expensive but affordable scheduled flights, shared with locals of the High Arctic going about their day-to-day lives. Undeniably, this striking distance would be a long way from ideal, evidenced by the fact that scheduled flights, unsurprisingly, do not tend to fly right into the wilderness. The time additions inherent in skiing a route that I would prefer to fly would cause headache after headache; it would test my knowledge, problem solving and research to the limit.

I came up with an idea. 'The Dark Ice Project' was born. The aim of the project was to open a new route, unsupported, to the North Pole – or, strictly speaking, to achieve the Pole from a new starting point, given the ever-changing nature of the Arctic Ocean with its covering of sea ice. Despite a modern trend to use artificially shortened routes to take advantage of convenient logistics hubs (examples include starting at Hercules Inlet or the 'Messner Start' in the Antarctic, flying over inconvenient crevasse fields on other icecaps and starting at the edge of good sea ice in the Far North), these journeys can only be considered full-distance in academic terms. Polar travel is a practical undertaking and so it follows that start points should reflect common sense. Coastal starting points are where land or permanent ice meets open water and for sea ice expeditions, stepping off land is the only truly legitimate start point. Otherwise, the goalposts will be forever moved to satisfy agendas. The pioneers never had the luxury of inventing their own rules and neither should we.

For 'The Dark Ice Project', having reached the Pole, we would then return, hauling the entire distance again, instead of meeting an aircraft at the Pole ... and we would do it mostly in the winter.

My appetite for something new was a driving force. The North Pole has never been attained unsupported in the winter, despite a master-class effort in 2006 by Børge Ousland and Mike Horn. It has only once been achieved in winter, in 2008, by Russians Matvey Shparo, son of the legend Dmitry, and Boris Smolin. This expedition was completed with resupplies.

I think most of the handful of polar travellers currently active would agree that the following are amongst the biggest challenges of the Arctic: man-hauling equipment, no resupplies, sea ice travel, new routes with little precedent, polar bear territory and darkness. Most remarkable expeditions combine two or three of these. 'The Dark Ice Project' would combine them all. The lure of the dark was too great to ignore. Usually one to scoff slightly at personifications of the wilderness; or suggestions that the presence of just one or two humans is of any concern to such a powerful place, I did wonder whether Robert Swan's words, 'Welcome to a place that wants you dead,' might one day take on a very real meaning for me. This was big.

I felt it was a worthy successor to 'The Long Haul' and the medium for travel would be sea ice, completely different to life on a permanent ice sheet. It was the spring of 2012 and if I was to waste no time, I only had nine months or so to turn a plan on a sheet of paper into something real.

That aim to waste no time has always resonated with me. Above all things, I have always loathed waste, waste of anything: food, materials, talent, but most of all, time. Everyday is full of waste at every turn and I truly believe that the next great challenge to face our species is to reduce it. What we have created already could go so much further. This is easily applicable to tangible things like fresh water, precious metals, plastics and fossil fuels but time requires more consideration.

Imagine what we could do, if every year we live allowed us to achieve much more than it does at present. Only we have control over this. Far from being a call to turn ourselves into highly-productive, almost robotic entities, it must apply to everything with value. This includes that which makes a truly rich life – time to relax and think, time to ponder with likeminded people and learn from them. It is the perpetual search for simplicity and modulation in the mundane parts of life and for extension and enrichment of the valuable parts.

Fear is something we all face in so many guises and for me, far, far beyond leaping across open crevasses or handling a tent in hurricane-force winds is the fear of wasting the opportunity and the time I have. My ultimate goals are to achieve legacy and influence in a broad sphere of activities, making a positive difference to the world I leave behind. There is, simply, no time to lose. Self-awareness of our own truths is something that may come to us all, perhaps in our teens, perhaps in our final days or perhaps not at all. A flaw of mine is my impatience and this is, I am sure, a direct reason for the fact that my greatest fear is that unrelenting passage of time and the possibility that I may not make enough of it. Logic tells us that fear is just a reaction, a protective measure taken by our minds to keep us safe. It can be switched off and controlled. How true that is for

147

some aspects of fear like jumping crevasses but how inadequate it is for others. All of this being taken into account, the nine months I had simply had to be enough. Another year would be torture.

It had taken me four years of work to prepare for 'The Long Haul' in 2008. Most of this had been solo work, though eventually I was joined by my teammates as the years went on. 'The Dark Ice Project' was, once again, down to me. This time, though, I did not have to learn everything from scratch. I had relationships with every supplier, craftsman and logistics provider I could ever need. In fact, the nine months seemed quite reasonable for putting together the nuts and bolts. More demanding, however, would be the completely original research into the route and finding someone daft and willing enough to accompany me.

If you were to describe the overall plan of another major attempt on the North Pole from the recent past, you might manage it in a short sentence – not a reflection of the difficulty, but of the relative simplicity of the journey's aims and timeline. In 2000, Rune Gjeldnes and Torry Larsen crossed the Arctic Ocean unsupported from Russia to Canada, the first and only time it has been done. In 2002, Briton, Pen Hadow, became the first soloist to ski unsupported to the Pole from Canada. From these simple sentences, you may have most of the information needed to visualise their journey.

In comparison, 'The Dark Ice Project' would launch from the Greenlandic settlement of Qaanaaq at around seventy-eight degrees north. This is around four hundred miles south of a normal coastal starting point. From Qaanaaq, in the very first days that safe sea ice forms off the Thule coastline, sledges full of supply depots would be man-hauled north and laid along the Nares Strait. Once at the Lincoln Sea, the first part of the Arctic Ocean after leaving Canada's Ellesmere Island and Greenland to the south, a final large depot would be laid on land before returning to Qaanaaq. A year later, this route to the Arctic Ocean from Qaanaaq would be retraced via those depots and an unsupported, near-thousand-mile journey would be made to the North Pole and back again to land. The final depot supplies would then feed the team for the last four hundred miles back to Qaanaaq and civilisation. A total of three hundred days on the ice would be required over more than two years.

If all that sounds like a bit of a mouthful, that is because it is. The planning and research about what was possible and when would take thousands of hours of phone calls, reading, thinking and discussion. Also, this was only Plan A. Such a long-term project would be at the mercy of circumstance and I needed to allow for other plans, some of which ended in Norway or Russia, with the associated bureaucracy and added work.

The main practical shift I had to make professionally was to prepare for travel on sea ice. Our main quarry, the North Pole, is, of course, positioned in the middle of the Arctic Ocean – ice-covered – more so in the winter and less so in the summer. This ocean is covered in a fractured, dynamic and ever-mobile skim of frozen sea ice, usually covered in a layer of snow. Needless to say, the challenges differ a great deal from travelling on vast, high elevation, permanent ice sheets like those covering Greenland and the Antarctic.

The North Pole is an academically defined position at ninety degrees north, which, in practical terms for a traveller, means very little beyond being a symbol. Every person lucky enough to stand at the position where the world's invisible lines of longitude meet will experience a unique Pole. Theirs might be a flat pan of ice, an open 'lead' of water or a pressure ridge. If they stand still for long, they will drift off the Pole and south in one direction or another. The winds and Arctic currents (mainly the Transpolar Drift towards the Atlantic and the Beaufort Gyre above Canada and Russia) make sure of that.

Although I was planning to work with a teammate once again, to share the load and also the memories of the journey, I could not call on my trusted former partners. The time commitments of 'The Dark Ice Project' were formidable and, although keen as mustard in principle, the numbers and dates were just not going to add up for them.

Undeterred, given the many months of time left until we flew and the fact that I generally undertake the lion's share of research anyhow, I put the word out. The art of finding a brilliant collaborator was not straightforward but I felt I had cracked it thus far. First and foremost must come personality, before any hard skills are even considered. Skills can be learned, experience can be gained but a good person is always a good person and a lazy, burdensome partner is always lazy and burdensome. I decided not to put the call out to the public as that would result in a deluge of emails from enthusiastic, no doubt honest, but wholly unsuitable people. The double-edged sword of the incredibly small polar community means that finding a companion for travel is far from easy. Some will be inactive or retired, some pure soloists and most only willing to work on their own projects.

I decided to use my friends and contacts in the community to circulate news of the project amongst polar people and mountaineers and see what came back. Satisfyingly, some really serious options appeared in my inbox from as close as London and as far afield as South Africa. Meetings, phone calls and Skype meetings were set up and I felt confident of success.

Following suggestions from friends and with a reasonable awareness of his past work, I met with Justin Miles near London's Euston Station. Short in stature yet well built, he came across as sensible, easy-going and with plenty of experience for his near-forty years.

I was aware that he had been involved with a couple of expeditions in the past which did not get off the ground. One was with a British man in apparent full mid-life crisis. This individual had made a real Horlicks of a South Pole attempt, sitting in his tent when it was anything less inviting than blue, calm and sunny and then trying, unsuccessfully, to fund a far more demanding venture. The grapevine indicated that Antarctic logistics experts would not let him travel even if he was to get the cash, for his own safety and those of rescue pilots. This rang alarm bells in my head, but I soon realised that Justin had come to the same conclusion and that was his reason for cutting ties. It is never fair to condemn someone purely by association.

As far as I was concerned, I had all the raw ingredients in Justin that I needed. These were an experienced pedigree, although the details of these past journeys were occasionally a little vague, an easy manner, good physical condition, motivation for the goal, availability and finally, the ability to make the likely personal contribution. After a few weeks we decided to work together on the project. Of course, a good person is far more than a combination of attributes and I was convinced I had made a great choice.

Justin was in the process of selling a business of his, a children's school education programme, and was also going through a tricky personal situation, extrication from which would involve a lot of time and emotional energy. This was not a problem from my point of view as I would continue to develop the project and get everything done, asking Justin periodically to undertake tasks he had an affinity for or enlisting his help when I became snowed under with work. These tasks were not often completed without a delay or a problem or two, but I remained optimistic. The fact that ninety-five per cent of the work was on my plate was partly my choice and made sense in context, but I did start to feel slightly uneasy about the professional dynamic our relationship had.

A journey as long as ours would require a mountain of equipment. The underlying urge of every polar skier, alpine climber or any other cutting-edge outdoor professional is to save weight. Titanium is chosen over steel or aluminium wherever possible; Kevlar and carbon fibre are chosen over heavy plastics and glass fibre. There is always an inherent cost with these decisions, especially since most items cannot be found on shop shelves in England. Instead, almost everything has to be researched and imported from Europe or North America, if not custom-built from scratch. What was unavoidable was that, with the best will in the world, and even with the very best gear on the market, the total weight of what we must haul edged higher and higher.

There are two major implications of travelling unsupported: there must be no resupplies from the air or pre-laid caches and no physical locomotive assistance like wind kites, dogs or vehicles. Firstly, every single thing an expedition needs to survive, succeed and solve breakages must be carried or hauled. There is no 'get out of jail free card' if vital items break or supplies run out. Secondly, the sheer load will always vastly reduce speed of travel. Some journeys involve physical assistance but shun resupplies, taking on the label 'without resupply' but lacking the added strain of fully unsupported travel.

What about the depots we planned to lay in the first year, Phase One of 'The Dark Ice Project', to feed the three subsequent legs up and down the Nares Strait in Phases One and Two? Are they not providing support for Phase Two since we would return home for the summer in between the phases? They are indeed. The journeys to and from Qaanaaq and the edge of the Arctic Ocean are simply transit, 'positioning' legs to take the place of aircraft. The unsupported attempt on the Pole, and the return, starts and finishes on that shoreline. The fifteen hundred miles or so of extra hard work will not go on record, yet may contain some of the most valuable experiences.

This raises a few questions about what counts, what is 'allowed' and what is not. There are, as has been stated ad nauseum, no rules or governing body, but common sense usually prevails and candid reporting is the unwritten code of honour. Some argue that wind support is not support since it is natural and a part of the environment. Unsurprisingly, these people are almost always those who use the wind and like the benefits of the unsupported label. Without doubt, comparing a wind-powered expedition with a man-hauled one is folly, rather like comparing a swimmer with a racing yacht. Kite-skiers can reach up to thirty miles an hour; it requires a skilled technique but is, nonetheless, supported.

Another bizarre distinction, which often gets glossed over by publicists employed to get newspaper column inches for expeditions, is that of stages. If you ran one mile per day for twenty-six days and then finished with a three hundred and eighty five-yard flurry on day twenty-seven, it is reasonable to say that you have not run a marathon. Unfortunately, the skewed logic which says otherwise is used more often than you would imagine. Roz Savage, the ocean rower, claims to be 'the first woman to row solo across the Pacific Ocean'. The facts are that she rowed from island to island in three stages over three years, returning home in between.

A polar traveller for whom I have great respect, the American Lonnie Dupre, claims to have circumnavigated Greenland. This he achieved over many years, using a non-continuous route and even travelling in opposite directions to prior stages. His journeys were, in reality, an epic series of brilliant expeditions that, I feel, are tarnished by the overall false claim.

The reason I believe this should be widely understood is not to denigrate the achievement of one person, but rather to give fair recognition to those who actually do exactly what they claim. For example, Chris Martin and Mick Dawson spent 189 days afloat to cross the Pacific for real in 2009. They did receive an airdrop as they neared the USA and have never claimed an unsupported status.

The point here is to retain the gravity of truly great achievements. If Greenland has not yet been truly circumnavigated, that is no problem. It simply means that such an achievement is impossible, nigh on impossible or yet to be achieved. Honesty is the key and it means that no-one is misled or denied fair recognition. We rely on the good will and trust of the public and we must not betray that trust.

The challenges for 'The Dark Ice Project' were many and significant and occupying my mind, as time went by, was the load which needed hauling. The overall projections would help to visualise the expectations I had. The entire project would involve three hundred days per person of food and fuel. Ninety of these days would fuel the Phase One depot laying up the Nares Strait and two hundred and ten would fuel the second phase from Qaanaaq to the Pole and back. For Phase One to be of any real use, as well as eating all of those ninety days of food as we went, a large proportion (one hundred and sixty days) of the remaining two hundred and ten would need to come too and then be laid as depots. What is not depoted during Phase One, perhaps only fifty days or so, would be the starting weight for Phase Two.

Why all this complication and repeats of travelling the same ice routes? The state of the Nares Strait ice would be critical to success and speed would be vital if we were to reach the Arctic Ocean early enough in the season to make it to the Pole and back. If we did everything in one massive go, we would have to haul two hundred and ten days of supplies the entire length of the strait, through some of the most turbulent and uncertain ice. We would most likely be thoroughly degraded physically by the time we could even think about the Pole attempt.

Quite plainly, we planned to use Phase One to make the opening four hundred miles, the positioning leg, of Phase Two a little easier. Once on the open frozen Arctic Ocean, we would be on our own since it is impossible to lay depots on mobile and temporary sea ice. We also intended to use the first phase for reconnaissance to assess feasible travel speeds. The lack of precedent for such a journey and the need for this reconnaissance was exciting; it was real exploration – perhaps not drawing maps, but travelling with physical uncertainty.

What do all these days mean in cold, hard kilograms? In 2008 'The Long Haul' meant one hundred and ten days of supplies all weighing a kilo each and containing a dense 5,600kcal. The shorter speed expeditions were more forgiving due to their duration and supplies contained up to two kilos of more palatable food containing between 5,000kcal and 9,000kcal per day.

The need to be energy dense and highly efficient would be even more vital on 'The Dark Ice Project'. I aimed to build a sub-kilo ration pack of nearly 6,000kcal per day but without the revolting ghee butter, which so ruined many a freeze-dried meal those years before. Weight loss at this intake level would be unavoidable but hopefully sustainable, given the extreme cold and daily toil.

A decision on sledges is just one of the many choices an expedition leader must take. It is a decision few will agree on. There are certainly more ways than one to crack this particular nut. Options range from glorified children's toboggans all the way up to vast space-age shells made from bulletproof materials. I had to match what we had to haul with what was available.

At the start of the first phase, we would need to move nigh on three hundred kilos; this would be a formidable nemesis. George Bullard and I had already surprised many and proved critics wrong as we each hauled two hundred kilos from sea level onto an eight-thousand-foot-high icecap and then made a return crossing. To haul half that weight again over sea ice was an utterly eye-watering prospect.

With the assistance of Craig Mathieson, a friend of Rich Smith (from 'The Journey South 2007'), who had been a great help in the past, I sourced two large Kevlar North Pole sledges. These would float on the water in between ice floes and prove near indestructible against the jumbled ice. Craig lived near Edinburgh and I was uncertain about the delivery cost and chance of damage from a courier. I travelled up from London to collect. This logistics trip would not be remarkable if it were not for the epic journey I undertook getting them back to my flat.

After a catch-up with my 'Long Haul' partner, George, who was still at university in Edinburgh, he dropped both sledges and me off at the station. I had to find a way of getting two human-height, bright white shells, somewhat resembling boats, onto the train. The passenger carriage was a no-go and so I tried my luck with the luggage carriage.

My slightly comical and conspicuous cargo had already attracted an audience when I attempted to shuffle it through the open doors. A large, grey-haired Scotsman barred my way. I was summarily informed that I had broken a string of rules, all with their own sub-section and clause; I should have registered everything in advance and seemingly should also have asked for personal permission from Her Majesty The Queen before daring to try and place my 'daft boats' on his train. I took a deep breath, smiled, apologised profusely and begged his leave to grant my 'daft boats' access. Having clearly decided he had projected his authority enough, he mumbled at me and ushered me through the wide-open doors. Expecting to see a carriage packed to the rafters with cargo, which had all been pre-registered, and thereby understanding the inconvenience I had put this man to, instead I was presented with a vast and totally empty space. Not even one item of luggage graced the corner. With a wry smile on my face, I was relieved to put down my awkward load and find some straps to stop them sliding around inside the empty carriage during the journey.

Things became even more amusing once in King's Cross Station in London. Unable to find a cab large and willing enough to transport me through Central to South-West London, I had always planned to give the Tube a go. Knowing already it would be a little bit of an adventure, I had also inadvertently chosen the best time to travel – rush hour. Imagine the sight of a man carrying these curious objects slowly along a corridor, down escalators, round corners and onto Tube trains whilst having to peer around their bulk to see where he was going. Almost every tenth person could be heard whispering to their companion about what they thought my sledges were. It became a bit of a game and everyone was actually very accommodating. Perhaps it broke the boredom of the commute.

Finally, as I got off the Tube at Victoria, a lady said to her husband, 'I think it's a sledge – you know one for the snow!' I simply had to stop, partly to give my arms and hands a rest but also to congratulate her on being the first to get it right. We then had a long chat about polar skiing and I finally got my Kevlar friends home, setting them down on my rug with a substantial sigh of relief. Job done!

Being nearly the length of a human being, these sledges would take a lot of our equipment and supplies and when two were rafted together, they were said to float with a total of two hundred and forty kilos plus a person sitting on top. This was excellent news and I had never had reason to doubt the word of Roger Daynes, whose work they were.

They would not, however, provide enough capacity. Tandem sledges were a fairly common solution to the problem of needing to negotiate complex mazes of broken sea ice and even ferry split loads over the worst areas. A second, usually smaller sledge, could be tied on behind to follow its bigger brother. Given that our depots of supplies would be pre-loaded into robust, sealed plastic kegs, a neat canvas cover would not be needed for the second sledge. I had used the low-cost and remarkably resilient blue plastic sledge shells from Daynes' Snowsled before and a larger 1.6 metre version was newly available. We chose these to be our tandems and they were readied to contain three or four large, thirty-kilo kegs. Roger even custom-made some 'high noses' for these low profile sledges to help them avoid getting caught on ice blocks and ridges.

Having made my weight estimates before settling on our exact kit list, it was clear the total would be close to nine hundred kilos including the protective wooden crates and the Phase Two supplies we would leave in Qaanaaq until 2014. Air Greenland, who would be our carriers for most of the long series of flights to Qaanaaq, charge around fifteen pounds per kilo of freight for that distance and besides, the smaller aircraft would not take a large crate. Even if we did decide to fly with our freight, the bill could be over thirteen thousand pounds one way. A far more sensible option would be to use sea freight with a total bill of a few hundred pounds.

CHAPTER ELEVEN

I have not really touched upon the climate and conditions in and around Qaanaaq, so perhaps there is no better time than now. Qaanaaq is, along with the tiny settlement of forty Greenlanders living nearby at Siorapaluk, almost alone in the far northwest of Arctic Greenland. Most of the Inuit and Danes living on the tiny halo of land around the vast ice sheet reside in the west and southwest. A few small villages exist on the southeast but the north coast and northeast is entirely uninhabited.

Qaanaaq, for one of the northernmost habitations on Earth, is comparatively large for a remote Inuit town with six hundred inhabitants, but their dogs outnumber this total. The Americans, who wanted the original location for an airbase – the same place where the B-52 crashed – relocated Qaanaaq during the Cold War to its current position. It is part of the Thule region (a widely used term meaning the Far North), one of the most ancient and constantly inhabited parts of the High Arctic, first settled in 2000BC by Paleo-Eskimos from the Canadian East. Some of the most fascinating, tragic and heroic stories of early Arctic history and exploration took place in the Thule and East Ellesmere Island region. A third Greenlandic dialect, Inuktun (Polar Eskimo), which is distinct from the western or eastern languages, Kalaallisut and Tunumiisut, is spoken by only a thousand people, all from the Thule region.

It is worth having a brief discussion about the word Eskimo. Although often considered to be pejorative and almost taboo, especially amongst Canadian Inuit (their preferred name), there is little evidence that it means 'eaters of raw meat'. Many consider that it is the result of other corrupted words. The history and migrations of those now called the Inuit and the Yupik (indigenous people of the Russian Far East and parts of Alaska) is complex and explain the reason for their diverse languages and traditions. My experience of polar identities is varied. In the Greenlandic East, there is a desire to be called Greenlandic or Greenlanders. They are the most isolated of all Inuit from other regions and their relative proximity to modern Europe may be a reason. Speaking to native people from the Thule region, some of whom remember life before the forced resettlement in the 1960s, they seem to have a greater affection for the turbulent history of this special territory. I asked one about the word Eskimo, expecting a dismissive reaction, but instead he said, 'Well, I **am** an Eskimo. I eat raw meat!' with a wide smile.

Famed, native Danish-Greenlandic explorer, Knud Rasmussen, travelled from and via Qaanaaq multiple times in the early twentieth century to test some of Robert Peary's claims about the nature of the northern coast of Canada and Greenland, part of which is humbly named Peary Land. As became a pattern of Peary's legacy, many found his claims to be exaggerated and in fact, evidence shows he merely made up whole areas of land.

American Peary's brutal and unflinching attempts to be the first to reach the North Pole followed Frederick Cook's fabricated claim and Peary set off from Qaanaaq, which became the favourite launch pad of many early explorers. The only real legacy Peary seems to have left in the Far North appears to be, apart from some admittedly genuinely pioneering and brave coastal mapping expeditions, a number of lineages of children fathered whilst apart from his wife back home. Many descendants of Peary and his assistant, Matthew Henson, live in Greenland to this day. His hubris and selfish obsession with claiming the Pole for himself at all costs is, most-likely, unparalleled in polar history. One attempt led to the loss of multiple toes from frostbite. 'A small price to pay,' he stated. I have often thought that sport, and in its own way polar travel, is a civilised alternative to warfare; a way for people to satisfy their basal urge for competition, tribalism, aspiration and the need to feel like a conqueror. Perhaps Peary was an early and extreme example.

As the debate still rages in Antarctic circles regarding Captain Robert Scott, his ill-fated race to the South Pole in 1911/12 with Norwegian Roald Amundsen, and whether he was an unlucky hero or a bumbling incompetent, so it does in the North.

A small but vocal faction, mostly American and not unlike the conspiracy theorists who claim the USA never sent a man to the Moon, continue to champion Peary's claim to the North Pole and some even support Cook's. Cook, initially a hero back home in New York, was also shown to have fabricated a claim to have climbed Denali, North America's highest mountain, in 1906, and was jailed for fraud and died with his reputation in tatters. These pressure groups tend to focus on destroying the credibility of others, like the British, Sir Wally Herbert and Sir Ranulph Fiennes, who, whilst not models of perfection or textbook polar travel, seem to bear the brunt of their fury. Herbert and his team were to make the first crossing of the Arctic Ocean in 1968/69, one of the greatest feats in polar history, but his vitriolic book, *The Noose of Laurels*, largely a broadside aimed at Peary, did little to endear him to many before his death in 2007.

Consensus amongst experts over many decades is that Cook's claims are almost unanimously rejected with Peary's not being a great deal more likely. A large portion of Peary's defence lay in a claim he could accurately estimate his daily mileage over moving ice whose speed and direction he had little idea of. Many of his navigational journal entries are conveniently missing and some daily claims of progress were double or quadruple the distances previously confirmed by those one could consider reliable witnesses.

In 2005, near the end of the pre-crash, UK-centric sponsorship frenzy when expeditions could find funding with relative ease, a team organised by Briton, Tom Avery, and then led and guided by the US-born and Canada-based professional dog-driver, Matty McNair, sought to support Peary's cause. In an inexplicable attempt to equate their expedition to Peary's, despite using modern clothing, modern navigation, regular airdrops, a commercial guide and no return journey to land, they narrowly beat Peary's claimed time of thirty-seven days to the Pole. This, apparently, was sole reason to vindicate Peary's claim. I do not think I have ever been so baffled in my life.

I believe it all comes down, again, to basic facts and honesty. Who really cares if Peary was the first to reach the North Pole or if it was another equally dedicated person? The point is that it has been achieved and that is a wonderful thing for human beings filled with wonder and adventurous spirit. We must be transparent and for that, there must be evidence or a lack of reasonable doubt.

There is a similar question on Everest about whether George Mallory's party may have climbed the mountain in 1924, decades before Hillary and Norgay. What is absent though, thankfully, is an attempt to degrade Hillary as a human being and discredit him in the face of the unlikely possibility that Mallory's camera is found with proof of his triumph before his and Irvine's death on the descent. As individuals I cannot help but notice the chasm between the ways in which Mallory's full 'because it is there' explanation and Herbert's 'those who need to ask, will never understand the answer' answer to why they lived as they did differ. When both placed in context, the former was elegant; Mallory was clearly aware of his human fragility, whilst Herbert's comment is an education in condescension.

The first person to lead a confirmed, successful surface journey to the North Pole was the American, Ralph Plaisted, much later in 1968, after the understandable indifference towards the Poles caused by two World Wars. Herbert's crossing, including a winter on the ice and a veritable town being built to shelter the large team and their dogs, followed a year later. It was by no means a lightweight triumph but a very British one – overshadowed in the press by the USA's first landing on the Moon. Perhaps Peary and Cook would at least be satisfied that the Stars and Stripes flew first at the Pole.

Cook co-founded the New York-based Explorers Club, a members-only organisation not unlike the London-based Royal Geographical Society (RGS). After my 2008 journey, I was, at first, genuinely honoured to be invited to become a Member of the former and Fellow of the latter. After four years of membership, however, I felt compelled to end both associations at the tail end of 2012.

Clubs are, by their very nature, cliquey sorts of places with lots of politics and internal crises. With the need to raise money to support their beautiful headquarters buildings, membership and fellowship recruitment grew to a level at which I felt their value became less justifiable. Realising the futility of a status symbol anyhow, let alone one that actually no longer conveyed any status or reflected any achievement beyond paying an annual fee, I resigned from both. There were no hard feelings towards either society; I could just no longer see the point. I continue to pay entrance fees and ticket prices happily to attend lectures and hire rooms at the RGS for events.

Why does this history and paraphernalia have any relevance to 'The Dark Ice Project' or anything else of note? I will attempt to explain why I believe it to be so. Polar expeditions past, present and future all have their place in the history of a special place on our planet. They are linked by their personal stories, triumphs, tragedies and their effects on our modern world, both physical and cultural.

On a practical side, 'The Dark Ice Project' would not have the chance of being the first expedition to reach the North Pole from Greenland if history had not been the way it is. On a personal level, I wanted to experience the same emotions that the pioneers felt on their quests, the same fear, the same fierce desire and the same joy in case of success. I wanted to think that, due to my desire to travel purely, honestly and without all-too-common shortcuts, my efforts would command the subtle nod of those giants I have always respected.

A person born in the 1980s can never enter the annals of history like those in the golden century of polar exploration, but we can strive to be the best of now. Celebrities are knighted these days, not explorers. Exploratory discovery is an original subset of exploration and even some of the pioneers were too late for it, really. Peary et al fully expected to find sea ice at the North Pole and Amundsen and Scott expected yet more polar plateau at the South Pole. Their expectations were right. They, even then, could not 'discover' a Pole as their existence and characteristics were already known.

The inclusion of discussion about colonial-era clubs in wealthy, temperate-climate countries may also seem curious. The truth is that as a Brit, especially one living in London, it is virtually impossible to ignore. This is especially true for a man with an inquiring mind and a desire to learn about and comment on what he sees as good and bad. Passion for something is hard to stifle.

•

Since the late 2000s, there has been a sort of evangelical, adventure movement growing, seemingly out of London rather than another specific origin. I find it a little unsettling. Gaining momentum from the anti-banker-bandwagon and drawn mostly from amongst the well-educated but slightly underachieving parts of the middle classes, the post-recession, hippy, 'quit your jobs and escape reality' movement is proving unsurprisingly infectious. A significant consequence of this, although there is no doubt those involved would instantly reject it, is to make people living normal lives feel bad about what they are missing out on; should not everyone be cycling around the world?

I think there is a real danger of writing off those who are genuinely happy with safe and reliable lives as the 'unenlightened'. I am all for inspiration, fresh thinking and freedom and the positive effects it can have on people's lives. When taken to a near-cult status, though, I think it can serve to depress those who cannot escape their 'mundane' lives due to responsibilities or those who actually do not wish to. They are pushed towards feeling less worthy.

What can be left is a trivalising evangelism which is, at its core, just naïve and smug, often peddled by those without responsibilities. They forget that the millions who cannot just quit their jobs and go and chase their dreams are the ones servicing their privileged freedom. Would their rose-tinted lifestyle be possible if the person driving the train to get them to the airport were to walk out on their job and family to seek adventure? Who would run the world?

For some it is not as easy as saying, 'let's do it' – they have the vision, consider it, but simply cannot. Given all of this, which can only be seen in a sadly negative light, the choice to keep a distance from the London adventure clique with their 'The North Face' gilets and ethnic bracelets is one I stick by. It does seem to be a peculiarly British trend. My experience is that, whilst not without their own problems, Italian alpinists or Norwegian skiers, for example, do not let potentially destructive things like this permeate. They just get out there, climb or ski and round it all off with beer and stories. Perhaps that is why they are, by and large, better at it!

An oft-used phrase about such attitudes is that they represent a 'call to arms'. 'A call to arms' against what: authority; reality? It sounds to me like childish rebellion without a true purpose and a manifestation of 'pointless inspiration' – something which might leave you buzzing immediately afterwards but with your long-term future unchanged.

This also has an effect on public perception of others and performance. I once heard a British adventure speaker seriously suggesting to a young, impressionable audience, amongst motivational clichés, that physical training is just for the old-fashioned, alpha-male explorers and all you really need is to come up with an idea and decide to do it. I would recommend that he try a demanding, self-sufficient, human-powered expedition with that outlook and see how it goes. The fact that Finn McCann, my Iceland partner, is climbing at an international standard is not because he wills it to be so. It is because he spends hours training, practising and yet more hours hanging off brick walls and anything else he can find.

Each to his own, though, as for religion or any other type of mass-indoctrination and 'grass is greener' movement driven by the agendas of the few. People should seek to consider all perspectives and draw their own conclusions after benefitting from the facts. Perhaps it is our equivalent of the various protest campaigns in the 1960s, which made cultural footprints but never changed nor saved the world. We are fortunate, people like myself who get to see special places in the manner in which we desire – fortunate, not enlightened. We must never forget that.

•

Sea ice movement, creation and melting are some of the major factors influencing High Arctic life. Everything and every decision is based on the state of the ice. The other major factor is the available sunlight, twenty-four hours in the spring and summer and none at all for months of the winter.

Every part of the Arctic and in particular, its waterways, differs depending on its location and what it is near to. The sea ice at the North Pole actually begins to melt earlier than other ice further south as spring turns to summer. Temperatures, weather systems and landscapes vary around any given line of latitude in the Arctic. Siberia is another world to Baffin Island and another again to the Bering Strait. Narrow inlets and straits often clog with pack ice late into melting seasons, yet more open parts are pushed clear of ice year-round.

Looking more closely at my area of interest, the Thule Region, Nares Strait and sea ice to the north to the Pole, there was a lot to learn. It would be difficult to identify a more unpredictable and multifaceted route. Qaanaaq itself is situated on the hillside and beach of a headland in a fjord that leads to the entranceway of the Nares Strait, the Smith Sound. This region has staged dozens of courageous, early explorations, many of them ill-fated.

Beyond the Smith Sound is the wide-open Kane Basin. To the west are the cliffs of Ellesmere Island and to the east, the seventy mile-wide Humboldt Glacier, the broadest tidewater glacier in the northern hemisphere. The southern shores are the rolling and rocky expanses of Inglefield Land, a rare part of the region, which is not covered by permanent icecap. Abandoned native settlements pepper the coastline; the most recently vacated of these is Etah whose derelict huts are still used for shelter by hunters on extended excursions.

The basin narrows dramatically again into the Kennedy Channel with the distance between Greenlandic and Canadian territory less than twenty miles in parts. Hans Island lies right in the centre and Ottawa and Copenhagen have disputed its ownership despite its small size and lack of real value.

A small widening is next, the Hall Basin, into which the fast-flowing Petermann Glacier runs, up to a kilometre of ice per year. Recent years have seen vast freshwater ice islands break off from this glacier and float into the straits.

The final Robeson Channel is all that is left before the Lincoln Sea and the Arctic Ocean itself is reached. On the Canadian Ellesmere Island side, Alert, a remote military listening station from Cold War times remains, although it is off-limits to civilians, and to the east stretch Greenland's Nansen Land and Peary Land.

Needless to say, the fact that all these channels, glaciers and basins exist, combined with the additional factor of the strait being one of three and by far the smallest exit route for Arctic Ocean water and ice, makes the sea ice changeable.

A polynya, an area of open water surrounded by sea ice and often open regardless of season, is usually caused by warm water upwelling from below or by winds and ocean currents. Their reliability has made some species of marine mammals, like walrus, seal and also birds rely on them for millions of years as well as being good news for early mariners. In the upper reaches of Baffin Bay as it merges into the Smith Sound, the water is, in fact, flowing south through the strait from the Extreme North and the North Water Polynya is one of the largest on Earth.

As the winter takes hold and the water within the Nares Strait begins to freeze from October each year, usual behaviour is for an ice arch to form at each narrowed end, locking, fixing and consolidating everything in between. For a traveller, both on foot or using dogs, this is perfect as there is no drift, limited compression and winds are less likely to fracture fragile, newly formed ice. Only when an arch at either end collapses in the spring or summer does movement restart and the ice in the month of May usually produces a true nightmare scenario of sharp, churned-up, broken pans of ice. Soon after, most of this will flow south and melt. Regardless, even in August and September, at the sea ice minimum extent, the straits are extremely hazardous even to ice-hardened ships. To raise awareness of global warming, Greenpeace sent a ship, *Arctic Sunrise*, to the Hall Basin in 2009 but its ability to reach that far north was not typical, aided by an early ice arch collapse some months before.

My particular interest was straightforward. When would the ice form safely enough for us to travel on it and when would it be likely to break up? The time window we would have to complete our journey in would need to lie within these inflexible and less than predictable constraints.

The ice off Qaanaaq itself is at the mercy of strong easterly winds and sea currents. It was this opening stretch of our route which needed to be workable for us. A decade ago, dog drivers were able to travel over the sea to and from Siorapaluk and even further north as early as November. Now, its feasibility is questionable even after Christmas. This was disappointing, but I was determined not to fall into the common trap of blaming the ice for our woes. We would work with what we had, as people have done for centuries.

CHAPTER TWELVE

The option of sea freight transport for the majority of our supplies, short of last minute items and valuables like satellite communications and other electronics, was very attractive but it created a time pressure. Only two sea shipments a year can be made to the Thule region, one in August and one in September. These transport the main resupply for the settlements for the entire year and so advance planning is needed by all who reside there. I would send up our crates in July for the September voyage.

I resolved to arrive in Qaanaaq with Justin in early December, ready to unpack and organise our supplies, familiarise ourselves with the environment and then set off as soon as the ice formed. With luck we could lay our depots up the Nares Strait within ninety days and return before April and the beginning of the break-up. The sun would rise towards the end of February for the first time and before that, darkness and then an eerie twilight would pervade. Bizarrely, temperatures at around minus twenty to minus thirty would drop another ten or more degrees as spring and the sun arrived. Whilst this may be counter-intuitive it is a function of the sun causing warming and cooling of the air which spells an end to the calm and clear conditions typical of the winter.

The next year on Phase Two, we would have yet more pressure on our shoulders, as we needed a window of time double that needed for Phase One. We would rely on speed and an aim to cover fractured ice with light sledges on the late spring return leg.

A flurry of activity continued in the run up to sending away the shipments. Friends and family worked for hours with us to pack and organise five hundred day bags of food in total. Another friend, Mike Lunn, who runs the Purvers International freighting company, offered to take care of the certification and safe packing of our more hazardous cargo. Along with the hundreds of kilos of inert food bags, we had a hundred litres of highly flammable stove fuel, hundreds of waterproof matches and an array of explosives, from flares to 'bear-scarer' charges.

On the day of the sailing, there was an air of relief that the packing was done but a slight tension due to the fact that if one thing went wrong, there were no second chances and our equipment would not reach Qaanaaq in time. It would all be over for 'The Dark Ice Project' if one delay or administration error occurred. First, Eimskip would ship our three enormous crates to Iceland, and then the Royal Arctic Line would take over for the multiple voyages north to Qaanaaq.

Weeks after our supplies were supposed to be safe and sound in Qaanaaq, the somewhat non-existent tracking and feedback from logistics in such remote locations, plus language barriers, gave me my first near-heart attack. Routinely calling to double-check all went well with customs clearance and storage, I was informed that 750kg of 860kg of our cargo was 'wanted' i.e. missing. No-one had seen fit to communicate this to me or even try to 'unwant' it.

Luckily, I had come across the most helpful lady in Greenland, Ivalu Kleist, at the Royal Arctic Line, who personally chased up the shipment and asked for a local in Qaanaaq to go and photograph everything in storage with my name on. I verified, with a sigh of utter relief, that it was all there. Quite obviously, someone had not ticked the right box on the internal company tracking system.

I had also begun to build a rapport via phone and email with Hans Jensen, a very worldly-wise Inuit in his early sixties. Hans had lived in Qaanaaq in its original location as well as its current position. Despite the tiny throughput of Westerners, mostly scientists, travellers and the odd film crew, he had, nonetheless, run the only guesthouse in Qaanaaq for over a decade. I would later learn that, due to peculiar anti-competition rules, even if another person wanted to open a guesthouse of their own in the village, it would require Hans' permission and blessing first.

'The Dark Ice Project' would be unique in so many ways from other expeditions and my own past experiences, but some practicalities stood out. An unavoidable menace for all those travelling in the coastal Arctic is the polar bear. A symbol for conservation groups and a special sighting, at a distance, for those visiting the Arctic recreationally, it takes on a different significance for others. Native communities of the Arctic have annual quotas for hunting polar bears, despite their IUCN Vulnerable status, which allows for traditional use of the pelt, fur and other body parts whilst not affecting population numbers. For travellers though, especially those without vehicles or permanent structure for protection, the polar bear is a hunter and we the potential prey. It is important not to overstate the risk or unnecessarily demonise these majestic animals, but they are one of very few predators on Earth to actively hunt humans as a source of food. Many other animal attacks around the world, from large sharks to elephants, are usually defensive when cornered or out of curiosity.

Though able to swim for miles at speed and run as fast as a horse, the life of a bear is tough; they starve throughout much of the year when a lack of sea ice makes hunting seals and other marine mammals impossible. Especially during the summer months or when hungry females and cubs emerge from dens in the early spring, any living or recently dead animal is fair game.

The overwhelming attraction for bears towards humans is curiosity. Humans have a particular scent and behaviour which intrigues polar bears. The main reason a polar bear will approach a campsite or a moving skier will be to find out what it is. In many Canadian hunting regions, Northern Greenland or East Greenland, the chances are that humans will represent danger for them and they will keep their distance. For this reason, the vast majority of encounters between bear and human are brief, at a distance and will sometimes even be undetected by the human.

The situation changes gravely, though, when a bear is hungry, injured or desperate for some reason. Any living thing will look like food and the animal will take more of a risk in order to get its much-needed meal.

Attacks on humans by bears are rare. The main reason for this is that people do not live in significant numbers where bears roam, live and hunt. With the exception of places like Churchill, Manitoba, an unfortunately positioned settlement where polar bears congregate to gain access to the newly frozen Hudson Bay, and some Inuit villages, there need be no reason for a confrontation. Any bears which stray into an inhabited place are either tranquilised and relocated when facilities are available or, more likely, shot. This is to protect children who might be walking to school and sled dogs that are chained up outdoors.

Where an overlap of territory is unavoidable, though, the risk remains. Education about how to deal with an inquisitive polar bear has improved the situation and many potentially lethal encounters for either person or bear, or both, can be de-escalated. Providing a bear is reasonably healthy and detected at a distance, all that is needed is for you to persuade it that you are a human. Nine times out of ten, it will have a sniff of your scent and wander off.

If that one bear persists, however, be under no illusion. The human will be firmly on the back foot. Polar bears are swift, stealthy, highly intelligent hunters and masters of their environment. Recent years have seen a number of attacks and most of these have been on groups or solo travellers who cannot jump into a vehicle or building for protection and who could not be on permanent lookout. Campsites and even a hauling skier will smell of various different foods and other scents which prove irresistible to bears.

Three recent examples have been on the Norwegian/ Russian side of the Arctic coastline. In 2006, the same season as the Ousland/Horn attempt for the North Pole in winter, Thomas Ulrich, a Swiss soloist, set off from the Russian Cape in March, months after the other pair. The ice conditions were poor and a storm rolled in. To add insult to injury, and the reason he had to call in a cripplingly expensive rescue from Russia, a polar bear had made its way through some of his sledge, leaving equipment and food bags strewn across the ice. He had to fire his revolver three times at its feet to force a retreat. Non-lethal camp invasions like this are not rare.

In 2011, a tragic attack occurred on the Norwegian territory of Svalbard, a group of islands increasingly popular with adventure tourists given its easy flights from mainland Norway and its stark, polar environment. Svalbard is home to a very large polar bear population; some suggest it is the highest density anywhere in the Arctic. BSES (the British Schools Exploring Society) leads youth groups to remote areas of the world and in 2011, their headline trip was to Svalbard during the summer. Operating from a static camp, a group came under attack from a starving bear, apparently with gum infections which had made hunting difficult; its situation was exacerbated by the lack of food in the summer. All in the camp were asleep in tents and by the end of the horrific incident one boy was dead, four were badly mauled and the bear was shot.

In the Norwegian and British inquiries, the facts of what happened were tragic but damning. The sole early-warning system, a trip-wire, was not set up correctly and failed to operate, there was no guard sentry system, no guard dog and the weapon misfired up to four times before killing the bear. The bear behaved as so many ill and starving animals would do at that time of year, aggressively and without the caution typical of a healthy animal. No criminal charges were brought against the leaders and it must be said that they were injured in the process of killing the bear and avoiding further deaths.

It is easy to make sweeping, knee-jerk reactions following emotive disasters such as this and in the aftermath it is vital to make changes and learn lessons which could potentially save lives. The BSES leaders, who, I have always felt due to the structure inherent in BSES trips should be supplemented by guides, were not professionals and were themselves gaining experience. There was a long list of questions about their preparation of a conspicuous and non-transitory camp against polar bears and the attack could certainly have been minimised or avoided, as the reports stated.

Some would say hindsight is a wonderful thing and that more deaths were avoided by truly brave actions, which I agree with. What remains as fact is that a dog with bear experience or a simple sentry rota could have warned the entire camp when the bear was hundreds of yards away. I also noticed from the aerial press photographs of the camp that the tents were in a circle. When in a large camp with multiple tents, the first anti-bear precaution to take is to pitch them in a line. This way, a bear that wanders into

172

camp out of inquisitiveness is less likely to feel surrounded and attack out of defence.

So, should there be more rules and legislation to keep people away from bears and limit expedition activity? I would argue a fervent, no. It should be noted that the issue only arose due to the fact that this episode occurred in that grey, murky zone where school groups and tourism cross into the fringes of the polar environment. In the ninety-nine per cent of the Arctic that is truly inaccessible, the problem will never arise. Driving a wedge between adventure and children who want to escape the cycle of games consoles and fast food would be criminal.

From my own point of view, I am already restricted in many areas of the Arctic by ever-tightening, 'one size fits all' permit conditions that are in place to stop the incompetent from costing the government vast sums of money. The Arctic is a wild, unpredictable yet magnificent place and to try and sanitise it with bureaucracy is a fate it, and we, do not deserve. It is inevitable that, occasionally, the price to pay for freedom befitting the wilderness itself will be a tragedy.

In 2012, Timo Palo and Audun Tholfsen, during their impeccably executed 'reverse' North Pole expedition back to land, encountered a bear which leapt out of the water of a lead they were about to cross. Only a few feet away, the bear jumped back into the water only when their gun was fired at the snow at its feet; it was a real close call with a bear clearly in hunting mode. For those wanting to see what an ambush from the water looks like, an identical attack on a seal was filmed for the BBC's 2011 series, *The Frozen Planet*.

These incidents invite the obvious question, what can be done about it? Deterrents are numerous and varied in their effectiveness. They also range in severity from a mild dissuasion to a lethal last resort. A colonialist, traditional reaction on meeting a bear on an expedition might have been to shoot it, regardless of its intention. Thankfully, modern expedition leaders have a great deal more knowledge and many more options to choose from.

The first course of action is to try and persuade the polar bear that you are not food. Making yourself as human-looking as possible i.e. not being in a seal-coloured sleeping bag and also making lots of loud, deep noises and waving arms can help when a bear is at a distance and clearly interested. Even this may not be necessary as a bear on a mission to get somewhere else might throw a cursory glance in your direction and nonchalantly wander off.

If a bear seems intent on a closer look at you or your sledges, the best deterrent is a flare, either fired from a pistol, shotgun or dedicated launcher. This is not to hurt a bear but instead, fired at its feet, to startle it enough that it runs off, considering you too dangerous to be worth bothering with. During the day, unless a bear is actively stalking you and using ice rubble as cover, in which case your chances of survival are slim, a vigilant skier who regularly checks behind can expect advance warning of some kind.

At night, the stakes are raised further. A soloist or small team cannot reasonably keep a watch system, especially in the cold winter or spring and must let their guard down to sleep. This time also coincides with cooking food and the smell of a camp must be inviting for bears for miles around. The best precautions are to set up a good perimeter trip-wire connected to alarm explosive charges, a time consuming chore to do every evening, or to bring along a sledge dog with polar bear experience. The drawback of the latter is the need to haul food for the dog or to have to hunt in order to feed it. A dog sledge-powered expedition need not worry as the weight of kibble is borne by the dogs themselves.

If a bear does invade a camp during the night and takes more of an interest in the curiously coloured and shaped tent instead of the sledges, a usual attack would come straight through the sides of the tent. If all alarms and precautions have failed, only a preloaded, strategically placed weapon and the wits of those inside will save them. In most cases, though, barking dogs (who seem to fearlessly and by some accounts successfully, want to attack the far larger polar bears) and detonating trip-wire charges is enough to scare a bear or buy time for the team to locate the bear and to ready the flares and weapon.

A last resort of having to kill an aggressive bear would be a tragedy for all involved and a stark reminder of what happens when we stumble across those to whom the Arctic really belongs. To this end, however, all members of a team would usually have a large-calibre rifle (such as a 30-06 or .303), a 12-gauge shotgun loaded with a solid-shot 'slug' (now inexplicably illegal in Greenland) or a revolver like a .45 Magnum (when legal) close to hand.

For 'The Dark Ice Project', our polar bear risk was severe. The Nares Strait, especially in the southern portions, is a hive of bear activity with plenty of broken ice allowing habitat for seals; the polynya attracts dozens of bears along its edge and the whole area is a relative safe haven from hunting in Canada or Greenland's Melville Bay. This danger would be less significant to the north, especially when far onto the Arctic Ocean, although a polar bear has been sighted near the North Pole itself. We would be travelling in the dark of winter when visibility is minimal yet bears are actively hunting, except those females who are nursing in dens. This made the risk of chancing upon and startling a bear behind a block of ice very real. The likelihood of spotting a bear which was stalking us, would be very slim in these conditions.

Short of the concern I had over Justin's compatibility with a meticulously organised expedition, it was the thought of bears that kept me awake into the early hours more than anything in the months leading up to December. The preparation phase was the time when I could actually do something about polar bears. Once on the ice, it would be too late to have a good idea. Had I thought of everything?

After long chats with my older and more experienced counterparts abroad, like Jerry Kobalenko from Canada and in particular, my friend and Norwegian polar guide, Inge Solheim, I had a plan I was comfortable with which would not hinder progress too badly. Particularly chilling, when hearing the advice from Jerry, was his understated observation, 'It'll be pretty interesting dealing with bears in the dark.' This was from a man with decades of High Arctic experience and a survivor of at least one bear attack.

Despite my own thousands of miles of experience in cold regions, it was vital that I sought advice and ideas from others. I was stepping into a region I was not familiar with, as is the entire point and nature of exploration, and it was no time for pride. I was glad I contacted those who I respected abroad: Weber, Kobalenko,

Dupre, Solheim and Ousland – the UK simply does not have any people like them whose deep and often humbly held knowledge outweighs their public profile and posturing.

I settled on a multi-layered approach. We would be constantly armed, both with pencil flares, flare cartridges and rocket flares and also with a shotgun able to make a certain kill. At night, if in high-risk areas, we would set up a four or five-post custom-made trip-wire. Each post would contain a black powder explosive charge with special fishing braid running in between.

As our main deterrent though, and a plan I was excited about and proud of, we would bring with us an Eskimo sledge dog – only one. He would not haul anything but just walk alongside, sniffing out any bears, day or night. I was sure he would also be a major boost to our morale and a great companion. All I had to consider was the fact that our already bulging sledges would have to have dog kibble added to them. The quantity needed would be a question for the hunters in Qaanaaq.

Determined not to fall into the Westerner's trap of giving him a slightly patronising, pretentious Inuit name like Nanoq (meaning polar bear) or the name of a pioneering explorer, I suggested to Justin we buck the trend and go with 'Dave'. He loved both the name and the reasoning behind it and so, although we had not even chosen or met Dave yet, his name was decided. That time would come once up in Qaanaaq and Hans had assured me we could go out and buy a young, healthy dog with bear experience for eight hundred Danish krone (DKK), around ninety pounds sterling.

Even before the difficult experience of the Vatnajökull and the damaged tunnel tent that contributed to the early end of that attempt, I had been thinking about tents. There are few things more important to the survival of a traveller than his or her shelter. Our tent is our home for many months. To that end, choosing the best one is more than a little important. In the same vein that I have alluded to previously, the crowd-following trends that are rife in commercial and adventure tourism polar travel have led to presumptions. Some are not even aware that brands other that Hilleberg, a specialist Swedish tentmaker, are available.

In reality, there is significant choice, mostly from amongst the mass-market mountaineering ranges which then have polar modifications made. The standard layout consists of a living area, either under a geodesic or tunnel frame, plus a large porch on the leeward end for cooking and admin and a smaller one at the windward end for added storage. A geodesic frame is better for all-round wind protection and can be free-standing without guy lines, but the interiors can be a little more cramped and they are slightly slower to erect than tunnels.

Although stock shortages for Hillebergs can create long lead times and vital additions like snow valances are optional extras, the European preference for their brand led to a number of other tents being discontinued. For example, the British-made Lightwave T3 Arctic, essentially a better-thought-out version of the Hilleberg Keron GT, was dropped because no-one was buying it. I was lucky to get hold of two of the last T3 Arctic tents in the warehouse. Musing on my acquisitions, I was reminded of the blind adherence to the Alfa boot system I have long questioned and began wondering if I was not missing out on better options and being a sheep myself?

Double-flysheet, siliconised, nylon tents with a matrix of narrow support poles have become the de facto standard. They are lightweight, easy to put up in practiced hands (a nightmare to put up in novice hands) and allow for good living arrangements. There are limitations aplenty, though. They are susceptible from ever-changing side-winds, a common occurrence in some polar regions. They are not breathable, which is not practical in the cold where hoarfrost forms on inner surfaces, ready to soak the occupants when the stove is switched on and if the frost is not wiped away. The silicone waterproofing is not optimised for cold locations where there is no rain and the ever-present snow will bounce off tents easily. In the same way, 'waterproof' clothing is not useful in truly cold conditions. Breathable, windproof fabrics are best for both tents and clothing. The narrow aluminum poles are easily bent or snapped by high winds and unless every gap around the valance line is sealed with piles of snow, winds will allow flying drift in between the flysheets, only to coat boots and possessions in the porch area. Even the smallest gap overnight can lead to a minor snowdrift in the porch on waking in the morning. Even though a sensible team will use oversized tents – a three or four-man tent for a pair, for example – they are still cramped and hard to manoeuvre within. Standing up is out of the question.

I looked back into the past in order to see the various ways people, both native and 'visiting', have taken shelter in the Polar Regions. Some are ingenious and some make the best of a lack of resources. Some are transitory for mobile expeditions and some are semi-permanent. Canvas pyramid tents have been used in the Antarctic for over a century, but they can weigh over thirty kilos. Snowholes dug into the surface have saved many a life, but are not exactly five-star living. Igloos take immense knowledge and skill, plus many hours of toil. Modern dome tents are a solution, but with the caveats I outlined.

A final option is nothing new at all – the tipi. Essentially a non-directional, single fly tent supported by a single vertical post, tipis have been used across the globe for centuries as reliable and practical shelters in places both hot and cold. Richard Weber (of 1995 North Pole return fame) had created a homemade nylon version a couple of decades ago with vertical walls, supported by skis and ski poles but I felt that the nylon let it down. Undeniably he was onto something, though – added to which he was not a man afraid of self-designing with his custom ski bindings and sledges – and his tent allowed for quick setup, a spacious interior and made use of otherwise redundant skis and ski poles.

With more research, I came across a Swedish company called Tentipi. They seemed to have combined the traditional canvas design of a tipi, modernised the materials and adapted them to cold climes. The single ply canvas was a lightweight and windproof polycotton and was, critically and excitingly, breathable. Could this reduce or even banish hoarfrost to history? The structure claimed to be fast to pitch, with only a single pole in the centre and eight guy points around the base. Interestingly for me, with my experience of brutally strong winds, the tent needed to be able to be fully anchored on all sides before being elevated with the centre pole. This final movement could be completed in no more than ten seconds, minimising the chances of the tent mimicking a kite at the vital moment, as tunnel and dome tents so often do. Finally, it would be tall enough to stand up inside, an absolute luxury if we could make the idea work, but not presenting a large enough surface area for the top to catch high winds.

Having met with Tony Stephenson, Tentipi's UK distributor, the company agreed to supply a Zirkon five-man tent (really only practical for two to three with equipment) with plenty of extras. Two questions had to be answered by testing: could this withstand high winds and could men wearing thick mitts handle it under pressure? The answer to both was 'Yes,' as was shown by impressive video footage and some comical practice sessions in local parks. Typically, a number of modifications would have to be made.

There were a load of superfluous cords and pulleys inside to operate clever vents and windows in the top point of the tent and there was one extra Velcro vent at the top. The clutter could go, making the inside far simpler and less likely to get tied up in knots during a storm in the dark. The extra vents and the 'top hat' of the tent would then be stitched closed and secure. Not having the equipment or skill for such a tricky job, I entrusted the tent to M Putt, Sailmakers in East London. They had been in business for generations and counted the *Cutty Sark* amongst their clients.

The central pole, I was assured, was made of the correct grade of aluminium that it would flex a great deal before snapping and this was gaffer-taped up to enable bare hands to hold it in the cold. Every small detail had to be pre-considered and solved in the comfort of the UK.

The breathability of the special polycotton would have to wait to be tested in the Arctic but the initial signs were good; it was totally windproof and repellant to splashes of water yet allowed steam and vapour to pass through without soaking the inner surface of the fabric. A complete change from the tent status quo was a commitment indeed, but there was one trade-off for all this convenience. The tent would weigh in at seven kilos compared to my Lightwave at four and a half. To be honest, even given the weight-saving efforts elsewhere, the decision was already enthusiastically made. The Zirkon would come to the High Arctic.

The dark and associated cold has a major effect on insulation. In sunny, or at least light conditions, moisture which has entered duck or goose-down clothing or padding can be dried out by sublimation in direct contact with the air and sun. In the dark this could not happen and every item would have to be nursed throughout. One mistake, leading to a damp or iced-up sleeping bag or jacket filling, would be suffered for horribly for the rest of the journey.

The solution was actually fairly simple and not a new decision for the handful of polar travellers willing to take on the winter or early spring. Down had to go. The lightweight and lofty comfort that came with it would have to be exchanged for the heavier but more forgiving synthetic equivalents, such as Driloft or Primaloft.

I researched, sourced and tested all the insulated pieces of clothing: tent booties, sleeping bags, over-sleeping bags (temperatures below minus forty Celsius would necessitate a second layer), over-mitts and jackets. The very best synthetic technology was found for each garment, although I conceded defeat with our massive over-jackets. I argued that they would be so far from our skin that moisture should not reach the filling, especially if our moisture management was up to scratch. Two enormous yellow 'Michelin man' down jackets were bought for those cold, static moments at food breaks and either end of the day. Even our 'if-it-is-bone-chillingly-cold' sleeveless gilets to go over our smocks were Primaloft filled.

Again, I opted for the unbeatable Montane Extreme smock and salopettes system which had performed so well for me since 2008. Montane, clothing sponsors for 'The Dark Ice Project' along with Bridgedale socks, provided almost everything from head to toe. The fibre pile and Pertex combination was simply brilliant; it was warm and comfortable as well as being supremely windproof and breathable. Waterproof it was not, but this would not be necessary. On previous expeditions I had noticed that perspiration on the harder days had passed so easily through my base layer and the smock soft-shell that 'tidemarks' had appeared on the outside fabric. In my opinion and having tried endless possibilities, the combination was peerless.

I have mentioned previously that the sledges floated to some degree or another. This flotation would be needed regularly through our sea ice expedition and increasingly so as we encountered the more mobile ice of the Arctic Ocean. Constant movement makes hundreds of tons of ice snap and crush like mere wafer biscuits, a truly stunning force of nature. For us, this meant encounters with notorious pressure ridges where two pans of ice have collided and pressed against each other. These can be twenty or more feet in height. At the opposite end of the spectrum are leads of open water or thin, recently refrozen ice caused by pans pulling apart. Sometimes one can gingerly ski over this thin ice but often it is unavoidable to take a dip.

Historic tactics for this hugely dangerous exercise have included using inflatable boats, rafts and ladders or waiting for days for them to close up again and even pure avoidance, skiing for hours along the lead edge until it narrows. Failure to keep dry, in most cases, leads to a rapid death for solo skiers like Dominick Arduin on the Russian side of the Arctic Ocean in 2004, possible loss of fingers and toes if saved by a teammate or at best, a compromised or curtailed expedition.

A new solution for this constant barrier on polar sea ice expeditions came when Børge Ousland began to use a modified Hansen sea survival suit as a swimming dry suit. A true innovator and elder statesman of polar travel to many, his was the solution for us, combined with the ability to raft our sledges for smaller leads or where we did not fancy the long process of 'suiting up'. It would be a judgement call every time.

Using a suit was not an easy procedure. They were enormous and fitted over our entire polar outfit, boots included. Having been zipped up into what was essentially a rubber bag, you would have to break through the likely skim of ice and then stabilise yourself in the water, all the time being vigilant for nearby polar bears. The best advice was to swim in a sort of ungainly backstroke, using elbows to crack through the ice ahead. Swimming forwards could lead to water leaking in around the face area and filling up the suit. If not corrected, and if the swimmer was not able to keep their feet lower than their upper half, it could lead to an unpleasant and undignified drowning in the dark, freezing waters of the Arctic.

As well as being awkward to use they were, due to their custom-made and niche nature, very expensive. In a rare show of real camaraderie amongst polar contemporaries, and typical of his kind yet professional nature, Inge Solheim contributed two of his suits, which Hansen had supplied him with for previous trips. These included the 'Walking With The Wounded' – a last degree North Pole event with wounded servicemen and briefly, Prince Harry, which Inge guided.

Typically Norwegian, Inge is direct and straight to the point. He lives with his British wife in London and some uninitiated Brits can take his manner to be rudeness, but soon it is obvious that the opposite is the case. Much like myself, Inge is also happy to call out dishonest or unacceptable behaviour by others and we both employ a 'credit where credit is due, but only when it is due' outlook. My own skepticism about the actions and comments of some self-styled 'polar guides' or 'explorers' has been backed up by eyebrow-raising but unrepeatable accounts from Inge's experiences.

The 'interesting' behaviour of two of the guides who, along with Inge, operate from the Russian Barneo base, which is temporarily and remarkably set up every April a degree from the North Pole, was evidenced on the television. In a slightly trivalising manner, in my opinion, Channel 5 made *North Pole: Ice Airport* for broadcast in 2012. The tourist-driven and circus-like conveyor belt of visitors there overshadows the immense skill and bravery needed to create this floating ice runway by people and equipment, including a tractor, parachuted onto the ice. The current base leader, Misha Malakhov, was Richard Weber's former 'polar brother' and is one of the all-time greats. But surely if there is anywhere on Earth that should be insulated from commercialisation, it is the Polar Regions?

One British guide, an individual I had long been warned had a bullish and slightly simple attitude, was filmed teaching his clients how to use the tent and what ski skins were, just a day prior to arrival. Another international guide had a full-on tantrum with

Malakhov over the use of the helicopter that could cost him just a few hours of travel. Storming out and refusing the flight window he was offered, his high-paying clients never reached the Pole and went home empty-handed. I watched in horror and disbelief – I vowed never to be part of the money-driven and trivalising polar tourism business. From many guides I know who have been in the mountains and on the ice for many years, the sense of wonder and positivity has been drained and replaced with a bitter cynicism.

In the last few months, a self-created 'governing body' called the IPGA (International Polar Guides Association) came into being with a few veteran guides at the helm. As a polar guide only when it is a sensible addition to my own journeys and therefore looking in somewhat from the outside, my view is fairly unbiased. I cannot really see much motivation for this organisation apart from looking after the commercial interests of those self-admitted to the club. As competition for polar tourism guiding has grown, I imagine it will not be long before clients are told that IPGA guides are the only 'safe' ones.

It should be reiterated that these adventure ski trips are not considered to be North Pole expeditions; they are up to ten times shorter than a full expedition, take place on the best ice and in the relatively benign month of April with daylong sunlight. Clients are led in large groups by guides and include the children of billionaires and city bankers keen for a new story to tell at parties.

Incredibly, some of these novice clients can later be seen on the motivational speaking circuit, marketed as polar explorers who have 'conquered the North Pole'. Equivalents would be if one were taken into surgery to be operated on by a second-year medical student or being taught to drive by someone still yet to shed their own L-plates. In comparison to ten to fourteen days, a well-conditioned professional polar traveller could cover the short route in only three or four days. I will let you draw your own conclusions.

Everyone knows that feeling of having to hide a wry smile when a new acquaintance starts telling you about his Uncle Larry who was in the SAS and on every major operation the regiment has ever been involved in. This modern influx of tourists I describe has brought a similar effect from the polar world. I can now barely attend a 'work do' or party where someone's second cousin or similarly unverifiable relative has not 'trekked to the North Pole'. A friendly nod is the only sensible reply.

The Russian team running the base cannot be criticised. They complete an operation of mind-boggling complexity and uncertainty each year and do so efficiently and safely. They are laughing all the way to the bank at the expense of the mostly ridiculous foreigners and are, in my experience, humble, skilled and I think the very best sort of polar people. In the most likely flawed, but intrinsically human tradition of categorising everything in sight, no matter how uncategorisable, perhaps there are three 'sorts': the first is the laissez-faire 'hippy' type who shuns training and believes that fate and a 'say yes' attitude will solve all. The second is the archaic, pseudo-Edwardian who sees no need for progression and uses bluster and the 'sledgehammer' approach to seize his/her colonial prizes. The third 'sort' is the professional who combines a modern passion and respect for his/her environment, grasps lessons hard-won by predecessors and seeks always to become more efficient and forward thinking.

What is interesting and I suppose a product of the sheer intensity of independent polar travel, the duration of most journeys and the fact that measurement of expertise is relative to others, is that someone who is wet behind the ears can become a highly effective operator in just a few expeditions. You learn fast when the stakes are so high.

It would be this base, Barneo, the only one of its kind, that would provide extraction support for my 'Dark Ice Project' during April and I had a contract agreed with the non-tourism side of the Russian team in case our plans had to change. Barneo also supports vital logistics for scientific research in the narrow April period.

A final logistical headache caused by 'The Dark Ice Project' would be, surprise, surprise, again due to the lack of light. The usual up-to-date method of generating electricity on multi-month expeditions is to use solar panels. These can be strapped to a sledge or tent and charge anything from GPS units to iPods via an intermediate reservoir battery.

Electrics in cold and remote locations are a true nightmare. Nothing electronic, or very little at least, is actually designed to thrive in low temperatures. Batteries are the worst, with most chemistries totally useless and only lithium varieties even worth considering. All batteries need to be kept warm in order to perform at all and the only saving grace is that they can be stored cold.

Electronics are a necessity on any expedition and without them, the safety of the team could be in unnecessary danger. There is a priority list for charging and battery supplies, which ranges from emergency to luxury. For me, this priority list would usually be as follows: EPLB (an emergency beacon, although these have built-in sealed batteries), GPS, satellite phones, tracking device, cameras and iPods. It would be a sorry situation indeed to find yourself clean out of power and in an emergency with an empty phone battery and a fully charged iPod.

Without this neat cycle of newly recharged batteries from the ever-present sun, we would have to make do with stored power. Some of the main resupply items for the Russian winter expedition in 2008 were battery packs. They are heavy in bulk and will drain far faster than at room temperature even when warmed in a sleeping bag or jacket. We did not have the luxury of resupplies and so would have to haul them. In one of the few moments when miniscule gram counting did appeal to me (usually I find weight-saving obsessions like chopping corners off food packs and shaving paint off poles fairly amusing) I was delighted that lithium AA batteries weighed 17g each compared to 23g for inferior alkaline alternatives. AA batteries, almost the world's default battery, would become, for us, the core energy store from which all other items charged or ran directly.

Having painstakingly done the maths regarding the power needs of every device and having estimated the degradation of the battery charge due to the cold, I found that we would need to take no less than eight hundred and twenty lithium batteries. These would give us a fighting chance of keeping the vital equipment powered up, especially the critical polar winter addition, high power torches.

One set would be used for all-day use as head torches, illuminating the ice twenty feet or so ahead. The other torch we had was a specially designed long distance model able to project a beam nearly three hundred yards. It would be with this spot lamp that I would scour the distance for polar bears. Our head torches would be useless – only alerting us to a bear when it was too late to save ourselves. We would have to use it with extra care when setting out a few yards from camp to answer the call of nature. Being caught by a bear literally with our pants down would be an embarrassing end.

I wondered what sort of effect the constant lighting we would use would have on any bears who happened to catch our scent or chance upon us. There was very little precedent for winter travel in the full darkness for me to refer to. The light could put the bears off if they associated it with humans and danger. Alternatively, and more likely, they would find us curious and approach for a closer look. We just had no idea; it was another unknown of the project I had created.

CHAPTER THIRTEEN

The final two or three months before our 10th December flying date went by like a flash. One moment I was thinking there was still time to adjust my mind slowly to what was to come and the next, our departure was nigh. The sheer workload of making sure the expedition was truly ready, reordering my London life to survive four months without me, and seeing friends and family, had taken every waking hour.

Justin had only just reached the closing stages of a business deal, which was clearly giving him some grief. I took up the slack as I had done throughout the whole lead up. With a week to go, ensuring we had the correct inventory of gear to fly up with – essentially everything bar that which was shipped up in the summer – I asked for a list of what he would arrive with. Somewhat aghast, I was informed that he usually did kit lists in his head. Trying to be diplomatic and understanding, I worked through the kit list, both for shared and personal equipment and through a process of elimination, wrote a 'bring to the airport' list for him. I hoped that this would help.

The day came and it was time to fly. I was ready, physically and in terms of preparations. It was to be the most ambitious, technical expedition of my career and with a massive spoonful of uncertainty thrown in. In the past, especially with a teammate I had not worked with on a big journey, I still felt like we had a united front and it gave me confidence. Now though, whilst I was assured of Justin's credentials and his intentions, something niggled.

Seeing us off were Justin's fiancée, Sharon, and my father. I remember the same moment back in 2008 with George and our families. Back then, I could not wait to get through check-in and security. I wanted to get out of the goodbyes mindset and into expedition-mode. I was twenty-one and very scared; it was a fear which manifested itself not in outward emotion but in a need to get on with the job. This time, however, I was altogether more relaxed. I was in control.

Justin arrived half an hour or so behind schedule, (something I had grown used to), with two enormous holdalls. Leaving everyone to say hello, I began the now slightly time-constrained process of integrating the contents into the shipping barrels, in which I had left space. Trying hard to contain my horror, I found the inevitable, two holdalls looking like they had been packed in a frenzied rush; it was almost as if everything in sight had been thrown in whilst leaving the house. I wondered how compatible this was with a major polar expedition, to put it mildly. Even after I had sorted it all out, I pondered on what the differences in mindsets would mean for our future.

Nutrition is, as I have explained, an exact, calculated and lifesaving thing to get right. I had spent dozens of hours balancing the weight of a daily ration pack with the calorific content. What I found in Justin's holdalls were about seven or eight kilos of random supplements and food packs I had never heard of before.

Personal choice is always to be expected on an expedition – I always choose a pair of foam pads to sleep on whereas Justin preferred a foam base and an inflatable Therm-a-rest. This was different though. It was random, unplanned and chaotic. I asked how he would integrate them into our food plan and what gaps they would fill and in return there were a few mumbles.

I think on something as risky and close-knit as a polar journey, the difficulty as a leader is to make sure equilibrium is kept between micro-managing and meddling in grown people's lives, and running a functional team. I tried to keep this in mind and not turn something solvable into a wedge between us. Our lives would soon be in each other's hands.

The barrels sealed and ready, with some of the unexpected additions, we were more than a little over our luggage allowance. As any traveller will attest, even those who pre-freight equipment out, part of life is the game of charm and diplomacy in reducing over-weight charges at airports. This can be quite fun, almost like a casino. Who of the check-in counter staff looks the friendliest? We triumphed at the British Airways counter with a lovely lady who was fascinated by our expedition. As we flew another five times via Copenhagen, we would incur nearly a thousand pounds of charges. Some of this was inevitable, but I could not clear it from my mind that some could have been avoided.

It was not just a case of jumping on flight after flight. Part of the myriad of arrangements I had to make included errands in almost every stop-over. In Copenhagen, the flights were so close together that instead of bothering with an overnight hotel, the departures lounge and a twenty-four hour pizza and pastry stall kept us comfortable and well enough fed. For about three weeks before our start date I had not started a concerted fattening regime, but had just loosened my athletic diet, opting for the full-fat option for everything and never saying no to a pudding, snack or good cheese – absolute bliss and a bonus of expedition life.

The long flight from Denmark to Greenland's South in Kangerlussuaq occurs just once a week in the winter and marked the real transition point. Kangerlussuaq, although hundreds of miles south of Qaanaaq, is still well within the Arctic Circle and so, once there, and given the proximity to the winter solstice, we would not see the sun for many months. That moment, as we climbed above the clouds in the aircraft to see the sun shining, was poignant. Soon it would set and be hidden from us until at least late February. We were entering the polar winter.

Kangerlussuaq was in a cycle of twilight during the day and darkness at night and it was there I had my first task. Unable to import specialist, anti-bear ammunition into Greenland due to their illegality in most countries and my lack of an international firearms licence, I had asked for my friend, Robert Peroni, to send some across from Tasiilaq. Even in Greenland, where children may purchase firearms in the local shop, there are understandable restrictions on their transport by air. Our weapons were waiting for us further up the coast but the shotgun ammunition was the headache. The Inuit hunters use large calibre rifles to hunt large mammals due to the lower damage to the pelt compared to a shotgun's solid slug. This made the chance of buying them up North unlikely.

After rushing up from the airstrip to the postal building, one of only a few buildings in Kangerlussuaq, it turned out there was no package with my name on it. I visited the Air Greenland freight office to see if they had ended up there but again, nothing. With little chance of luck finding these precious items in Ilulissat, Upernavik or Qaanaaq, I tried the hunting supplies store that only stocked rifles and finally a Danish guesthouse that I had dealt with in the past for 'Point 660' pickups.

Kim, the moustached Dane who ran the business was helpful as always. Whilst not able to sell me slugs, he was able to find a box of similar shotgun cartridges also rated to be lethal against a polar bear at five metres. Beggars cannot be choosers and I gratefully accepted, only to be told by the uncharacteristically bureaucratic airport staff that they did not like the box we had the ammunition in. They would not fly and we continued our journey empty-handed.

As we took off again, this time exchanging the large Airbus for a small propeller-driven Dash 8 aeroplane, it would be our last proper view of the coastline and icecap beyond. By the time we landed in Ilulissat, on the shores of the world-famous, iceberg-strewn Disko Bay, our latitude would ensure the light would be too dim to see without artificial lights. Justin and I peered out of the window almost continuously, taking in the sight of the open water leads, frozen sea, fjords, mountains and the featureless icecap inland.

The repeat at each ever-more remote airstrip of collecting our twenty-kilo barrels from the freight area and lugging them out of the way of the locals also flying with us was always a 'fingers crossed' moment. It is so easy, especially given where we were, for freight to go missing or get damaged.

A sigh of relief followed each successful collection. In Ilulissat we loaded them into a pickup and made our way through the relative metropolis, home to four and a half thousand Greenlanders, to the guesthouse I had booked. Justin took charge of getting our gear sorted and shifted to the foyer as I set off with a rough mental map of the town to find our weapons. My plethora of emails and phone calls months before had finally come up with what we needed: two new single-barrel Russian shotguns with lightweight plastic stocks. These cheap and reliable Baikal shotguns, which are surprisingly hard to get hold of, are ideal for a robust expedition in the extreme cold where handguns are banned. The Inuit preference for rifles was the same throughout the Arctic.

I finally found a petrol and fuel shack that fitted the description of my destination which I had been given, but I had to be redirected to their sister-shop further up the hill. I discovered my contact, Malik, in the doorway of his store and without a word, he ushered me inside. There must have been a hundred boxes containing every variety of weaponry an Arctic inhabitant could ever need. Malik, without any questions and in a scene I chuckled about ever happening in Europe, handed over the two shotguns in return for a handful of Danish Krone. More or less remembering my way through the dark streets past buildings that were all built to the same design and therefore hard to differentiate, I met Justin back in our room.

During the fifteen-minute walk, I started to notice things were becoming more Arctic. In Kangerlussuaq it was minus five degrees or so and I barely needed gloves or a hat whilst running errands. Now, further north, I found my hands, just covered with thin liner gloves, were feeling the cold a little. It was still mild by polar winter standards: around fifteen degrees below zero.

I have always been, since my teens, keen not to overdo my clothing, especially when around locals of the Arctic. Westerners have a bad enough name whilst in their world and emerging from an aircraft cabin overdressed to the nines in brand new gear instantly screams 'tourist'. You may not think this has any significance beyond personal pride but their perception means a great deal. Giving the first impression of being a tourist would lead only to villagers trying to sell us overpriced tusk or bone carvings which most kept in their pockets on the off-chance. Conversely, showing comfort, ease and conservative use of equipment and clothing can often break down barriers. I have received a great deal of advice, local knowledge and reports of conditions from these generous but often shy people over the years – all it takes is a little effort, thought and a smile.

The next day, after our now-familiar negotiation with the freight manager from the aircraft operator, there was some confusion. Due to the unsurprising lack of demand for flights to the extreme north of the territory, especially in the winter, we would stop only momentarily in Upernavik, in fact, not too far from 'The Long Haul' turn around point in 2008. This would be to exchange two or three Greenlanders, refuel and then carry on to Qaanaaq, vastly further north than any other scheduled destination. Villages north of Ilulissat are measured in hundreds or even just dozens of inhabitants and few have the funds to afford the expensive airfares.

The problem came because, after speaking to the pilot, it turned out that there was cloud cover and snow over Upernavik but clear skies in Qaanaaq. Landing in the dark on short and bumpy runways perched precipitously on the edge of cliffs is a feat in itself, but doing so in poor weather would be asking for trouble. Over the years I have become so used to the rumour mill of whether an aircraft will fly or not that I just sat back and waited. A lot rode on the outcome, since schedules are always tight and aircraft only fly at best every week or fortnight; it was not the thrice-daily shuttle from London to Edinburgh. I suppose at least part of the reasoning behind the title of this book is becoming apparent.

In a bittersweet moment, the news came through that the good conditions in Qaanaaq, typically cold, calm and clear in the winter and the reason Thule has been a favourite of the Inuit for centuries, meant we would fly. However, we could not land in Upernavik, halfway up the coast, and this meant more fuel would have to be carried. More fuel meant less cargo and as the owners of by far the most freight, ours might be the first to be left behind, only to follow days or weeks later.

Mercifully, no cargo had to be abandoned in the end and we began to embark. The plan was for the one family destined for Upernavik to fly all the way to Qaanaaq and then hope for good landing conditions at Upernavik on the return leg.

Needless to say, we were so far north by now that once the landing lights on the side of the Dash 8 had been switched off, only the Moon could provide any illumination of what lay below. In between short naps, I glanced down out of the small window and saw icebergs running along the rugged coast, eerie and ghostly in the murk and both captured in the sea ice and floating free further off shore.

As is so often the case, the sheer workload of expedition planning and disconnection with the reality of what was to come had enveloped me up until that flight. Qaanaaq had always been a dream for me. I always knew it existed and remember musing over a map with George in our tent, saying I would like to launch a journey from there. The time had come and all the tales and stories, which had stirred my imagination about this absurdly remote outpost of human civilisation, were about to have a face put to the name. It was a shame we would not be able to see much of it until our return.

Only a minute or so after spying the dim lights of Qaanaaq ahead, the wheels dropped down from beneath the twin engines and we made a masterful yet bumpy landing moments after. I had never before in my life seen that kind of total commitment and steep descent into a routine landing.

Our freight appeared through a hole in the wall of the tiny arrivals/departures/air traffic control building, which comprised only a couple of rooms. There was a common design throughout Greenlandic buildings like shops and airstrip terminals, since these modern parts of Greenlandic life invariably had one source.

•

The fact that the modern airstrip buildings made such an impression in the face of an otherwise pristine wilderness and traditionally attractive local settlement was because they seemed out of place. They represented a practical way to get things done, in this case allowing Greenlanders to get around their impossibly sparse nation; their value ended at that point.

I have noticed that the people of the Arctic, whilst embracing modernity, value knowledge and their families above all else. Their whole frame of reference as to what is normal is different from ours. Outside of the capital, Nuuk, employment is a minority occupation and subsistence from hunting, fishing and crafts is commonplace, although in decline. In the Western World, there is very little potential to live in this way and because the type of alternative value present in the Far North does not exist here, those outside of employment are stigmatised.

We have actually driven our society into an unwitting and unrecoverable situation where money is so much more valuable than other forms of 'value', that employment is the only feasible way to behave. Without it, there is no life worth living for our families and us. Seeing this wholly different way of leading an ordinary life, I was taken aback and reassessed my own foundations. I also noted and had mixed emotions about the pressure on even the remotest outposts like Qaanaaq to conform to our ways.

•

A quiet and unassuming man, perhaps in his fifties or early sixties, stood in the corner of the airstrip building. He wore spectacles and a large, green, fur-lined parka. Putting two and two together and since he was clearly not welcoming members of his family in time for Christmas, I decided it must be Hans. Walking over and offering my hand, the man took it and shook it firmly.

'Alex! We have spoken a lot. Welcome!' he said. I introduced Hans to Justin and we began to load the barrels and our bags into the back of his aging Toyota 4x4. The temperature was barely below minus fifteen, very mild, and although the ice charts I had been following from various government meteorological services had been promising, warm temperatures were not the best news. The weather was, as I believe is universal, our first topic of conversation as Hans drove us back along the snow and gravel track from the airstrip to Qaanaaq itself. The heater in the 4x4 had broken, as had most of the controls and dials, and so a noisy, plug-in heater whirred away in the back.

It goes without saying that getting a vehicle up to Qaanaaq is no mean, or cheap, feat and the few residents of Qaanaaq with trucks can be counted amongst the wealthiest. Completely in contrast to the throw away attitude of many at home, even cars are bought by other locals perhaps four or five times as they age and degrade, before finally giving up altogether.

In the same way that Georg Utuaq in Kulusuk was certainly the Inuit villager most adept at embracing the benefits of working with those from abroad, Hans was his contemporary in Qaanaaq. We were brought into Hans' guesthouse, a six-room building in the style of all other brightly coloured wooden houses but far larger. We immediately felt at home. Running hot water, showers and even internet (via a massive satellite dish high up on the hill) are never to be taken for granted in the Arctic, but Hans had it all. Not that there were any alternatives, but we could not have chosen a more perfect HQ prior to our launch onto the ice.

Before getting down to the nitty-gritty of unpacking our equipment and setting to work, we familiarised ourselves with our temporary home and Qaanaaq itself. After all, I had allowed for at least three days of preparation time and maybe more if the ice was not playing ball.

Apart from a couple of Siorapaluk residents waiting for their helicopter to be repaired before flying up the coast to their families for Christmas, we were to be the sole occupants of the guesthouse. It was not exactly tourist season and even in the summer visitors number fewer than ten at any given time; they are usually travellers, wealthy artists or scientists. The walls of the corridor were covered in signed photographs from expeditions which had started from, passed through or finished in Qaanaaq. Hans had played host to them all and the warmth and regard with which he was clearly held was clear from the messages. Lonnie Dupre, Bruce Parry and Alain Hubert have all enjoyed the comforts of Hans' guesthouse and benefitted from his advice and connections in town.

Hans' spoken English was excellent compared to many Greenlanders I have met, although his wife, who turned out to be a descendent of Knud Rasmussen, made up for her lack of English with ear-to-ear smiles and enthusiastic pointing. Emails exchanged between Hans and I had been slightly hit and miss detail-wise over the previous months and I later found out he used Google Translate to turn my English into Danish and vice versa. It was remarkable that, using this crude tool, we had achieved what we did. I had, as ever, enormous respect for a man who spoke so many languages and held no grudge against those who could not grasp each local tongue wherever we travel. He spoke the local Thule dialect, Western Greenlandic, Danish and English.

Hans would be far more than just our host. As an inclusion for our staying in his guesthouse, which I grant you was not cheap (and according to Hans was still not enough to secure its future), he would be our local 'fixer'. There was so much to do and as a newcomer to the area, he was my only contact. We needed to collect our shipped freight, move the eight hundred kilos of it up the hill, buy lots of odds and ends, source more ammunition, buy a dog and food for it, plus so much more.

Having failed to locate any solid slug ammunition in Qaanaaq, even after asking the sole policeman who was keen to help, I had to come up with a backup plan. One of my main concerns for our safety revolved around our ability to repel polar bear attacks and having to compromise on this before we even set out was worrying. It was an illustration of the fact that even with a good plan in place to solve a problem, sometimes life can conspire to throw a spanner in the works; I still had no idea why our slugs from Robert had not appeared in Kangerlussuaq. It was a mystery and to this day, neither Robert nor I have a clue where they ended up.

In place of two Baikal shotguns with twenty solid cartridges per man, our arsenal had to fit in with what we could lay our hands on. I would carry one Baikal with four high-energy cartridges and two flare cartridges for deterring a curious bear. These would be carried in a neoprene holder on the plastic stock to aid fast reloading. Justin would carry a .308 rifle, lent to us by Hans, with a five-round magazine and thus the ability to engage an aggressive bear more rapidly and at a greater range than myself.

Both very experienced weapons handlers, we nonetheless hoped that the only shots fired on our journey would be to test the weapons. In spite of this, we always chose to have them close enough to grab and fire in a couple of seconds. In the dark a bear in 'hunt' mode could easily outwit us.

Belying the tiny size of Qaanaaq, barely larger than a hamlet, the docks and shop down near the beach had a modern array of machinery to call upon. Clearly bored by the monotony of the winter, the villagers needed no persuasion to fire their JCB into action and help transport our crates, which had sat safely in a shipping container since August, up to our 'home from home'. It was just as well; I did not fancy manhandling three quarters of a ton of boxes up a steep, icy hill.

The inevitable pre-expedition admin had to be done. Everything had been packed for transit and not for expedition use so the job was long and laborious. It was critical, though, to have the chance to double-check everything was there and to vindicate my stringent approach to logistics. We repacked food day bags into depot barrels, placed every piece of equipment into the correct box or bag and then started to load up the sledges. Soon, they were far too heavy to lift; a bead of sweat made its way down my forehead. Could we haul all this, even in shuttles?

Finally, and intentionally, I had left the navigational details to the last minute. I had all of the maps and charts we needed but wanted to integrate local advice and knowledge into our initial route. Once beyond the Smith Sound and into the Kane Basin, it would be fairly simple. Either we would use the Canadian or Greenlandic side of the strait. Initially, however, the ice was more complex and unpredictable, near to the North Water Polynya and Kap Alexander in the Smith Sound where thick ice rarely formed at any time of year.

There was a chance that if the ice was broken, thin or missing altogether, we could use the thin 'ice foot' that clung to the shoreline. Hunters have used these for centuries at the extreme ends of the hunting season and they might provide a precarious 'get out of jail free card' should we need it. Far better was the option of avoiding the sound altogether and skipping quickly overland. This meant climbing a glacier onto the icecap protrusion on Inglefield Land and descending the other side towards Etah, the abandoned settlement, or straight towards the Kane Basin. There were question marks over each possibility and no-one had a clue what the conditions were like yet.

The prospect of a reasonably benign glacier like the Clements Markham Glacier and a little bit of icecap seemed like the obvious choice, even in the dark, when compared to potentially fatal sea ice. It was not that simple though. Nothing in the Arctic ever is. The permit restrictions issued by Greenland Home Rule in Nuuk meant that we had to travel without a permit and with that our hands were tied to a certain extent. We could ski outside of Greenlandic territorial waters (three nautical miles, at odds with the twelve nautical mile universal norm) on the sea ice without problems. We could use the Canadian territory as well since I had worked with Stephen Hoyt and Alex Stubbing from the Canadian government to be granted access across the Canadian border. What we could not do was to travel in the majority of Greenland's coastal territories or land for more than twenty-four hours out of every week. Any cross-country scamper would have to last less than a day.

I spoke to Hans and local hunters about their thoughts and there was, predictably, a wide spread of views. One doubted there would be any ice north of Siorapaluk, one suggested that we should climb the glacier directly north of Qaanaaq and only join the sea ice in Kane Basin and another that we could use the sea ice all the way up and use the ice foot near Kap Alexander.

After discussions with Justin, a plan was born and GPS waypoints loaded into our handsets. We would move up the coast via Siorapaluk, shuttling depot barrels there and using the hamlet for a little recuperation before making for the Smith Sound. Once we started to get a bad feeling about the ice or found significantly fractured sections, we would pick the nearest glacier tongue (in reality one of three options) and camp on its foot. Once rested we then planned to make a long and rapid ascent of the slope, avoiding crevasses in the dark, nip across the ice and descend towards Etah or the north coast of Inglefield Land, depending on what the latest ice charts said. It was a high-pressure and risky plan but none of the options would be easy. We had hardly signed up for an adventure ski holiday and our plan would hopefully allow us to waste the minimum amount of time.

I must admit that the hospitality of Hans, his family and the people of Qaanaaq in general made me somewhat reluctant to give it all up for the cold! Their stories were fascinating and the home cooking an adventure in itself. One day would be raw narwhal, called matak, and the next, a leg of lamb shipped up from Europe. Everything was cooked and prepared using freshwater collected from vast person-high chunks of trapped icebergs in the fjord. The children would go off with axes to break off blocks and bring them back to their mothers so they could melt in a large pot in the kitchen. Justin and I joked that some people in London pay forty pounds for a litre of glacier or iceberg water. How ridiculous it seemed given what we were seeing day to day.

Apart from the odd setback, easily overcome, things appeared to be going as hoped. Justin and I were bonding well, the ice in the straits was thickening by the day and the ice off Qaanaaq was not far behind. I continued to finalise details for the trip and stay in touch with Europe via Hans' computer. It was then that I received an email from the British guide from the *Ice Airport* show, Alan Chambers. On reading it, I was slightly shocked. Chambers was a former Royal Marine who had reached the North Pole from Canada with teammate, Charlie Paton, in 2000, using it as his sole springboard into a post-Marines career in guiding and speaking. I had never met Chambers but had heard reports from far and wide; some used the words 'salt of the Earth' but others described him as 'arrogant and easily riled'. Save for the alarming guiding practices of his I saw on television, I knew little of him. I had reserved judgement as I knew how often agendas and egos can fuel stories to spread.

The email read as follows, with no 'Dear Alex' or even 'Hi':

'Doing research

Could you Alex please explain and list what units and who you served with and commanded as a Royal Marines Officer
Being a former Marine myself of some 16 years I am struggling to trace your time in the Corps

This would be helpful'

I do not know about anyone else, but I took the email to be quite aggressive and felt it was insinuating that something was amiss with my story. I was not sure I wanted my time anywhere 'traced'. My time as a Royal Marines Young Officer lasted only twelve months and ended with a series of infuriating injuries and my eventual withdrawal from the service; it was a period of my life the memory of which will always disappoint and frustrate me. The whole episode was, in fact, too raw to expand upon a great deal in *The Long Haul*, which I began to write whilst still on the payroll. I do not like not finishing what I begin. I wanted to serve, along with the other forty or so in my batch, on operations abroad.

Soldiering was something that was vastly more to me that a knee-jerk, post-university thirst for excitement. I had the elite service in my sights since my early teens and for me it was to be a form of expression with a great deal of inherent purpose. Any journey without such purpose holds little interest for me, no matter how difficult for others to grasp. Using practical means to send a strong message to some around the globe that their behaviour is unacceptable without mitigation was the way I wished to spend my early years.

Whilst not erasing the year of my life from memory, I firmly believe against using military backgrounds as a marketing tool once back in 'civvy street' and so only mention it in passing or in a few words on a 'bio'. I did not serve abroad and so did not consider it proper to mention my time alongside those who have fought – some injured and even killed. Given all of this, I did find Alan's email to be quite accusatory.

This message was sent on the eve of the greatest challenge of my life. I, and Justin when I showed it to him, could only imagine that Chambers was trying to put me off and knock my confidence.

My response was, I admit, irritable:

'Hi Alan,

Not entirely sure [of] the purpose [behind] your research, but if it is of interest, I did not serve abroad or command since I only stayed in the Corps 12 months before injury and leaving.

If you have something unpleasant planned I'd ask you to think twice.

Thank you.
Alex'

I had nothing to hide, despite my disappointment, and I was keen to make sure that my time away would not be used as an opportunity to spread stories that might affect my credibility. I have to say it reminded me of the sort of worries a boy might have in a playground, a 'pit of the stomach' worry which I had not felt for over a decade.

Clearly enraged by my response, his reply was a claim that he was researching an article on ex-Royal Marines involved in exploration. The opening sentence said it all:

'Unpleasant –? a disappointing , strange and in itself very unpleasant , unnecessary and distasteful comment ? !' (sic)

I have to say, I had never come under such scrutiny from someone whom I had never met and his almost unintelligible messages backed up the warnings of those who suggested I be wary of him. My only assumption was that either he had a fanatical possessiveness about the coveted nature of the commando green beret or something against the fact that I was a Young Officer, similar to one of my training team whose first words to us were, 'I fucking hate Officers.'

Although I will always feel a great pride towards the Corps, I did not miss that sort of person one bit. The combined unity of a highly selective and proud organisation of its sort certainly translates into strength as a whole. I would argue, though, that this could leave some of the constituent parts weaker as individuals, almost like part of them has been amalgamated into the machine. Being unable to fully regain ownership of one's identity and purpose once outside that machine was something I was always wary of.

As I am afraid I have seen in many with similar outlooks to Chambers, the self-styled 'old and bold' or 'elder statesmen' of a given occupation can often assume a 'grumpy old bugger' deportment, habitually jaded and keen to denigrate those of the next generation. In the climbing world, the great Reinhold Messner is well known to claim that, on mountains he pioneered routes on, any future efforts, no matter how demanding, are somehow inferior.

Some of the more prolific alpine guides I have met who are based in France or Italy have been equally dismissive, a contrast which is unexpected from people with such a passion for their lifestyle.

I sent a final, diplomatic email to try and douse the flames, citing crossed wires and apologising for any offence caused but unsurprisingly, nothing came back. I have to concede that Chambers had succeeded in rattling me. I am not immune from normal human emotions and I needed to put the negativity to the back of my mind. We had a colossal trial ahead of us. The four or five-dozen emails of support from friends, polar colleagues, family and strangers alike returned the smile to my face.

The last job before we set out was one of the most important. We needed Dave, our anti-bear dog and our companion. We had already bought him a few dozen kilos of top-quality sledge dog kibble and all that was left was to select him. Hans took us down the hill towards the beach where most of the hundreds of dogs were staked out for the winter and introduced us to Rasmus. Rasmus was something of a TV star, having spent time with Bruce Parry during his BBC *Arctic* series. He certainly came across as the same amiable and smiley hunter, perhaps in his forties, and with next to no grasp of English. Instead of using my feeble attempts at Danish, Hans interpreted. Rasmus found us a male dog, around three or four years old and with two seasons of bear hunting under his collar. The dog was handsome; his thick winter coat was mostly black with some white highlights. He had a keen face and bright eyes. We checked his teeth and got the general feeling he was a healthy dog, sadly unlike many dogs of the Arctic that receive less than reasonable care and treatment.

Delighted with Rasmus' offer and with Hans' knowing nod of approval, we handed over another wad of bank notes. Dave, as he was now to be known, was ours and we were thrilled. Using dogs was a slight step into the unknown for me and his welfare was now our responsibility. We stayed around for a while in the cold, allowing Dave to get to know us better and asking Rasmus questions about feeding regimens and the fact he did not 'speak' the Eastern Greenlandic dialect I have been used to hearing hunters command their dogs with. Undeniably, Dave was a little taken aback by our presence and took a short while to relax around us. This was, after all, the end of a six-month or longer period when dogs could not be used and just lived on the hillside with little physical contact with other dogs or humans. I wondered how I would feel if three or four men appeared from the dark with dazzling head torches and started chatting and inspecting me. At any rate, the noise of hundreds of excited sledge dogs barking and tugging on their chains given the slightest excuse needs to be heard to be believed.

A couple of days were still to play out until we planned to set off on an initial depot-laying shuttle and during this time, we studied the latest weather and ice reports and took Dave out onto the ice for training. We also travelled some way down the shoreline to test-fire our weapons, not wanting to cause a false alert in Qaanaaq from our flares and gunshots.

CHAPTER FOURTEEN

D-Day finally came. I called home, sent some last emails and lent my phone to Justin to do the same. He was leaving behind his new fiancée after all, another emotional strain after what had been a dramatic six months or so for him. With the opening leg of the expedition having no other goal than the laying of depots, we did not have to worry about accepting assistance and Hans kindly offered to see us off from his 4x4 after driving us down the shoreline to the west as far as possible. We gratefully accepted; there was nothing too difficult for Hans and he genuinely seemed to adore being part of other people's journeys.

It was not going to be possible to shift all of our equipment, plus Dave, to the shoreline in one move. This took into account Hans' kind offer to drive us down in his 4x4, filling up the boot and a large trailer. In total, there were four near-human-length sledges, two Kevlar and two plastic, plus skis and poles which are awkward to stow. Dave had never been in a car and would most likely become quite stressed. Both because it might undo the work we had done to gain Dave's trust over the past few days and also to avoid a mess in Hans' vehicle, we opted to walk him down from Qaanaaq. The three of us would first head down with the sledges and leave them safely on the snow-covered beach and then drive back. There we would say our farewells to Hans, collect Dave from the hillside and walk him along the track, out of view of the orange glow of Qaanaaq and on to our temporary stash. Here our journey would begin.

The track was reasonably snow-free due to use by the occasional vehicle and the general lack of snowfall Qaanaaq experiences; it was a few miles long and took thirty or forty minutes to walk. Of course, there was no natural light so head torches were the order of the day and the surface was loose and gravelly, like much of the rest of the sliver of Greenland not covered by ice or seasonal snow. There were large areas of slippery ice (Qaanaaq has a year-round permafrost) and so we donned our rubber microspikes which gave our boots better grip.

Having received Hans' wishes of good luck and given his wife a big hug and thanks for her cooking and general good cheer, we wandered down the hill. Hans had told me that the whole of Qaanaaq had heard about our plans to travel far north on foot and that we were regarded as very brave. I found this very difficult to take in; firstly, that the infinitely more experienced local hunters considered our journey to be risky and secondly, because I did not feel we had earned even the smallest plaudits yet, least of all from the people I so admired.

•

Bravery, heroism and greatness are all enormously powerful and emotive words. Modern society, and in particular the media, is very keen to overuse superlatives so that every person of note is now 'a great' and every public servant 'a hero'. It now becomes so very hard for true titans amongst men and women to be identified so their characters can be held up as an example. There are so many unresolved questions about this matter on which I think we should all muse: can heroism be sought and achieved? Can a sportsman or entertainer, who essentially plays for a living, ever be great? Is bravery different if acted upon voluntarily as opposed to when there is no other alternative? Is greatness bestowed upon someone who commits one great act but is inconsistent and otherwise flawed? What about heroism or greatness in one era which, in another, would be villainous or criminal? I maintain that a person should do what they must, driven by their own judgement and morals, and the end product is for others to assess. The consequences of greatness are only indirect, in terms of providing inspiration or guidance to others. Some who are considered heroic may have not the slightest care in the world, going about their business regardless, and perhaps this is the greatest accolade of them all.

•

It was true that, with some of the ice offshore being broken, only a fraction of hunters had taken their dog teams seal-hunting yet. The rest were waiting until the New Year as twilight grew before the return of the sun some weeks after. As if to confirm the difficult conditions, Justin had suffered two or three quite nasty slips and falls on the sometimes steep and icy paths, his Sorel boot soles apparently less effective than my Baffins, and so our final walk was completed with care.

I also used the time for a little reflection, firstly, to do an 'idiot check' to ensure I had everything on me I needed, and then to shift into expedition-mode. Just hours before, we had enjoyed a warm bed, showers and the ability to check our emails and radar ice charts. Now we faced months of little, rather than plenty. It is a strange contrast to experience so dramatically.

We found Dave at his usual staking point and swapped his very tired looking collar, belonging to Rasmus, for a nice, new, shiny red one. I had taken great pains to research and source him the best quality and most comfortable collar possible. He would most likely save our lives over the weeks to come and it was the least we could do. Connected to his equally new and shiny, stainless steel chain, I attached one end to my hip with a karabiner. Even though Dave knew us, he was not a domestic animal and would grasp unintended freedom with all four paws, likely never to be recovered once loose. In Qaanaaq, his fate would almost certainly be sealed through the barrel of a gun.

It was late morning, fairly still and the village seemed sleepy and quiet as ever. The dim, blue glow in the sky was as much help as we would get from nature. Still, there were no storms forecast, the temperatures were mild at twenty below zero and there was sea ice. Luck was, thus far, on our side or rather chance was – my not being a believer in luck or fate.

We left the sight of wooden houses and dim, lamp-post lighting behind as we dipped below a rise and relied only on the beams of two bobbing head torches to find our way. We passed the airstrip, which only opened for the once-weekly flights, and found the shore, which was, at times, hard to pinpoint against the snow and ice.

In another mile or so, at the end of the 4x4 tracks, would be our sledges. Just a couple of hundred yards short of reaching the real start point of 'The Dark Ice Project', Justin again fell heavily on the ground, grimacing on the ice below as I helped him to his feet. I had to put it down to his boots; Justin had suffered a major car crash years back but he had not indicated that his balance or sure-footedness were a cause for concern. It was then that we noticed one of his microspikes was missing. A sinking feeling descended on me and I hoped out loud that they had become caught on the rocky and snowy ground just behind us. Surely otherwise he would have fallen or noticed earlier on? The sensation of walking with microspikes differs compared to without.

Without much discussion, we turned around and began walking back, scouring the footprints ahead for a sign of the shiny metal spikes. I could not fathom how it would be possible not to notice the loss of our main source of traction with the ground, but accidents happen. One of the main messages I communicate to audiences back home is of tolerance. Little things can seem more significant than they really are when on stressful journeys and I was sure I would test Justin's tolerance over the coming months also. It was time to practice what I preached, however baffled I may have been.

It became abundantly obvious that the shoreline was clear and we climbed up onto the track to Qaanaaq. The track itself was less rocky and uneven than the snowy beach and so, frankly, they could be anywhere. They were just as likely to be in Qaanaaq as a few steps ahead of us. All we could do was walk and talk as if nothing had happened and it was all part of the plan. A couple of lost hours, the worst-case scenario, mattered little when put in the context of a ninety-day or longer journey. In the short term, though, I had waypoints in mind between us and Siorapaluk and missing these first targets would not be ideal.

The glow of Qaanaaq began to grow in the sky and stepping onto the final rise, we saw the buildings on the outskirts of the settlement once again. I had not expected to see Qaanaaq again for many days, until we returned for the second load of depot barrels.

Then, barely fifty yards short of the first hut, glistening in the light of our torches, we spotted the spikes. They had become caught on a large rock protruding from the track and had parted company. Given the effort required to pull these rubberised fittings onto our oversized boots, I could only guess at how they could have come off so easily.

To be honest, there was not a great deal to say. I pointed to them on the floor and Justin put them back on. He sensed that I was not ecstatic at the lost time and effort and he pre-emptively said, 'It could have happened to anyone.' I smiled to try and lighten the mood and said it did not matter, unwisely adding that I had considered being annoyed but that it would achieve little. We turned around once again and set a brisk pace back to the shoreline. A while later we arrived again at our ever-patient train of sledges and supplies. This really was the start of the expedition and I wanted to start as we meant to go on – united. Trying to crack a few jokes and making positive predictions about our initial targets for the next few days, I was feeling ready. I sensed that Justin felt differently.

We had got on well over the preceding week, the longest period of time we had spent together in a purely expedition setting. We were gelling and the atmosphere was light and upbeat, both when we were working on our equipment and relaxing with a Danish Tuborg beer in the evening. Justin had been particularly supportive when Alan Chambers had got under my skin and said exactly what I needed to hear. I had noticed he was not one to shirk hard work and I never had to wonder where he had got to whilst I was doing something or other with the kit out the back of Hans' guesthouse. He did certainly let me take the lead, though, unsurprising given the dynamic we had in the preceding months and the differences that existed in our Arctic experience despite the thirteen year age gap. It was this hesitancy I saw at the start of the expedition and which I had seen at other times that began to ring an alarm bell in my head.

Harnesses on, sledges pointing the right way, skis strapped to the canvasses and Dave clipped safely onto my waist, we looked out at the sea ice. The first job was to take a wide sweep of the area ahead with our powerful torch to find a route across the tide crack. As in all coastal Polar Regions in the cold seasons, there is a sequence of features. First is the rocky shore or cliff itself then, potentially, if conditions are right, a narrow, stable ice foot attached to the land. Beyond that is a ten or twenty-foot-wide tide crack which is very uneven, fractured by the moving tide and often has a shallow puddle of unfrozen sea water on top of the ice. The actual sea ice which is beyond is then at the mercy of a thousand factors; it may be flat as a pancake or perhaps mashed into millions of shards. Its condition was uncertain, but that was the game we played.

The tide crack can actually look quite intimidating, especially in the dark when the view yonder is unknown and black, but it is, usually, surprisingly straightforward to cross. Providing the water on top of the ice is not too deep and the pack itself is stable, it is almost unnoticeable. Our plan was to hop across the tide crack, move a few hundred yards offshore, past most of the trapped icebergs and dramatic protrusions through the ice caused by frozen water pressing down on rocks under the waterline, and then follow the coast. This would allow us to enjoy the best of the ice, avoid the broken ice floes a couple of miles offshore which the hunters had warned us about and navigate fairly easily.

First though, we had to tackle one of the more confusing sides of winter travel: when to go to bed. With no visual cues as to when it was night or day, we had to trust in our watches. The advice I had gleaned from the handful with experience of the polar darkness was that it was hard to overcome the urge not to get up the morning and not to stop travelling in the evening. Mastering this would allow us to remain healthy and not to degrade physically any faster than necessary.

Given the delays caused by getting Dave down to the start point and the microspikes incident, it was fast approaching the evening. To avoid eating into the night-time and delaying the next day, I suggested that we settle into a haul and get onto a nice big pan before camping for the night. My reasoning for wanting a good view, unobstructed by icebergs or risen cracks, was to be safe and secure on our first night on such unfamiliar terrain. I wanted the job of scanning the full three hundred and sixty degree vista for unwanted visitors to be easy as I was finding my feet.

Having found a suitable site for us to pitch the tent, I noticed we were not alone. Not all of the hunters had resigned themselves to waiting in Qaanaaq until the New Year (the recent reluctance being due to the death of a number of Inuit on thin ice over a short period of time). A small, white light and the outline of a dog sled gave away the presence of a local man fishing through a hole in the ice, perhaps nearly a mile away. It was hard to judge distance in the dark. Dog food or kibble is very expensive in any remote settlement and fish represent a much cheaper way of feeding a large team of ten or twelve dogs.

Pulling our sledges into a horseshoe and removing our harnesses and rucksacks, the first job was to look after Dave. He had been exceptionally well behaved so far, walking out to the left of me with a little slack in the chain, not lagging behind or tugging ahead as we had feared. As the best way I knew to make friends with a new dog, I emptied his daily ration of kibble onto the snow and clipped his chain onto an ice screw I had placed into the surface. After a whimsical glance up at me, as if to say, 'Really? No seal?' he downed the mound of kibble before I had time to put the scoop back in the sledge. At least he had an appetite.

The Thule region was famous for its cold, calm, clear and relatively snow-free climate. Whilst great news for winter and springtime sea ice travellers and the reason for its continuous Inuit inhabitation for centuries, it did throw a spanner in the works when it came to pitching a tent. Already having to get used to the new design of tent, I was also used to using skis, poles and occasionally snow-stakes to anchor a tent to the surface. However, I had predicted this barren, almost snow-free surface and so we had come armed with a stack of ice screws. There was literally a smattering of snow and beneath that, rock-hard ice.

The single drawback of the Zirkon tipi tent was that, instead of four anchors minimum around a tunnel tent, eight points in an octagon were needed for securing the canvas. This was good news for all-round wind protection but took a little time. Luckily, the rest of its operation was so simple that it more than made up for the initial inconvenience. Justin and I set about placing the screws around the flattened canvas. Most were brand new but the one or two that had blunted slightly over a couple of seasons of use found it harder to bite into the solid ice. This was especially the case if they had to be moved slightly to improve tension and I was relieved that my 'Oh Shit' box had a tooth sharpener in it. One omission like this and anyone can see how an audacious expedition like ours could crumble over a tiny detail. No screws, no tent. No tent, no shelter and no survival.

Just seconds after each screw was clipped to a tent loop, the pole was placed into the 'top hat' and the tent erected. With just a few adjustments to the tension to make it symmetrical, we were very happy with our new home and began to throw in the two or three bags we needed for the night.

The beginning of the day had been fairly static with a lot of waiting around and so I had worn a few layers: a merino wool base, Montane Jackal mid-layer, with nifty built-in wristlets to stop draughts, and the main windproof smock. As the hauling intensified with over two hundred and fifty kilos per man, I had vented and removed the Jackal to manage my moisture levels and warmth. It became obvious that Justin had not done the same and although my legs and body were gently emanating a fine mist of vapour, Justin was literally steaming to the extent that I could not see across the inside of the tent.

He had overheated massively and the resulting sweat had soaked his clothes. This basic error confounded me and I just suggested we get the stove on and let his body heat drive the moisture out. Taking the clothes off would result only in a block of ice and useless clothing by morning, with only a single spare left, meant for rapid emergency changes following a dunk in the sea. The last thing to do would be to get in his sleeping bag, shivering as he was, as that would either soak the insulation on our first day or create a humid atmosphere inside his VBL.

Thankfully, any excess use of fuel to get a little heat into the tent could be replenished when we returned to Qaanaaq for more gear – a lifeline, but not one to rely on. It was only minus twenty after all and we should have been very comfortable. Another saving grace was the breathable polycotton of the tent, which would hopefully let a lot of Justin's vapour escape and not form hoarfrost.

After a rapidly devoured meal it was time for bed. Although not really that hungry – we had only hauled for a few hours and were still full from Hans' guesthouse, after all – I knew we would need to get into the habit of eating regularly and build strength for the coming days.

After shutting off the stove and hearing the reassuring roar die away with a flicker, the door to the tent was zipped closed after a glance outside to check on the sledges (that they were closed and no other novice mistakes had crept in) and that Dave was ok. He was indeed; he was curled up fast asleep in a furry ball.

Having let the humidity in the tent drop, out came our enormous synthetic sleeping bags, their even larger overbags not yet required due to the mild temperatures. My final move before bedtime was to load a live shotgun cartridge into the barrel of my weapon and leave it, still safe and open, above my head and within easy reach. If we were disturbed in the night we would not want to draw attention to ourselves by fiddling around with head torches on. Justin ensured that his rifle was loaded and also close to hand.

It is true that many North Pole expeditions have a more relaxed attitude towards bear protection, many wrapping their weapons, unloaded, in plastic overnight or even outside the tent itself. Even with Dave outside as an early warning, our risk was significantly higher than others for a few reasons: we were travelling just as the ice was forming, meaning that bears, which had starved over the summer and autumn, were ravenous and only just starting to hunt again; additionally, our ability to spot stalking bears and tracks was limited by the darkness. Finally, there are simply far more bears in the Thule region than there are offshore on the Arctic Ocean.

Nice and warm and dry in my sleeping bag, I nodded off fairly easily, only to wake a few hours later to an odd scratching and grunting sound. Instantly shooting my hands out of my sleeping bag, and without switching a light on, I grabbed my weapon and silently closed the gun, ready for action.

The sounds outside continued and were in the direction of our sledges. I counted out the possibility of it being Dave snoring, but there were two other possibilities. Either it was the sea ice, dynamic and ever-moving as it is, groaning and cracking around us, or it was a bear sniffing around our supplies. I could not decide and so gave Justin a couple of gentle kicks and as he came round, asked him what he thought.

A moment of complacency could be a disaster and although highly unlikely, an attack on day one was not impossible. At the very least, I owed it to Justin to wake him. Both satisfied that it was just the ice, I settled back into my bag and tried to sleep. My heart was still racing and the adrenaline surging, so it took a while. I was relieved that I had woken up to the noise and had not slept through what could have been a lot more sinister.

The horrible moment came when my alarm began to beep and signalled the start of a brand new day. I went through my normal few minutes of 'pain' as I resigned myself to my predicament and built up my motivation to move and get things done. Justin was also stirring and so I called across, 'Fancy some brekkie?' I was nearest to the stove and so took on the responsibility for food. Unlike the usual glow of morning shining through the tent, there was darkness. This was something – a daily disappointment we would have to get used to for many weeks yet.

As our head torches were switched on, and before I fetched a waterproof match to light the stove, I wanted to inspect the inner surface of the canvas. Were we about to be showered in wet and freezing hoarfrost? With almost a shriek of delight, I saw there was barely anything, perhaps the odd feathery thread of frost but nothing that was going to melt onto our bags or flake off and cover us from head to toe – our first victory.

Having got the stove into action and melting some of the tiny amount of snow available, which I had scraped off the ice outside, it was time to eat and get ready for the day ahead. Whilst very slightly damp in a couple of areas, my sleeping arrangement had worked well for me. Looking over at Justin, I was horrified. Looking at me in shock, he emerged from the sleeping bag, sodden wet. His hands were clammy and prune-like, as if he had spent too long in a bath, and his clothing was sticking to him. He was, once again, steaming heavily into the cold tent air.

I had been under the impression that Justin had vented enough the night before and would sleep in reasonably dry clothes. This was clearly not the case. Something was very definitely wrong; he did not seem himself. It was day one, we had over eight hundred miles to haul on just this phase and Justin was off-balance and not performing basic self-care. His eyes were screaming, 'Help!' at me. Thinking logically, the only explanations were that he had not released enough moisture before sleeping or that his core body temperature was elevated, i.e. that he was not well.

The only thing to do was to get on the move and allow his movement to dry the clothes. Mercifully, his VBL had saved his sleeping bag from too much degradation. I did most of the outdoor duties that morning to allow Justin to stay as warm as possible until we got moving and use the residual heat of the tent 'inner' to get ready. Preparations included going for my customary morning 'answer to the call of nature'. I headed a few yards from the tent, armed with a shotgun, roll of loo paper and single latex glove, and quickly scanned the surroundings with my torch. I did not want to be interrupted. The latter item was for a new technique I was using. Not wanting to use bare hands in the cold, despite the lack of wind-chill, and only having three changes of thin liner gloves, they had to be protected from mishaps. An oversized latex glove over the top each time would ensure a swift and effective result and could then be discarded in our rubbish bags.

We both warmed up by having a quick run around and set about dropping the tent. It took just seconds and before long, the tent was back in my sledge and the ice screws collected up. Through all of this commotion, Dave had stayed firmly curled up and disinterested. As I harnessed up and pulled my sledges into line, though, he sprang into action, ears pricked and bright eyes keenly staring into the dark.

It was in this way that we began our journey along the fjord and towards the Smith Sound. Each seventy-five minutes or so we would stop for food and water and I could occasionally jump up onto an iceberg or piece of rubble raised up into the air by the pressure. From my vantage point I could scan for bears, bear tracks and for the best route forward. Although the surface was smooth and fast, relative to the weight of our monstrous loads, there were certainly better areas and broken sections to avoid. All in all, though, we could not complain. The ice was not going to be our limiting factor, here at least. Once past the Smith Sound and heading due north towards the Arctic Ocean, ice reports suggested good news; arches had formed at both ends of the Nares Strait and ice consolidated within.

Having taken bearings every hour or so, we kept a minute-by-minute grasp of our heading by using the stars in the sky as rough guides. Calls like, 'Just to the left of the low red one and the right of the super-bright pair of white ones higher up,' were common and we found, successful. My main job was to control our direction and maintain a safe distance from the shore on one side and the edge of the ice pack on the other. In the middle there would be, theoretically, a path of reasonably flat ice.

It was Justin's turn to be out in the lead with Dave and I following on behind. The landscape, or icescape, or whatever its name was, is hard to describe. Apart from the infinitesimally small glow in the sky around midday, which allowed us to just make out the hills to the north, our only view was from our torches, flicking from side to side as we walked and glanced around. The ice was a light grey with a dusting of snow-cover. Parts were almost impossibly flat, yet other parts had suffered from pressure. It was as if a giant were poking a finger up from beneath the brittle surface, leaving abrupt piles of rubble up to twelve feet high with cracks emanating in each direction. I was used to travelling on featureless icecaps with few reference points for keeping a straight line and so actually, these hummocks of ice helped. They were far enough apart not to force us to snake around too much.

Life was good. I was hauling the heaviest sledges of my career at a near mile-per-hour pace, Dave was behaving, Justin was moving well, the wind was non-existent, the ice reports were good and it was not too punishingly cold yet. I knew this would change in time; there would be open water leads, storms, pressure ridges and bear encounters. For the time though, I had learnt to enjoy the good moments and make the best of them.

As Justin picked his route, I was double-checking his direction, as is normal, and noticed a constant pull to the left. This was not unusual; it is very hard to navigate using subtle visual cues and I had experienced the same with George, Wilki, Finn and others. Over time the pull became different, though, far more extreme. I became concerned. I wondered if Justin had fixated on the wrong star and so called ahead. He corrected, but within a minute he was hauling over to the side. Was he avoiding a patch of bad ice I could not see? Apparently not.

Again and again this pull to the left became more marked and eventually I had to stop Justin. We were wasting energy and it had to end. As I pulled up alongside, I turned to look at Justin, his face was covered, as was mine, with a frost-encased mask. I asked whether he was looking at the right star and if he was ok.

Justin removed his mask and immediately, I could see the excruciating pain on his face; it was hard to misinterpret. My powerful headlamp was dazzling him so I angled it down. He told me that he felt extremely sick, could not actually see any stars and his belly was so painful he was bending over almost double. Here, Justin's account (with tense alterations for clarity) takes over:

'We took our first bearing of the day and identified a distant star as our marker. With plenty of space on the flat pan of ice we headed away from our campsite following our marker in the sky.

The ice became a little more jumbled in patches as we headed on so we were scanning the way ahead and picking our route through. We reached a point where the route ahead through the ice eruptions broke off to our left slightly which corralled us into single file with me at the front.

I had developed a niggling, 'stitch-like' pain at the bottom of the ribs a few days before; it ebbed and flowed but was generally constant as I moved. It wasn't enough to hamper my progress, but I was aware of it. I put it down to a slip that I'd had a few days before and decided that it would eventually pass.

Even when you train for several hours a day for an expedition you do discover 'new muscles' and aches and pains when you first set out hauling a heavy pulk in the first few days of a trip – but when you're fit enough, adaptation is generally very fast and relatively painless.

As I pressed on the pain grew, but living with bouts of trigeminal neuralgia for the last fourteen years has led me to a position where I can block out, to a point, 'creeping' pain. The pain was increasing but my mind was successfully blocking it out.

Alex shouted to me. 'Just, where are you heading?' A wave of my ski pole gave an undefined answer.

A little while later he called out again. 'Just, are you ok, mate?'

'Yep. You?' I called back over my shoulder.

'Just, how are you feeling?'
'Just, we're off course a little.'
'Just, are you ok?'

When you're in the field, one of the first rules of safety is to be constantly monitoring your teammates for unusual behaviour. Alex and I had bonded quite well over the previous few weeks so he could tell that, despite my vague answers to the contrary, something was wrong. My words were saying one thing, but my actions and movements were indicating the exact opposite.

'Just, STOP!' As he approached me he led with the question 'Which star are you heading for now?'

I looked up and could see nothing but black. I rubbed my eyes, looked down and then back up at the dark sky and could still see nothing but *black. Then one light in the sky slowly came in to view, followed by another and then another.*

As Alex talked it was as though someone had thrown a whole bucket of something nasty over me as my mind opened up and the pain flooded in. My body was wracked in agony.

'Al, I'm in pain' was as much as I could manage as the realisation grew that I was in absolute agony.

The spoken admittance gave my body permission to feel its full effect as I doubled over my ski poles heaving for breath, nausea causing me to bend further over and retch and any sensible activity ground to a halt as I struggled to regain control.

The pain was hard to describe, but the closest that I can get is a hot and searing, tearing sensation combined with a 'heavy, knot-like' feeling.

Alex stopped talking and looked at me for a few seconds before speaking again. I couldn't really hear his words but I understood his intent.

Although Alex and I are both confident in our ability to cope with most medical situations that we were likely to encounter, there is always a slim chance that something may happen which requires medical advice. To that end, the emergency medical charity that I support, MAGPAS, had offered us a 'reach back' facility whereby we could speak with the emergency doctor on call should we need to.

Alex placed a call to our UK support team who wasted no time in setting up a call between us on the Arctic sea ice and Dr. Rod Mackenzie, the MAGPAS doctor on call thousands of miles away in the UK at the time.

Rod spoke with me about how I felt and then spoke with Alex about what his version was. I stripped to the waist (Author's note – I remember just lifting up his smock and baselayer) as Alex slowly and methodically poked and prodded my abdomen with direction from the doctor on the phone, reporting back every lump and bump as he went.

Rod spoke with me again. I didn't want to listen to it. I couldn't, or wouldn't, hear what he was saying so I passed the handset back to Alex. He spoke with Rod for a few minutes and then turned to look at me. I could tell by the look on his face that it wasn't good news.

Rod explained to Alex that it sounded very much like the 'tearing' pain followed by the pain that I had now, combined with the feelings of nausea – and the fact that there was a gaping hole in my abs and my insides were clearly hanging out – suggested that I had a rather nasty epigastric hernia which would only get worse.

Alex spoke with Rod as he explained that if I continued to haul the chances were that this would lead very quickly to a life-threatening condition requiring emergency surgery, or I would perish on the ice.

Alex took the news and passed it on. I have to say that he was brilliant – I was not.

In my mind, the 'pig headed' part of me wanted to just rest for a little while and continue and I can understand that for Alex that must have been such a tempting option – to tempt fate and see what happened – but he 'stuck to his guns' and gave me no option.

A tear or two trickled over my cheeks as I looked north. I really wasn't ready to go home. Alex gave me a quick 'man hug' and we turned to retrace our steps. Alex took the lead so that all I had to do was walk along his tracks. My head hung low, my motivation was below rock-bottom and every slow step was causing me pain and discomfort.

By the time we crossed back over the tidal crack I was done. The pain was draining but the emotion of knowing that this first part of 'The Dark Ice Project' was over, and because of me, was devastating. Alex had put thousands of hours of work into preparing this trip, from inception to taking our first steps and knowing that all of that work had, for this year, come to an end because my body had let us down was, and is, a huge emotional burden.

Tears of frustration froze my eyelashes together as I plodded and stumbled on. Alex dropped in the odd conversational piece, quirky comment and even a few jokes to try to lift my spirits but I was in my own little world

The biggest 'thank you' has to go to Alex. I can only begin to imagine his disappointment and frustration at having to turn back, but despite all of that he put his personal feeling aside and remained buoyant, trying to lift my spirits through conversation and jokes.

I have to admit that I learned a lot from Alex too. His planning for the trip was absolutely meticulous, right down to weighing absolutely everything that he carried to make sure that every gram was worth the calorie output to carry it which is a far cry from my approach of 'just do it', so I think I will be adopting a few of his techniques.'

When I first read Justin's version of events it made sense. The facts mostly matched my recollection and in the parts where it did not, the reasons were obvious. It was my first real glimpse into Justin's internal monologue and it explained a lot. I knew I was not working with a knowingly dishonest or bad person, just one who, I realised, I found it nigh on impossible to work with, hernia or no hernia. It was tough and frankly, a new experience for me.

We stepped across the tide crack once again, our footprints and sledge marks barely faded from our outward journey. What a bizarre feeling. It just all seemed wrong. I was so utterly determined not to let anything affect the running of the project, remembering the compromises of the last couple of years, and I felt like it was happening to someone else.

The waves of frustration, anger and sadness that surged through me in the space of a few seconds were almost too much. Despite this, standing shell-shocked on the snowy beach, I had to control them entirely. Justin did not need to be made to feel any worse about what his illness had caused, apart from the physical pain he was in. Emotions had to be capped, put in a box and kept for my time in private. My job, as the leader, was to get Justin back safely and plan logistics once again.

Leaving the gear by the sea ice, the first job was to walk Justin and Dave back to Qaanaaq before returning with Hans for the equipment. The hauling was over and so the chance of the abdominal tear getting larger or Justin's intestines strangulating were reduced but still possible. We were not out of the woods yet.

Dave was still attached to my hip via a chain and karabiner at each end and I kept a hand loosely on the chain to control his direction. Suddenly, he sprinted forward. I expected him to stop at the end of the chain, but instead he continued on. Clearly expecting to be yanked to a standstill, he stopped and looked back, as confused as I was. Glancing down at the ground, I saw my end of the chain lying in the snow. We must have come to the realisation at the same time because as I flung myself to the ground in a vain attempt to grab the chain, Dave sensed freedom and ran into the dark. The chain had run through my mitt and in seconds, he was nowhere to be seen.

That was the last straw. There were no histrionics, just a silent dejection. We both knew what this meant. Dave, the animal we had taken responsibility for and removed from his normal life, would either run back to Qaanaaq and get himself shot or follow scents of wildlife out onto the ice or into the hills. His chance of survival was nil.

Wracked with guilt and anger at myself, I tried to find out what on Earth had happened. The karabiner, a snap-gate and not a screwing lock gate, had failed and the gate was fixed in the open position, letting the chain slip off. Heads metaphorically down but physically raised, we scanned the distance for anything moving or shiny and reflective. Five minutes passed, then ten, then twenty.

I cannot remember who saw it first, but something could be made out beside the track about a hundred yards ahead. Justin said, 'It's Dave!' and we stopped. Our lights again reflected a chain and there, lying on the ground, was Dave.

Leaving Justin to walk slowly and quietly along behind, I softly made my way over, desperate not to spook him or set him off running again. Incredibly, he let me walk right up to him barely raising a look to me. He was far more interested in whatever he was furiously trying to dig out of the ice: the rear third of a large flatfish. It must have been left there from the last summer and frozen into the surface. With zero trouble, I grabbed his collar to get firm control of what was, potentially, a very powerful dog and then clipped him back onto my belt with two new karabiners.

The relief was extraordinary and it had been the most extreme set of contrasting emotions in such a short time; despair and elation mixed into the most confusing cocktail. Finding Dave again almost lifted our spirits for a while but soon the pensiveness returned.

Only half a mile from Qaanaaq and as that familiar glow once again reappeared, I joked that at least it was the last time we had to walk that damn track. Then I felt a tug on the chain. Dave had sat down and as I looked round, he lay down fully. He did not look tired or curl up into a ball; he simply looked up at me. This staring contest dragged on a little and so I gave the chain a light pull and egged him on. Dave stood up and carried on walking, only to lie down again barely ten steps further on. This time a tug did not help and I practically had to lift him up – same result. Eventually, he became so stubborn that I gave up and picked him up and began to carry him. I am not sure what I was hoping to achieve but after putting him back on his feet, again he stopped.

We were in sight of Qaanaaq but why would our dog not move? Perhaps he liked the freedom of the sea ice and associated Qaanaaq with other mean dogs and a Spartan life chained to the hill. Then I had a brainwave. I wondered whether he always ran on a particular side of a dog team and did not like the change of being out of his comfort zone? Some humans have such odd traits, so why not a dog? I recalled that he tended to stick to the left as we hauled on the ice and now he was on the right of me. Maybe, just maybe... I stepped over the immobile lump of dark fur, his eyes following me as I went. Instantly, Dave stood up and began trotting along happily. At least we had cause for almost hysterical laughter as we re-entered Qaanaaq. I would have been mortified if a local had witnessed that performance. We had an insane dog but I was already very fond of him.

I took Dave back to the hill once again and suggested Justin went up to the guesthouse to let Hans know the situation and rest. The hard work coming back must have been very painful but it would have been nonsensical and highly irresponsible to request assistance when we could feasibly return on foot.

The next few days were a whirlwind of last minute arrangements with a sporadic and unreliable Air Greenland booking system which finally, due to the determination of our UK team, got us a couple of seats before a fortnight's cessation of flights altogether. We were lucky indeed to have to wait only three days before setting off back home, our only option. There was nothing much that we could do, beyond securing and storing our equipment in a shed. I could not travel alone that season and so accompanying Justin back was the sole option I had. I was so busy with the planning and contingency work, I barely had a moment to vent, hit something or feel upset. Perhaps it was best that way. I talk a lot about perspective; I had lost a year, a season of good sea ice and potentially, a shot at the North Pole. On reflection though, Justin was alive and the expedition could be postponed, not cancelled. There was something good to take from the false start despite the almost humiliating act of having to tell our audience we were coming home. A number of tweaks, which could only have been learnt by being on the ice in the dark, could be integrated into my systems to make the restart even more proficient.

'The Dark Ice Project' would survive and in time, return safe and triumphant. Of that I was certain.

CHAPTER FIFTEEN

To action the reincarnation of 'Dark Ice' the following winter I would need to build a new team. Quite apart from anything else, Justin's surgery would make his retention a risky affair for both safety and insurance. The story was not just one of health, though.

I think it would be suspicious and unfair simply to breeze over the replacement of one important teammate with another, so a brief explanation is reasonable. It pains me a great deal since, with every other previous teammate, I would happily re-embark on a project, as well as head to the pub to recall experiences over a beer and by all accounts, they feel the same.

The key is that there was no bickering on the ice or battle of wills between Justin and me. Instead, I suppose the parting of ways was the inevitable conclusion of a vastly different approach to business, planning and life in general. Although I only occasionally mentioned my concerns in past chapters, I had experienced problems even six months before the 'Dark Ice Project' launched. I have always expected fluid communications and an 'if you say you'll do it, you'll do it' attitude towards all aspects of an expedition from my team. This way things get done, the atmosphere stays positive, productive and above all, happy.

Sadly by the late summer, a seemingly endless and inexplicable series of communication black-outs, missed deadlines and excuses pushed me to issuing a 'you're either in or you're out' speech which led to an improvement. Weeks later, some of the problems did resurface, but because the vast majority of the expedition tasks were on my desk, I pushed on with them so that the project could fly in December 2012. I still had the feeling in the bottom of my stomach which I imagine those employing 'cowboy builders' must face – a growing sense of impending doom you cannot easily halt.

I think at the core of the problem was the discrepancy between my desire to plan and think through all the various parts of the project, as is professional, and Justin's rather chaotic 'it'll all be ok if I pretend it's not happening' viewpoint. He openly admitted that he did his kit lists in his head. There was also the issue of painful ribs (the future hernia) he complained about prior to the expedition. I suggested that he must see a doctor and have it checked that close to the off. He is a grown man and I did not feel I should or could follow-up or check on this. Hindsight would show that I should have pushed harder.

I suppose amid all the immediate pressures and trying to keep the metaphorical house in order, I lost track of how ridiculous the situation had become. I was losing more sleep over Justin's reliability than I was over the polar bear threat or broken ice. The point of a team was to share challenges and workload, not to add to them.

Of course, life is not black and white but sometimes it is not far off. For my own part I felt I had done all I could possibly do to support and help, but fully admit that the personal financial contributions did exceed the estimate window I made very early on by a small margin. Some costs did increase beyond my projections, but we were both in the same boat and I had, without much choice, become Justin's creditor – not a productive state of affairs in an expedition team. In the weeks after our return from Qaanaaq, I had to make a final, firm push to resolve final balances and arrangements. This was not met with a helpful or rational response, surprising to say the least given what I had done for him, and so I said we would have to go our separate ways. You can only try to be so patient and generous before enough is enough.

Fundamentally Justin is not an intentionally deceitful person, but perhaps one who finds it difficult to grasp or empathise with others' points of view and admit to the consequences of his actions. Thankfully, we were able to tie up loose ends after a fashion. I just knew I could never wholeheartedly rely on someone that haphazard when it came to a life-threatening expedition. Although feeling let down, I did feel like a weight lifted off my shoulders once the deed was done and I think I had given Justin the way out he actually may have craved subconsciously.

It reminded me of the situation experienced by polar veterans, Richard Weber and Misha Malakhov, in their first, unsuccessful, North Pole return attempt in 1992. They started with a third member, Bob Mantell, who ended up turning back alone some way through their first leg across the Arctic Ocean (a fourth member backed out, way out of his depth, on a training week). Despite obvious, tell-tale signs weeks before the launch that Bob's administration was dated and chaotic and his attitude very stubborn, Richard and Misha softly tried to coax him to reason. Eventually, they had to become firmer and firmer until it became unworkable. When I first read their account years ago I wondered how they had let it go that far – now I understand.

Through all this though, I continue to reject utterly the oft-quoted claims by Ran Fiennes that it is inevitable to 'start to hate' everyone on an expedition team due to the cold and the stress. Expeditions do not cause friction – people do. I know of a guided pair, remaining anonymous, who were openly yelling at each other within two days of a summer glacier climb – it was because they lacked maturity and self-control, not because of the difficult conditions. I certainly intend to continue to relish the company and fellowship of those I work with on the ice and am never tempted to travel solo.

Having to repopulate the team seemed almost like starting again from scratch, despite the fact that the incumbents would hopefully slide with minimum fuss into an already mature framework. Some might say, given the experiences with Justin and regardless of my personal aversion for the style, 'Why **not** just travel solo?' My answer to that is simple. That difficulty was an aberration, a minor road bump, as I have always felt past companions have been a massive addition to both the spirit and the practical side of my ventures. In particular, a journey with the dangers of the 'Dark Ice Project' would be nigh on suicide for a soloist.

Weber writes that soloists have a special mind-set, almost elevating them above team travellers as those with additional strength and ability. Weber's outlook on the polar world often mirrors my own but I do feel he was inconsistent in this respect. He does state his own desire for and pleasure in sharing his journeys with others, but he almost admits this as a failing of his, which I think is unfairly self-critical. A soloist may have to deal with many things alone, like open water, bears and crevasses, but I would suggest that the ability to unite and motivate a team to achieve something greater than the sum of the parts is a special skill too, especially when the odds are not in its favour. I would also say that, for a social animal, an urge for solitude can hardly be seen as an accomplishment.

So, when looking at a select group of potentials for a major polar expedition, what is the aim? What sort of men and women are polar explorers of the modern day? We are in a new era of polar expeditions and a brief examination of the history of polar exploration and the types of polar traveller may inform the quest for the modern-day expert.

Firstly, there was the Heroic or Golden Age of polar exploration. Then followed the wartime hiatus. Funds and motivations were needed elsewhere and so interest waned in the more symbolic achievements around the Poles. The Cold War saw a rise in nationalistic competitiveness across the world and the posturing made its way to both the Arctic and Antarctic. Americans, Soviets and many other nations began to set up stations and launched flag-planting expeditions. The renaissance era began in the 1980s and this coincided with an increasingly commercialised world and the rise of advanced new breathable fabrics and satellite navigation and communication. The frequency of expeditions with purely geographical goals, not science-based or similar, increased from one per five years to up to half a dozen per year in the early 2000s.

The pre-credit-crisis spending spree on sponsorship meant that 2000 to 2005 saw a boom in ventures and even those novices considered borderline were able to secure backing. The new era of exploration, which I refer to, emerged from the glowing embers of the global recession. Money is scarce, the media has grown to be both gullible and at times, jaded and most of the 'playboy' explorers have dropped off the map, moving onto easier games. A core of professionals has remained, annual expedition numbers are down and the future is looking challenging in the extreme but there is potential for the credibility, romance and 'specialness' of polar travel to return.

To my mind there are three clear categories of polar traveller. First come the original pioneering explorers: the true explorers in most people's minds and in mine too. They travelled with next to no outside support or hope of rescue in search of places for which they had no map – most drawing them as they went along. Many still had dreams or beliefs about what was to be found there which might amuse us now, but seemed plausible then, for example an open polar sea, openings into an inner Earth or giant basalt columns. These are the men, Ross, Mawson and Rasmussen, to name just three, for whom we should have deep reverence and whose opinion I would always try and consider when deciding whether an expedition, a policy or even a comment is a good idea.

Then there are those who wish to see the great polar expanses of the world and have neither the motivation, nor the skill, nor the time or health to reasonably attain their dreams independently. Their ambitions are as valid as anyone's and they have the same rights as even the earliest explorers. These people can include the cruise ship travellers, the adventure tourists and the guided adventurers who rely heavily on others in their quest for an experience of a magical place. These I would deem visitors or tourists – not in a patronising way but purely in a descriptive way.

Finally, there are the modern explorers. Explorer is a big word and not one I use in my literature for fear of causing misunderstanding, but I believe it has its place, even in the modern era. Those who independently develop their goals, plans, inventories, logistics, hard skills on the ice and then undertake a journey, whether in a team or solo, should be classed as modern explorers. They are the ones not necessarily drawing maps, but testing boundaries and not being tempted by shortcuts. I have seen some try to use the word explorer whilst evading the scorn of others by adding things like 'explorer of the mind' or 'explorer of personal limits', which must surely be laughable. Explorer is a word with a dictionary meaning, which these people have technically used correctly, but it also has a common-sense real world meaning and to manipulate this is disingenuous. Modern explorers can count a variety of men and women amongst their ranks, for example the Shparos, Weber, Malakhov, Skog, Ousland, Gjeldnes, Fiennes (whose Antarctic journeys were far more remarkable than those in the far North), Hadow, Horn and their various teams and companions. These are the men and women whom I identify with most closely in terms of outlook.

What of the personal characteristics of the individuals and the ideal teammate? Should he or she be single-minded and determined mentally, physically robust and naturally athletic, loners with an aversion for people so extreme that they seek absolute solitude, alpha-types who have to feel conquistador-like, those with a starry-eyed wonder for the natural world? Probably they should be all of these, or a combination of a few or, maybe, none at all. In my experience, the cream of the crop does not conform to a stereotype or a pattern. This makes the search for a partner not one to be rushed and one that is forever surprising and utterly fascinating.

Some will uncover a way of finding the worst in every person and every situation. These are the jaded, the pessimistic and often the ill-informed – those unwilling to scratch beneath the surface. The parallels between personal and national politics intrigues me and occupies my mind given that I had considered a later political career. We currently find ourselves in a time when even the most intelligent, well-balanced and well-intentioned politicians are instantly marked out by the electorate as bad news because of their affiliations and identity. I wonder how many less entrenched voters would find themselves actually believing in the man or woman standing in front of them if presented with nothing more than their philosophies, hopes and dreams and intentions? Stripped of their party badge and tribal allegiance, perhaps this unthinkable situation could lead to a positive feedback loop for confidence in political leadership and away from generations-old assumptions that either they are all, or just ones from a single party, to be reviled. I cannot think of anything more exciting than being able to influence the policymakers without the constraints of partisanship and for good, not simply being one of the pawns.

At present in the UK, it does seem that people find it is less taxing on the mind just to hate them all. Any need to think about policies is consequently negated and we are locked into having another generation of good people avoid political life like the plague, leaving those attracted like moths to the flame of power and corruption to stay in command. Whilst personally attracted to political life, it is this negative trend which makes me unwilling to pursue a political goal in later decades of my life. Logic, reason and basic decency are so easily stamped out or lost in the mire when those who are already in dominant positions see them as threatening and unhelpful. Until such time as this balance is redressed, much talent will reside in other industries and those in politics will find themselves curiously relying on those people who would be better suited to guiding our national and global destiny, for lobbying support and cold, hard cash.

Despite previously making active moves towards a vocation in politics, in preparation for a time in the future when the draw of the cold has loosened its grasp over me and creating legacy becomes my focus, these realisations brought me to my senses. Instead, for now, my sole drive is to try and use the perspectives generated by the uniqueness of my experiences to date to have a positive impact for generations and across nations rather than making a transitory contribution on the political seesaw. This consideration of personalities has its equivalent in the outdoor world and it would be my job to identify whom to bring on-board – people who have that special, dynamic ingredient which just makes things happen and contributes to a buoyant yet realistic mood.

Long ago, my father told me the fundamental he kept in mind whilst in positions of leadership: 'When choosing who to place around you, choose those of strength who will complement the gaps in your own skills. Do not pick the weak, who make you feel powerful – this is, in fact, the feebleness of the leader and a recipe for failure.' I took this to heart in my teenage years and it runs strongly through my thoughts, writing and speaking like a wide vein in a leaf of strategy.

The goal I sought was to find someone or some people, perhaps different from those your mind might conjure up when asked to design a polar explorer, with some combination of the following: a willingness to work, a physicality which survives repeated degradation, a calm demeanour, tolerance, self-awareness of fallibility, talented 'ideas' without a resignation to fate and finally a sense of humour that jumps to the fore at the moment most needed.

It is these people who I live for and will remember through every phase of my life; these are the people who enrich and make existence more than just a sequence of necessary progressions. They will form the backbone of 'Dark Ice' and beyond.

EPILOGUE

Why is this book called *Maybe*?

On an immediate level, maybe is probably the most regularly used word I have heard spoken by the native people of the Arctic I have had the privilege to know. The weather, the ice and the sheer amount of uncertainty that contribute to life in this remote, frozen world make its people arch-pragmatists and fundamentally unbothered by disappointments or delays. It therefore seems appropriate to borrow this term to describe a book which is not a clean and simple journey from the birth of an idea, through struggles to ultimate success.

Above all, I wanted *Maybe* to be about a passionate aspiration for real achievement and honesty, a common theme throughout. For it to be authentic, I had to lift the lid on the less clean-cut sides of polar travel, the disappointing moments and the raw and at times, uncomfortable facts. I wanted it to be a window into the inner workings and often intentionally private world of the polar traveller. Without these additions, I simply would not be telling you the full story. They are the reflections of the myriad of positives which accompany my life choices – the cerebral blank canvas that the cold wilderness represents, the utterly special moments they allow me to share with some remarkable people and the very deep affection I have for the places that provide the backdrop to it all.

Maybe was a difficult book to write. 'The Long Haul' journey was such a triumph that this book, which has come out of the ups and downs of the following years, could seem like it was written by a man with his back against the wall rather than one basking in the glory of accomplishment. That is not the case, though. In contrast, my awareness of value, the truth and my future is far more assured now than when penning my first work as a mere twenty-three year old. The future is bright, focused and positive.

'*Harrowing and shattering defeats are good for you*' – A well-known British politician. But only for a moment – they just teach you how to win even better. I never used to believe this, being convinced that every moment must be an indication of your mettle, but time has shown the many colours of life and its fluctuations. It is the overall drive which bursts through all this and wins through that matters in the end and the difficult times and failures can do much to inform those later joys.

In another sense, *Maybe* is a reminder for me of the inherent uncertainties of life in its original context. I think in a world where a car's lifetime warranty can matter more to a customer than what the car actually is, the word represents the ubiquitous uncertainty that accompanies all polar endeavour. Without this, almost every shred of value is lost from such journeys. I suppose this is why expedition guides can, on occasions, stare in disbelief at clients who want some form of guarantee of success, Pole or summit. The lack of control over the outcome, once willpower and talent are negated, is so alien to what society seems to favour that to actively seek it out seems just plain wrong. This, along with a long list of other reasons, explains why there are only a few of us trudging the long, virgin trails of the extreme latitudes. I am not sure I would have it any other way.

'The Long Haul', both the journey and my first book, began with a dream. That dream was then dealt a series of blows before morphing into reality. Our ultimate triumph was a story of teamwork in the face of physical struggle and setbacks on the ice. There could not have been a more textbook tale of adventure and motivation, in terms of the concept therein. In comparison, *Maybe* is not one thing like it.

Sometimes I have told you the answers, the truths, and sometimes only hinted at a notion which may allow some to reassess their own viewpoint. Above all, I hope I have provoked reactions; doubtless some will be critical and negative; others I hope are positive and encouraging. Perhaps many will be content just to have had the opportunity to think through someone else's eyes.

Why the book has the title it has might be eclipsed by the wider issue of why do it at all? It is one which, in context, I have touched on as the journeys progressed but a more universal explanation might do well to put such a fundamental question to bed.

It is a question I carefully sidestepped in *The Long Haul*, the real response I had being almost like an invention not yet prepared to be uncovered; I did not feel ready to share my thoughts. I have noticed that so many are terrified of being asked this, the most important question of all. I wanted something definitive and as devoid of subjectivity as is possible, but yet achingly personal. After all, it requires me to question the hopes, desires and efforts of every day I have lived for nearly a decade. Some of those days involved putting myself in situations where my survival was no sure thing – making it a brutal self-appraisal with nowhere to hide.

You will often hear about motivating youth, about raising awareness for causes, whether environmental or charitable. In most cases – except occasionally where there is overwhelming commercial motivation or lack of thought – these are not a façade; they are real. However, they represent only one layer of motivation. Once swept aside and after delving deeper, there is always more: the raw, human desire to do something. My studies of biology, behaviour and evolution in the context of society, pull me towards seeking the human truth behind 'why?' and not the complex set of excuses we might instead offer an inquisitor.

Charity can be put to one side. It is a bonus but difficult to voice as an overriding motivator. We all know the feeling of being bombarded with requests to sponsor people to do every conceivable 'challenge' in aid of a cause close to their heart. However, in an expedition context, the lines become blurred and we must assess the actual goal. Is it to gain support to do a challenge you want to do whilst feeling justified or unselfish at the same time, or is it to make a significant contribution to fighting cancer or poverty? If the latter, much of the large sums spent on the actual expedition could be better used if given directly to the charity. I often feel that the real motivation is the former and the broadcast motivation is the latter. I know of one £50,000 adventure challenge which raised just £5,000 for the charity in contrast to a humble marathon runner who raised £500,000. The enterprise with the most objective impact is clear, yet it was less exciting for the participant. Motives are complex, though, and I fully grasp that often the mere creation of a small memorial charity with indistinct practical aims can be a powerful part of the grieving process for families and friends who have suffered tragedy. The less honourable will regrettably use association with a cause, charity or topical subject to further their promotional aims which serve to satisfy ambition – dressing up a personal quest as a charity expedition and using goodwill as an unwitting vehicle.

The polar world is uniquely bigger than us. Physically, of course, but more importantly in terms of its utter indifference to our individual presence and in its extra-terrestrial nature – divorced in every way from the world we have shaped and created to satisfy our every need and comfort. Given this, my response to 'why?' is:

•

The Point Is... (a brief essay)

The first question I face at every public speech or at the head of every enquiring email is consistent: 'Why?' This can be in the most innocent form of curiosity or in the more challenging tone of 'What's the point?' What is the point of polar travel? Even after considering the responses of countless polar travellers, I still did not have an answer when writing my first book, *The Long Haul*. I sidestepped the question clumsily. My mind was drawn back to the question by discussion following the supersonic free-fall by Felix Baumgartner and the ignorant commentary from one or two with the privilege of writing for national newspapers.

Finally, I feel ready to answer. **This** is the point:

-       Firstly, we must strip away the easy additions which can give a polar expedition purpose – charity, medical research and the like. Let us just consider the expedition on its own as an end in itself.

- If someone is to say that a polar expedition has no point, he or she must also ask themselves the following questions: do they listen to music, watch or play sport or visit the cinema? If the answer is yes, they must instantly boycott all of these things. That includes reading this book or any website apart from the news, weather or Wikipedia. None of these things have ANY biological purpose of any sort – they are pointless too.

- You can say that a polar expedition costs a great deal and so is different to kicking a ball around in the park, added to which it can commit vast government resources in the event of an emergency. Compare this cost, though, to that of policing and treating injuries at major sports events worldwide and we can safely say it would not even show up on a pie chart.

- We are all different. I loathe football but I do not, even for a moment, suggest it should be banned on the basis of being pointless. I accept that plenty of people find inspiration and intrigue in the game and leave it at that. The exact same is true for polar travel and for its own audience which reads the books and watches the footage.

- Music originated as a way for cultures to pass on vital information and stories to benefit the subsequent generations – something which has mostly become absent from modern music. The origins of polar travel involved a desire to find new living space and natural resources and to add to our knowledge of the world. Both of these historic bases are biologically important to individuals as living entities. Now, most music has nothing more than entertainment value and polar travel has morphed since our discovery and documentation of the Poles. Does this

236

mean that polar expeditions are now reduced to banal forms of alternative entertainment? Absolutely not. These 'pointless' uses of our time lead to creativity, progress, culture and empathy.

- Wally Herbert, a British polar explorer of the 1960s, said 'and what of those who ask? It is as well for them that there are others who feel the answer and never need to ask.' For all that one might object to his superior tone, in essence he was right. There is something intangible about the lure of the Poles, as there is with so many valuable parts of life.

- In general terms then, if you accept that there is a need for something in life apart from those functions necessary to survive, you agree that there is a point to polar travel. Life would be a colourless and insufferable experience without the experiences which take us beyond the mundane.

- If you first overcome the hurdle and accept that there are worthwhile endeavours that transcend our natural history – survival and securing the immortality of our bloodline (whilst feeding, sheltering and launching them into the world on their front foot) – you open the door to an endless and wonderful array of otherwise pointless geniuses and spectacles. Whether these impress you or not, is up to you.

I am usually of the opinion that every view held should be subject to counter-arguments and new perspectives. Without this, we have only stubbornness and no progress. In this case however, I will place my neck on the block and say that I would be very surprised to hear a view which does not find the above inherently definitive. Thank goodness there is a point in the pointless.

•

What of the balance I expressed between robust endeavour on the ice and enough brain food and stimulation to keep all sides of the individual satiated?

Let us face it – genius or visionary does not truly describe even the most innovative polar explorer of times past or present. I would argue that the regimented backgrounds of so many of the most active of them have contributed significantly to their 'toeing the line'. The occupation itself exists within a known framework and the most ambitious individuals do no more than peek their heads out from this frame, the majority still encased within. Some expeditioners are repetitive and some are inventive but they run along the same train tracks at the basal level.

The real divergence between characters comes afterwards, in terms of how they apply the lessons learned to the rest of their world. The potential for vision comes later, in infinite guises.

This open-ended and unconstrained potential for a free life is alluring. For me it invites responsibility and comes with a yearning to deliver something of value to the world; it is an enthusing vision indeed.

Over time I have gathered subtle life lessons, such as that a simple mind will seek to overcomplicate the mundane in an attempt to bamboozle and the bright will seek to simplify the complex, making communication a breeze. I learned, even at university, lucky enough to be surrounded with thousands of exceptional minds, that I craved an academic and cerebral yet unchained and non-institutionalised setting. This, I found I could create with just an idea and the drive to see it through.

And what about the future? I have my own eyes set on some special polar journeys, all of which are pure and original in nature. However, my own projects do not occur in isolation and only really have relevance in the company of other activity in the cold regions. Every significant journey has its place in history and it is impossible for the protagonists not to occasionally glance left and right in awe of the achievements of their contemporaries. The trend for publicity stunts which grew after the millennium continues apace but some audacious journeys and leaps of faith have come to fruition as well, both in polar work and in the sister-disciplines in the mountains, the air and elsewhere.

•

An endeavour, which recently captured the world with its human story, sheer ambition and masterful use of online video streaming and suspense, was the Red Bull Stratos jump of 2012. Felix Baumgartner made the first supersonic, free-fall jump from a high-altitude balloon twenty-four miles high over Nevada, in near-space conditions. The cameras were, of course, rolling throughout and we followed the stresses and personal relationship strains in the lead up and then the uncertainty and fear on the day itself. Was it a public relations triumph or a truly valuable contribution to wanderlust and science? Probably a little bit of both.

What interested me most was the dynamic between Baumgartner and his mentor, US Colonel Joseph Kittinger, who, since 1960, held the previous free-fall altitude record of nineteen miles. Kittinger clearly held a real affection for Baumgartner, who had a mixed relationship with other senior staff on the project, and there was none of the selfishness that might be expected of a man who held the coveted record for so long. He was actively seeking to hand over the mantle to his successor and it was hard not to warm to this larger than life character.

These men were very different in their background and approach; Kittinger is a military man who had an eye for honour, duty and service to his country. Baumgartner is a daredevil who clearly covets freedom and independence; it would be fair to say that he wanted the jump firstly as an accolade for himself and secondly for his team. The documentary showed that the Austrian felt that it was his project, his jump suit and that his return after a falling out with the team was driven partly through his jealously at seeing his replacement in his suit.

The 1960 jump was US government-driven and the 2012 one an unashamed commercial endeavour for Red Bull but both had a common thread of a desire to test out extreme-condition protective clothing. These could have real applications for space travel and high altitude flights closer to Earth.

The crux of my curiosity was in comparing the two characters – Baumgartner and Kittinger. Whose jump was more significant? Baumgartner fell further and faster and he, most likely, recorded more data in his instrument-strewn space suit. Kittinger was jumping into a vastly more unknown space, for which there was even less precedent. His equipment was a far cry from that of the modern day and his survival chances were similar to many test pilots of his day – not assured. On paper, Baumgartner's jump was more impressive, but I cannot help but give an additional nod of respect to the sheer bravery Kittinger showed jumping literally into the unknown in the infancy of his craft.

Why comment on something seemingly unrelated to polar travel? Well, a great deal of the spirit of each aim is the same and the applications for furthering space travel are inherent in both high altitude and cold regions of the world. The ape that stood on two legs and went on to shape our world is outgrowing its planet. The future of exploration lies in the stars.

Conversely, the Antarctic has seen two recent endeavours which are difficult to evaluate. Almost as if skiing has become too boring for some, a few attempts to cycle to the South Pole have been suggested, but show little potential for completing a full coast to Pole route. Mostly tested on flat and compacted ice and snow, the converted bikes are slow and bogged down when presented with crevasses, any snow of note or sastrugi snow ridges. I do not expect the latest craze to last long. Eric Larsen gave the journey a try from an artificial start point far from the coast and abandoned the attempt along an oft-used route, quoting the obvious obstacles I listed.

Vehicles are also making a return to the South in the exploratory rather than just scientific field, with the enormously expensive and typically grandiose 'Coldest Journey' by Ran Fiennes and co. The aim is to cross the Antarctic (a true crossing from coast to coast) in the winter months for the first time, with resupply and power support. At the time of *Maybe* going to press this journey is still underway, albeit having lost Fiennes himself to another dose of frostbitten fingers. It had to be Fiennes at the helm if this behemoth of a logistical exercise, complete with its own ship, was to gain any traction, for he is the only polar man with the profile capable of attracting the necessary mid-seven figure funding.

The project attracted a great deal of criticism from home and abroad; many saw it as being grossly overfunded (drawing funding away from multiple other cheaper ventures), environmentally polluting and otherwise without purpose as a swansong for an aging explorer from a past era. I am less condemning. Whilst the style does not particularly attract me, using a heated living quarter hauled behind tractors, I appreciate that one size does not fit all. It does represent a creative goal, embraces the true geography of the Antarctic region and takes real risks by taking place in the dark, winter months – albeit without the sea ice, polar bears or tent-life that the 'Dark Ice Project' encapsulates. It does take the proverbial sledgehammer to crack their chosen nut, though.

The future is rosy also for our contemporaries in the mountains. The lid has finally been lifted in the mainstream media on the ludicrous egotism of the Everest tourism market and instead, the humility and talent of special combinations such as Simone Moro and Ueli Steck are driving the sport forward. As this book goes to press, this duo announced their partnership to achieve something genuine and new on that same mountain. Sadly, their climb was quickly halted following a high-altitude conflict with Sherpas.

•

I used to write philosophy off as a fluffy hiding to nothing, a waste of time with no purpose. This was most likely as a product of the science-heavy education of my own choosing. How wrong I was. Nothing has any meaning unless placed within the framework of a philosophy. It helps to explain the reasons behind the otherwise inexplicable. Hard science or endeavour can occur without, but they gain their value when the human element is returned to them; information becomes knowledge.

Polar travel, in an extension of the 'The Point Is...' essay, is an art. I think that, despite the many disciplines encompassed within (sports science, geography and meteorology etc.), they all reside together as part of the uncategorisable desire to experience the extraordinary, learn from it and then express what is created to other people. I wonder how different this endeavour is in reality from that of other artists? Authors, songwriters (as distinct from singers who can be the vehicle for the creative visions or observations of others) or photographers all do the same thing in their particular ways as a professional expedition leader might via imagery, film, voice or the written word.

There is a tempering observation to make, though, and it is a word of caution about how our society has grown to reward and recognise art and entertainment. In a counter-culture spiral, amongst the most wealthy and celebrated, there are often those who perform other people's work, pretend to be other people in front of the camera or play a mainstream sport which has only a shallow direct influence. This often leaves the scholars, the creatives and the productive engineers of our world in the relative shadows. This is no new observation, but it is a cause for concern that instead of progressing to champion the true innovators, we applaud their inverses and the demonstrators of the idea, not the creators, more with each year that passes.

In a similar way, in the area of polar travel, a recent media-driven trend to place emphasis on the irrelevant and contrived components of an expedition rather than the actual journey being undertaken is regressive. It is almost as if the polar journey is a sideshow to a desire by someone to prove a point – often a point which does not really need to be proved. An all-female team showing their equal ability 'in the face of male chauvinism' or someone with a physical hindrance that actually has little impact on their ability to travel often serve to damage the cause of those they claim to champion. This is driving a wedge yet further and making double standards a self-fulfilled prophecy, just as the new generation is showing promise.

My view is very clear. If people achieve something of significance, they should be celebrated on the strength of their achievement regardless of anything else. I would be the first to give a standing ovation to a person from a country with zero polar heritage or with a disability who stands in front of an audience and speaks, just for a while, without reference to their perceived disadvantage. I have listened with utmost respect to those who have suffered enormous misfortune and then refuse to be defined by that experience – instead they wish to be compared on an equal footing. I assert that we should all take note. Quotas and special treatment prolong discrimination instead of reversing it.

●

I believe firmly that not everyone has the 'right' to see the Arctic or any other special place on Earth. I do not believe in unlimited open access. I believe firmly that the Polar Regions should be closed, save for those native to them, to all but the elite. Shocking you may say? Outrageous? Let me qualify that statement. In this context I define the elite as those with the inherent desire, determination, persistence and lateral thought to get them there. Forget the usual definition of elite as being those with inherited wealth or 'connections in high places'. It does not matter to me where someone was born, how they were educated or how much wealth they have accrued. If they have the initiative to make their way to the world's remotest places, they are the elite in my mind – the deserved elite.

Ultimately I believe in a crucible of perspective drawn from experience, passion grown from acceptance of our humanity and a purpose driven by conscience. Into the pot also needs to flow an impassioned hope for the ultimate triumph of standards and honest egalitarian merit over all else. The harvest of this powerful concoction can, if nurtured, be so explosively creative and affirming that the future is full of inherent optimism with no need for divinity nor delusion.

I do not expect everyone to share my passion for the Polar Regions or even every view, but I would be satisfied for it to kindle and reignite your passion, and even your fight, in whatever it is that means everything to you.

Informed conviction compelling you to act.

243

THANKS TO

George Bullard, Andrew Wilkinson and Finn McCann – the most magnificent companions one could hope for.

My family and friends – forever understanding and supportive.

Heidi Houlihan, *my ever-patient editor*
Steve Fowler and Carolyn Dunn *at Bridgedale Outdoor*
Paul Cosgrove, Jo Allen and Jake Doxat *at Montane*
Mike Madylus *at Blackfriars Bakery*
Nick Farrell *at Yellowbrick Tracking*
Tony Stephenson and Tentipi
Paul Holtom *at The Outdoor Shop*
Oskar, Brando and the volunteers at ICE-SAR
Andrew White and Chris O'Donoghue, *for your unwavering efforts on my behalf*
Piers Currie and Gary Marshall *at Aberdeen Asset Management*
Stephen Hoyt *at the Canadian Border Services Agency*
Alex Stubbing *at Parks Canada*
Talea Weissang and Finn L. Nielsen *at the Greenland Expeditions Office*
Marcus Agar
Captain Chris Page RN
Mike Lunn *at Purvers International*
Inge Solheim
Dan Bernard and Gail Baird
Kees de Nijs and Dave Annandale *at Be-Well*
Jim House *of Portsmouth University*
Jenna Phipps *at GTC Comms*
Hans and Birthe Jensen and the people of Qaanaaq
The people of Siorapaluk
Dr. Rod Mackenzie *at MAGPAS*

Robert Peroni
Georg Utuaq
Lars Bianco
Matt Spenceley
Robert Mirsky *at KPMG*
David Stickels and Sandra Mallia *at Hedge Funds Care*
Charlie Starmer-Smith *at The Daily Telegraph*
Joel Massey *at Five News*
Ian Gibbs *at G Comm UK*
Douglas Scott Henningsen and Sanne Eline Wennerberg
Malik Eriksen and the people of Ilulissat
Denise Prior *at the Royal Geographical Society*
Marc Van Der Veen
Bernard Duguay *at Environment Canada*
Victor Boyaresky and Victoria Redyaeva *at VICAAR*
Margarita Tertitskaia
The staff at Air Greenland
Chris Paton
Val Surrey *at D & V Fuels*
Ivalu Kleist and Jeanette Nielsen *at the Royal Arctic Line*
Charlotte Lee-Field and Leanne Hall *at Dogtag Insurance*
Siv Upsahl Hafsmo *at Helly Hansen*
Alain Hubert
Lonnie Dupre
Børge Ousland
Sir Ranulph Fiennes
Pen Hadow
Roger Daynes *at Snowsled*
Jane French
Eric Philips
The Hon. Alexandra Foley
Emma at PH Designs
Guy *at Braemar Mountain Sports*
Craig Mathieson
Andreas Muenchow
Trudy Wohlleben *at the Canadian Ice Service*
Humfrey Melling *at Fisheries and Oceans Canada*

Jemma Phayre
Jamie Korner *at the ACMF*
Erin Sheridan *at the US Coast Guard*
Peter Frederick Lyberth
Jerry Kobalenko
Eimskip UK
M Putt Sailmakers
Kim Michael Petersen
Niall McCann
Rich Smith
Bethany Steer *at the Financial Ombudsman Service*
Max Buttinger *at Fischer*
Mikael Strandberg
Rune Gjeldnes
Frissi Adolfsson *at Norland Air*
Christian Fensbo *at IF Insurance*
Einar, Gav, Will, Neil and Scott – *it was a pleasure!*
Odd Harald Hauge
Steve Jones *at ALE*
Kenyon Ellis
Col Stocker

There are countless others who have contributed in so many ways
and my thanks goes to them also.

OTHER BOOKS BY
ALEX HIBBERT

The Long Haul, 2010, Tricorn Books, £8.99

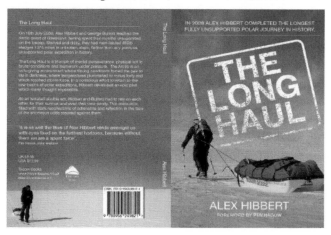

Kalaallit Nunaat, 2012, Tricorn Books, £25